IMAGES
of America

KENTUCKY'S HORSE-DRAWN ERA

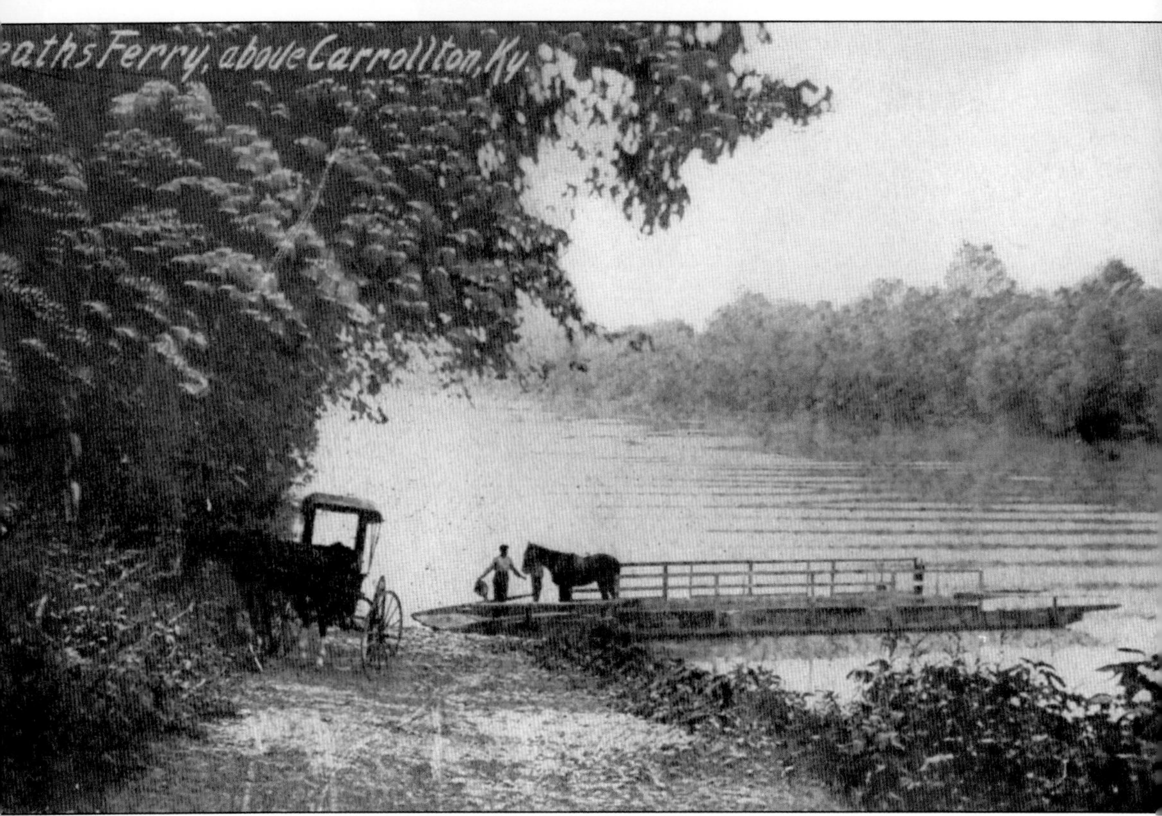

A QUIET MOMENT IN 1900. This scene at Heath's Ferry, on the Kentucky River above Carrollton, illustrates a couple of major differences between Kentucky's horse-drawn era and today. Life was quieter and much slower then. Except for emergencies, horses and mules rarely traveled faster than a trot, and speeding was not an option. A horse and buggy can be seen on the bank of the river, and a man is holding a horse's bridle on the ferry, which was powered only by the river's current. (Courtesy of the Kentucky Historical Society, item # CAO.1990ph2.12CAO16.)

ON THE COVER: This photograph from the Barker and Faulconer Fayette County Public Education photographic collection at the University of Kentucky Special Collections embodies the spirit of this book. It is a scene that could only have been captured during Kentucky's horse-drawn era. The complete photograph of the Greendale students and teachers in their mule-drawn school bus, as well as additional information about the image, can be found on page 94. (Courtesy of the University of Kentucky Special Collections.)

IMAGES
of America

KENTUCKY'S HORSE-DRAWN ERA

Jeanine and Berkeley Scott

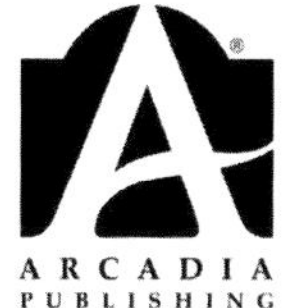

ISBN 978-1-4671-1186-7

Published by Arcadia Publishing
Charleston, South Carolina

Printed in the United States of America

Library of Congress Control Number: 2013952035

For all general information, please contact Arcadia Publishing:
Telephone 843-853-2070
Fax 843-853-0044
E-mail sales@arcadiapublishing.com
For customer service and orders:
Toll-Free 1-888-313-2665

Visit us on the Internet at www.arcadiapublishing.com

We would like to dedicate this book to our children and grandchildren, who make us proud and happy every day: sons Sean and Robert, daughter-in-law Rebecca, grandson Noah, and granddaughter Alison.

Contents

ACKNOWLEDGMENTS

We would like to thank all the helpful people who assisted us in gathering the historical images for this book: Sharyn Mitchell at Berea College Special Collections; Kent Whitworth and Jennifer Duplaga at the Kentucky Historical Society; Deirdre Scaggs at the University of Kentucky Special Collections; Russ Hatter at the Capital City Museum; Nancy Smith at the Hopewell Museum; Nancy Richey at the Western Kentucky University Special Collections; Shane Gilreath at the McCreary County Museum; Mike O'Bradovich; Ted and Betsy Kuster; Betty Witt; Chris Morris; Mary Ellen Hamilton at the Oscar Getz Whiskey Museum; Rebra Perkins and the US Forest Service; and Bill Cooke at the International Museum of the Horse, Kentucky Horse Park. Also, we owe a debt of gratitude to the legion of unnamed photographers who were out in the state during this period, working away capturing numerous scenes for posterity. Without them, there would be no "images of America."

Image credits for the following institutions appear in abbreviated form in the courtesy lines: the Kentucky Historical Society (KHS), the Library of Congress (LOC), the University of Kentucky Special Collections (UK Special Collections), and the Western Kentucky University Special Collections (WKU Special Collections).

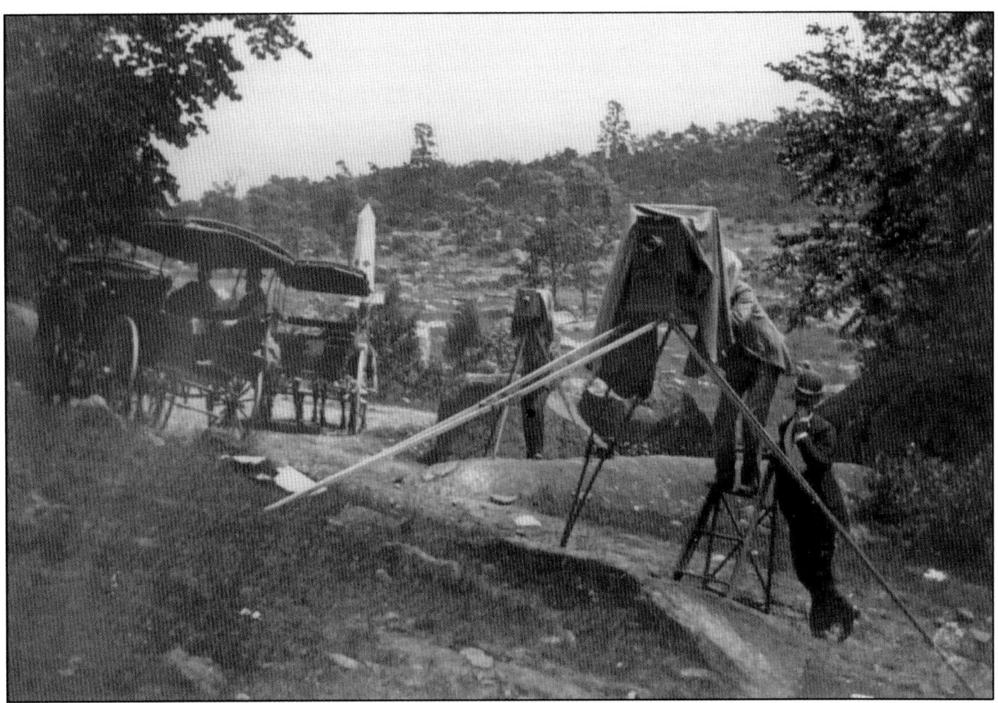

NOT AN EASY JOB. Taking photographs outdoors during the horse-drawn era meant lugging heavy equipment, tripods, and fragile glass-plate negatives down bumpy, unpaved roads in buggies or wagons. Luckily for historians and everyone who enjoys old photographs, many photographers like the ones seen here were willing to do the necessary hard work to get the perfect shot. (UK Special Collections.)

INTRODUCTION

Before the sounds of the day included the continual roar of internal combustion engines, the screeching of tires, and the distant grinding of a semi's gears from a four-lane highway, there was the gentle clip-clop, clip-clop of shod horses and the jangle of loose brass on a harness. Horses and mules were the living machines that made civilization work for centuries, and the time of their dominance has been gone for only a few short decades.

Kentucky and horses go together like peanut butter and jelly, or like bourbon and branch water. The state has been linked to equines of all types for more than two centuries, and Kentucky is alone in having a state park dedicated to the horse: the Kentucky Horse Park. This book covers the era from around 1880 to 1930, a time marked by the close connection between the people of Kentucky and their horses, mules, and oxen.

When this book was first envisioned, horses alone were to be the subject of the photographs: horses pulling fire engines, plows, carriages, parade wagons, and buggies; horses carrying men, women, and children of all colors and sizes. This book includes many fascinating photographs of those subjects. But, as we uncovered the variety of historical photographs from this period, it became clear that the horse would have to share this book with mules and, to a lesser extent, oxen. This was true partly because of the availability of numerous photographs from the mountainous areas of Eastern Kentucky, thanks to the assistance of the staffs at the Berea College Special Collections and the Kentucky Historical Society. The mule was often the animal of choice for small farmers and homesteaders throughout the Eastern Kentucky mountains. The animals ate less, could work harder, and often handled the rocky, difficult-to-travel terrain better than horses. However, for really tough or heavy loads, oxen were used, and there are some great photographs in this book of teams of oxen pulling huge loads. Another photograph shows an ox being shod, something not often seen.

While the word "horse" is in the book's title, and a horse, mule, ox, or some combination of those animals is featured in almost every photograph, the most interesting aspect of the book is the people of this period. Not only were they riding horses and mules, lots of them were turning out to celebrate victories, attend church, watch parades, and even go sledding behind horse-drawn buggies. People used horses or mules to farm, whether the crop was tobacco, hemp, bluegrass seeds, corn, hay, or sorghum cane, and historical photographs bring to life this part of Kentucky's past. Farming has changed radically since the horse-drawn era, making it even more interesting to see historical photographs of hemp being cut and brought in from the field, tobacco being sold and moved in giant wooden hogsheads, and bluegrass seed being harvested.

There are photographs from more than 30 of Kentucky's 120 counties in this book, and they display all types of landscapes. City scenes show huge crowds gathered in their buggies and on horseback, as well as horse-drawn trolleys and spiffy fire engines pulled by teams of horses. Rural photographs include a river baptism, life on small farms, and whole families on the back of a single horse or mule.

This, the authors' fifth book in Arcadia Publishing's Images of America series, contains a chapter that has appeared in all of their previous books and that is always one of their favorites: "Fascinating Faces." This time, some of the "faces" referred to in the chapter title belong to animals. Several horses deserved to be recognized for their faces, as well as for their carrying or pulling power. This chapter includes photographs of people and horses, a photograph of twin babies on a burro, another of a little girl on a pony, and a photograph of a wedding party on mule-back.

Horses and mules did not just help deliver the mail, the laundry, the milk, and the butter. They also took Kentuckians to war. Horses carried officers on their backs, and horses and mules were used to haul ammunition and supplies, both at home and on foreign soil when Kentucky units were deployed. Numerous photographs in the book show soldiers using their animals in daily military life.

The really uncommon sights from this era are featured in the final chapter in the book, "Special Ocassions and Unusual Sights." It includes a diving horse in Maysville, a circus wagon with lions and an elephant in Bowling Green, and the winners of the Mule Derby at Renfro Valley, in Rockcastle County. During the 1920s and 1930s, the Barnum & Bailey Circus required 90 to 100 railroad cars to carry everything, used 300 to 350 Percheron horses to move everything to and from the sites, and had an additional 300 performing horses. One photograph in this chapter features a parade of horses in a spectacular five-ring circus.

Historians have often ignored the tremendous influence of the horse, economically as well as culturally, in agriculture, industry, transportation, sport, war, and as a companion to humans. Many historians view the horse as merely a relic of the pre-industrial era. Mechanization has been given most of the credit for modernization, while little credit has been given to what preceded modernity for many centuries: the "living machines," horses and other beasts of burden. It should be remembered that horses carried and hauled civilization into the modern age and into the 20th century.

During the collection and research of this book's photographs and the writing of the text, the overall impression was how important horses, mules, and oxen were to almost every Kentuckian alive during this period. It is easy to be nostalgic and to think that, by replacing live animals with exhaust-spewing automobiles, trucks, and tractors, something valuable has been lost: a connection to the earth. But, on the other hand, what is also obvious from this collection of photographs is that change is inevitable, and, while we can enjoy looking at vignettes of the past, we have to live in the present.

One

ON THE ROAD

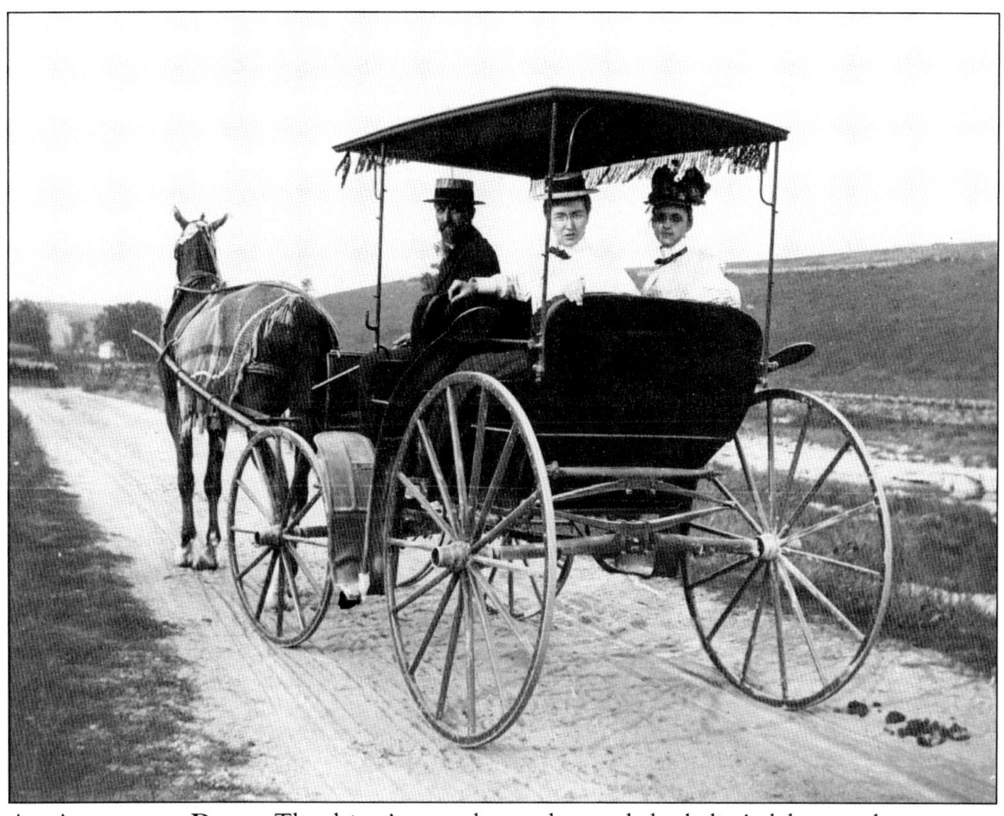

AN AFTERNOON DRIVE. The driver's straw boater hat and the ladies' elaborate chapeaus are iconic symbols of Kentucky's horse-drawn era, as is the "one-horse surrey with a fringe on top." This photograph was taken in Mason County in 1899. In the next century, such vignettes would disappear forever. (KHS, MAS.1990ph2.13MAS55.)

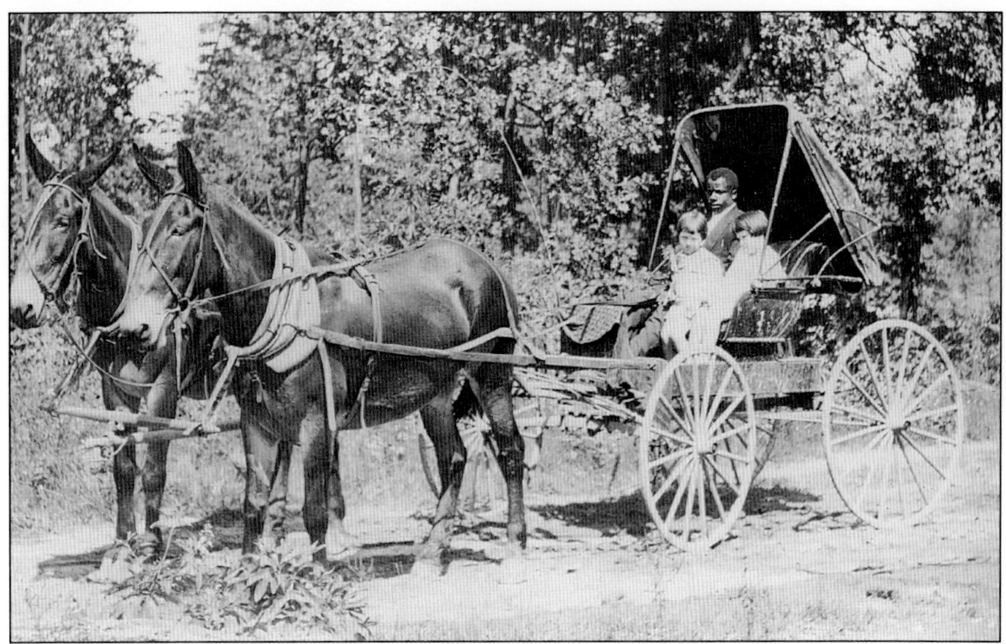

Mule-Drawn Carriage. This African American driver, Charlie Overton, probably worked for the Sugg family of Warren County in the 1890s, when Jim and Helen Sugg were photographed while out for a ride with him. Some may have described this as a buggy, but a four-wheeled vehicle built primarily for passengers and pulled by two horses or mules would more properly be referred to as a carriage. (WKU Special Collections.)

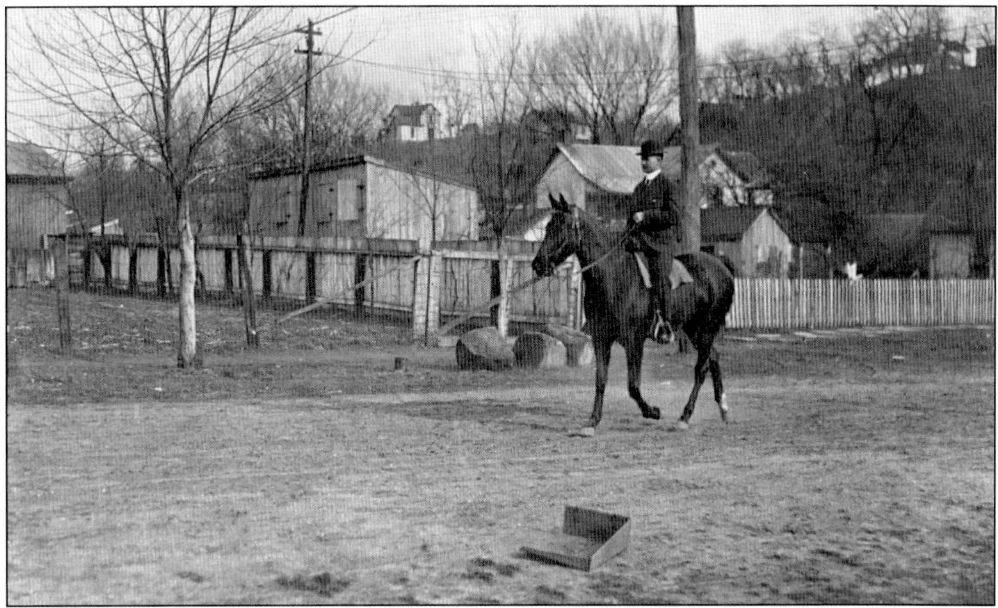

Making the Rounds. Dr. E.C. McDonald, of Cloverport in Breckinridge County, probably spent much of his day in the saddle, visiting his patients and rushing to emergencies. This photograph, taken between 1910 and 1915, shows the doctor's excellent riding posture. In 1930, house calls accounted for 40 percent of a physician's patient interactions. By 1980, it had dropped to 1 percent. Few doctors make house calls today. (KHS, JFA.1990ph2.4JEFA12.)

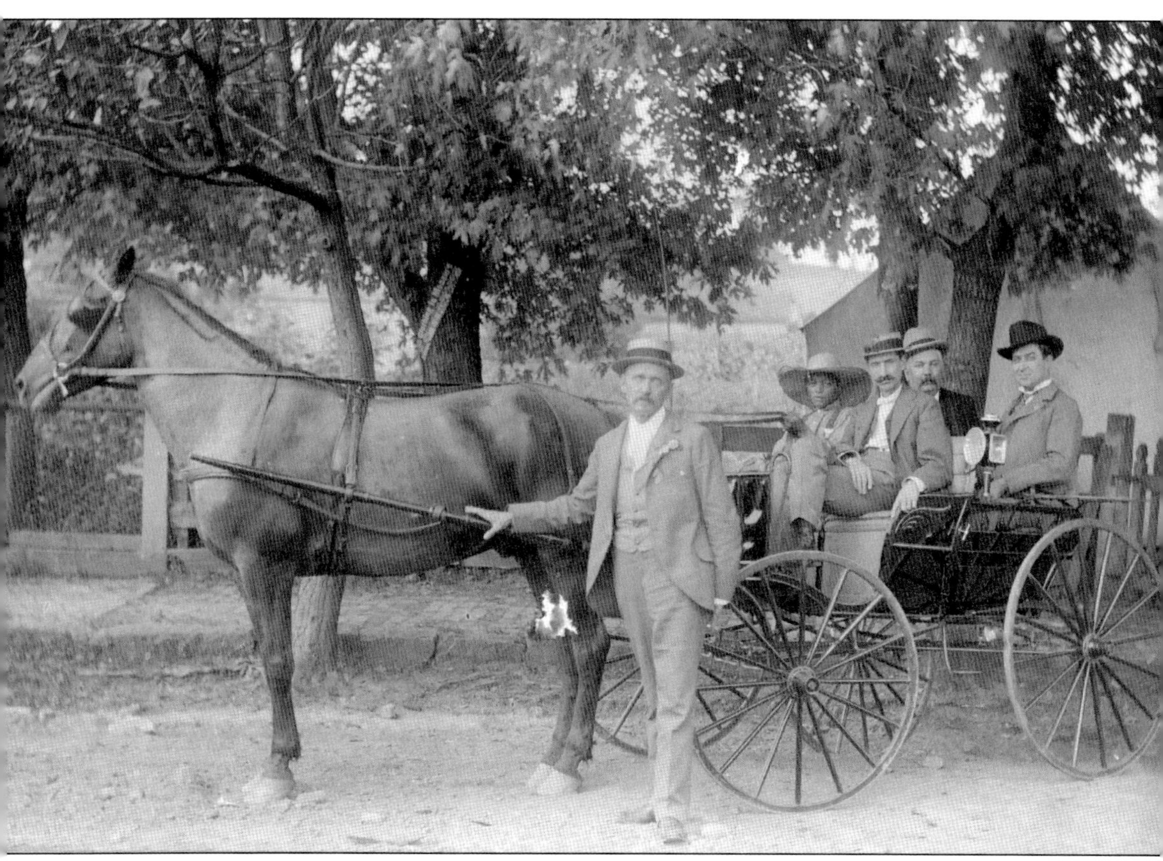

Short-Term Governor. William Goebel, 43, is seated in the back right of this buggy, wearing a dark hat, in the summer of 1899. Less than a year later, he was shot by a sniper as he left the Old State Capitol in Frankfort during a raucous election dispute. The Republicans said he had lost the Kentucky governor's race, and the Democrats said he had won. The wounded Goebel was sworn in on his deathbed and died four days later. He is recorded as the only state governor to be assassinated while in office. The two political factions soon had their own separate Home Guard units facing each other, armed with machine guns, on the Old Capitol grounds in downtown Frankfort. The incident was finally settled without further bloodshed, but it attracted national attention and further enhanced Kentucky's reputation as a violent place. (KHS, 2009MO3.B31.F1.11.)

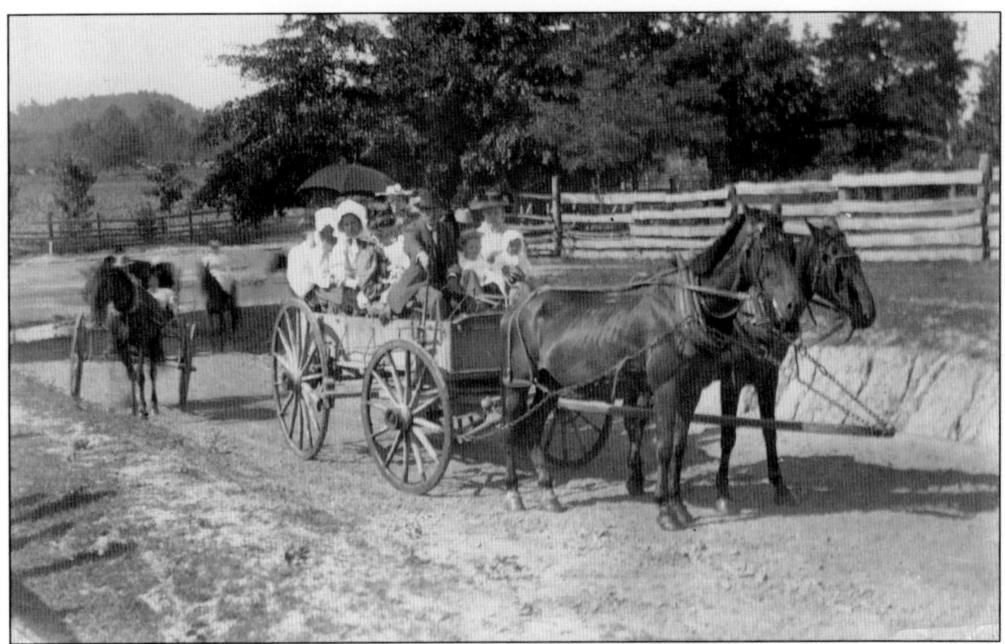

Churchgoing Folks. These Madison County residents were probably on their way to church during the first decade of the 1900s. Their sturdy carriage/wagon was made to withstand the rougher country and hilly roads of the area. Rural churches and camp meetings were partly religious and partly social in nature, much as they are today. (Berea College Special Collections.)

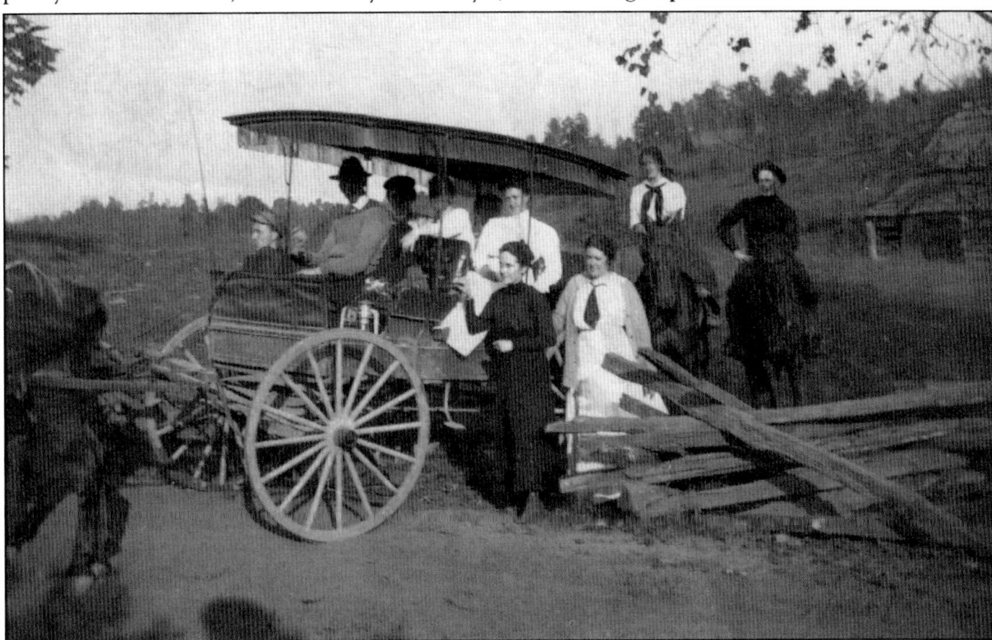

Wagon with a Fringe on Top. This photograph from around 1900 shows young Eastern Kentucky women with bright, smiling faces as they prepare to go somewhere. At this time in Kentucky, as elsewhere in America, women were transitioning from the Victorian era, when they were both subservient to their men and placed on a pedestal by society, to a new century that presented fresh opportunities and challenges. (Berea College Special Collections.)

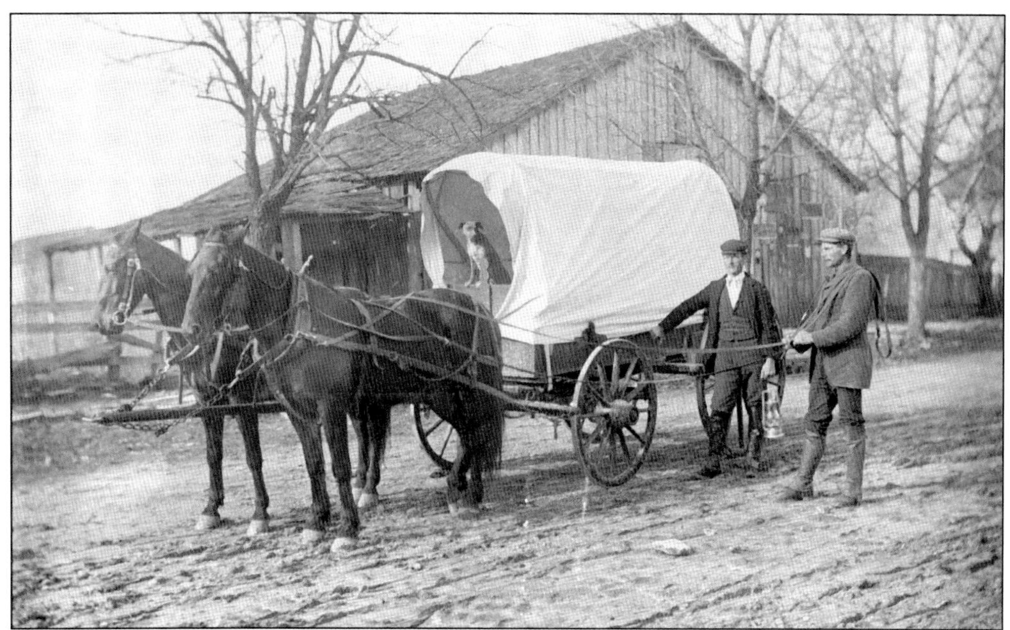

Covered Wagon to Tennessee. In 1911, Frank Butler of Carroll County was told that he should move to Tates Springs, Tennessee, the site of a well-known Victorian-era health spa, because of his consumption. Butler and his dog apparently chose a long, dusty wagon trip over a train. Although similar in appearance, this wagon was not as large as the sturdy Conestoga wagons that took pioneers out west. (KHS, CAO.1990ph2.15CAO3.)

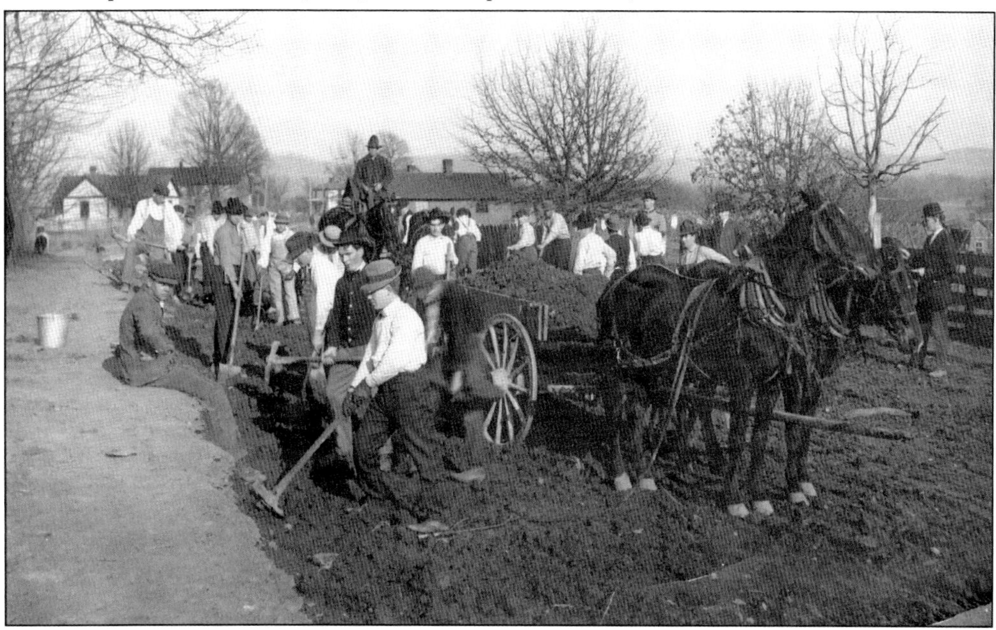

Students Building a Road. At the turn of the 20th century, road construction was the responsibility of local governments and organizations. In this photograph, well-dressed male students from Berea College are shown building a road on or near campus. The power used for construction came from the strong backs of the young men and from the limbs of their mules and horses. (Berea College Special Collections.)

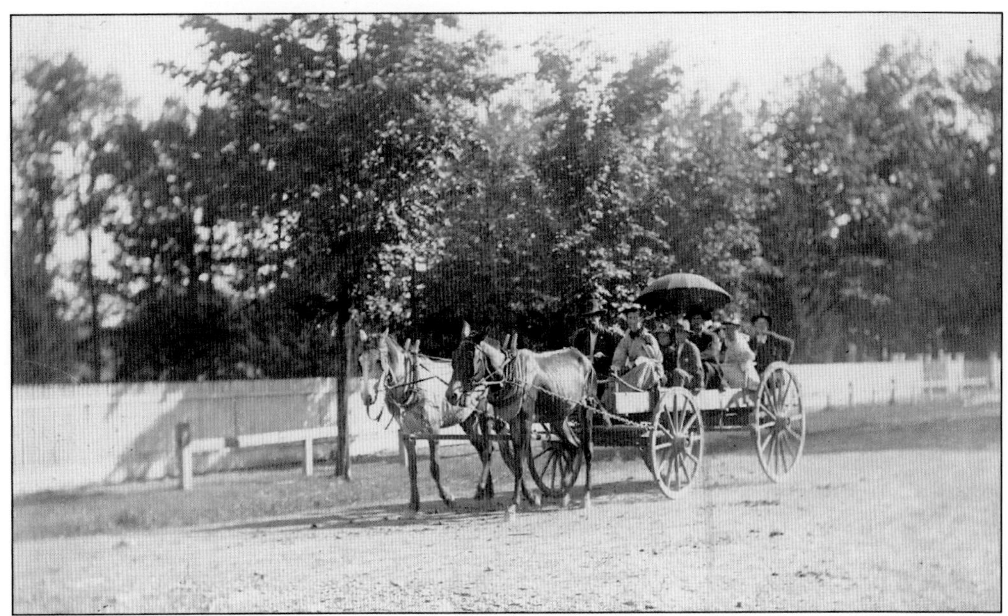

Wagonload for Commencement. These folks are on their way to commencement ceremonies at Berea College, in Eastern Kentucky, around 1918. Founded in 1855 as the first interracial and coeducational college in the South, Berea College continues to charge no tuition and admits only academically promising students, primarily from Appalachia, who have limited economic resources. (Berea College Special Collections.)

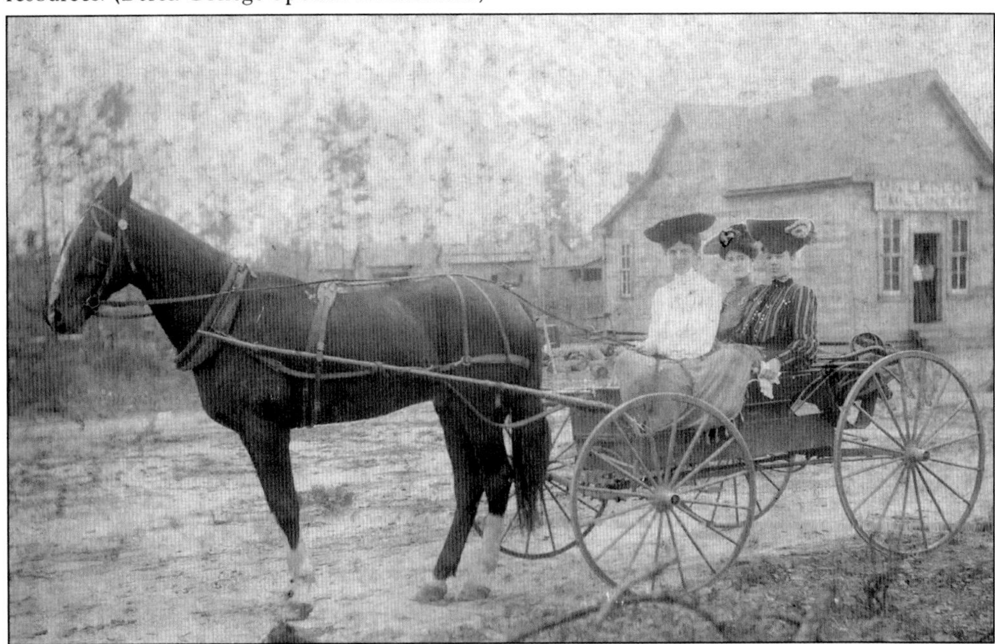

Millinery Shop Ladies. Here, Mrs. Ledlow and two other ladies are shown in front of Ledlow's millinery shop in Russellville, in Logan County, around 1895. Millinery shops, then and now, were all about ladies' hats, although in that era they also carried clothes for the entire family. As any reader of this book must notice, ladies' hats were a booming business at the time. (WKU Special Collections.)

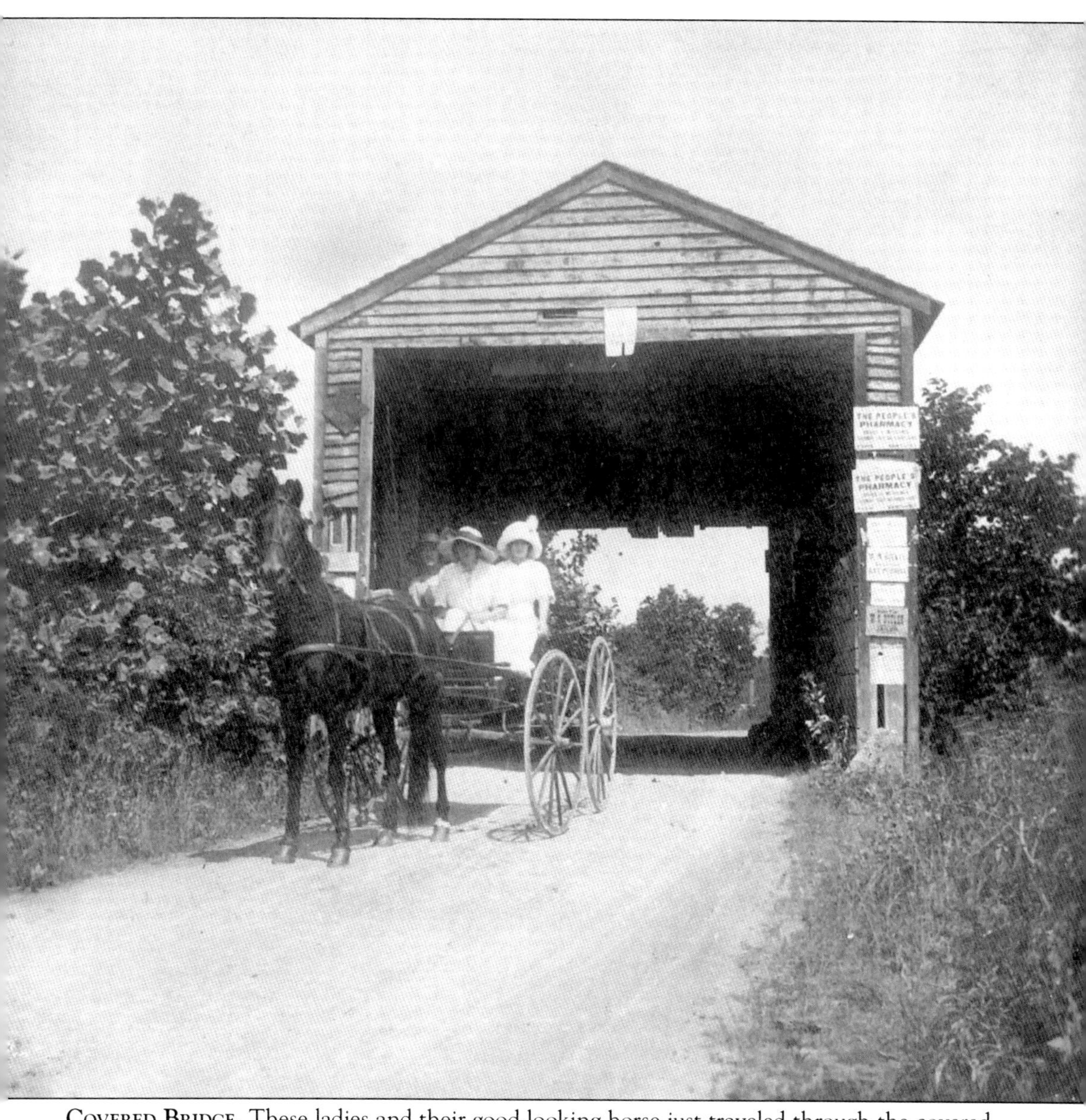

COVERED BRIDGE. These ladies and their good-looking horse just traveled through the covered bridge across Kennedy Creek in Bourbon County. Posters advertising the People's Pharmacy and political candidates cover the side of the long-gone bridge. Covered bridges of the time were mainly timber-truss structures with a roof and siding that formed a nearly complete enclosure. The purpose of the covering was to protect the wooden structural parts from the weather. Uncovered wooden bridges had a life span of only 10 to 15 years because of the effects of rain and sun. At one time, Kentucky had more than 700 covered bridges. By the mid-1920s, it is estimated that some 400 were still in use. At the end of World War II, approximately 65 still stood. Since 1986, only 13 of the treasured bridges remain in the state. (Betty Witt.)

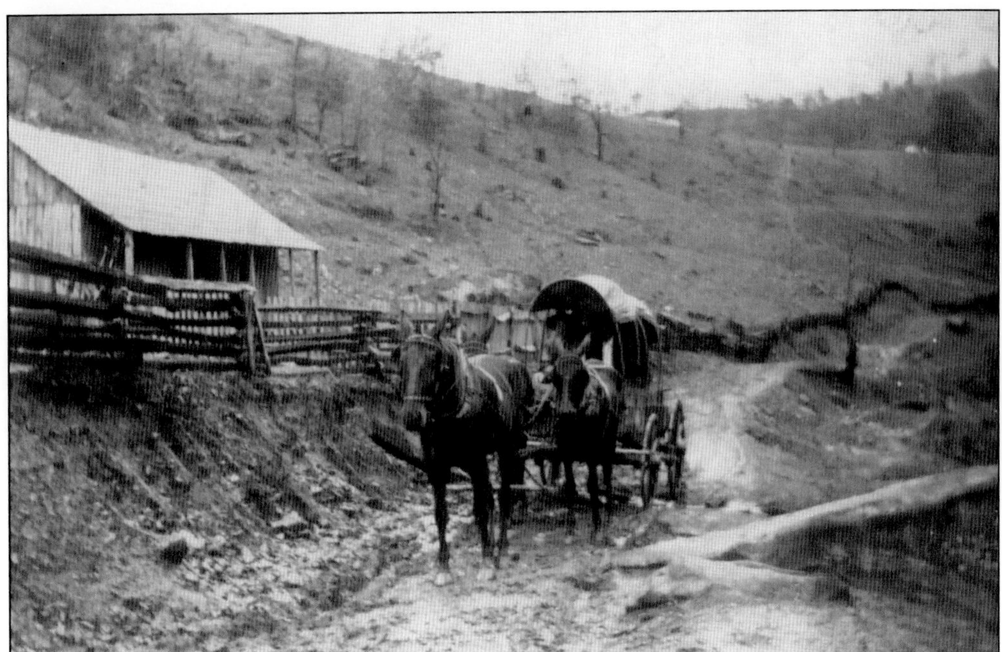

"Horrible Roads." Future president Franklin D. Roosevelt, during a trip to Eastern Kentucky in 1908, wrote about the "horrible roads" leading to Harlan. He traveled over a "so-called wagon road – positively the worst road I have ever seen or imagined and one which was not very easy to traverse on horseback." Kentucky's mountain counties, with difficult terrain and systemic poverty, continued to suffer with poor roads for many years. (Berea College Special Collections.)

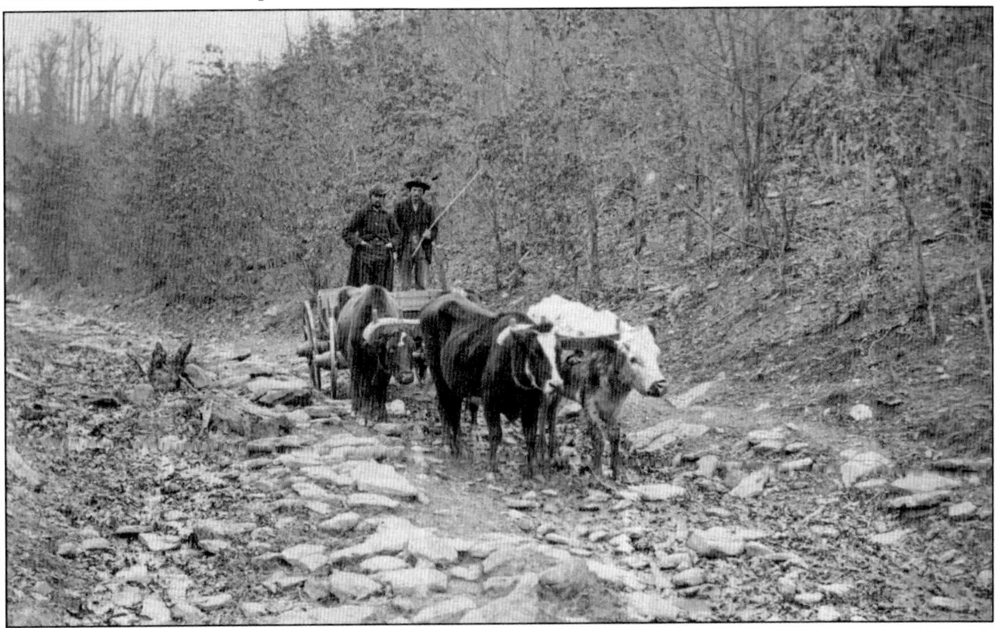

Oxen Power. Many mountaineers depended on the steady, brute power of oxen to traverse mountain roads and to farm the hilly slopes. These men needed a four-oxen team to travel this "road" to McKee in Jackson County. This right-of-way, as many others did, followed a creek bed that could become a raging torrent a few hours after a storm. (Berea College Special Collections.)

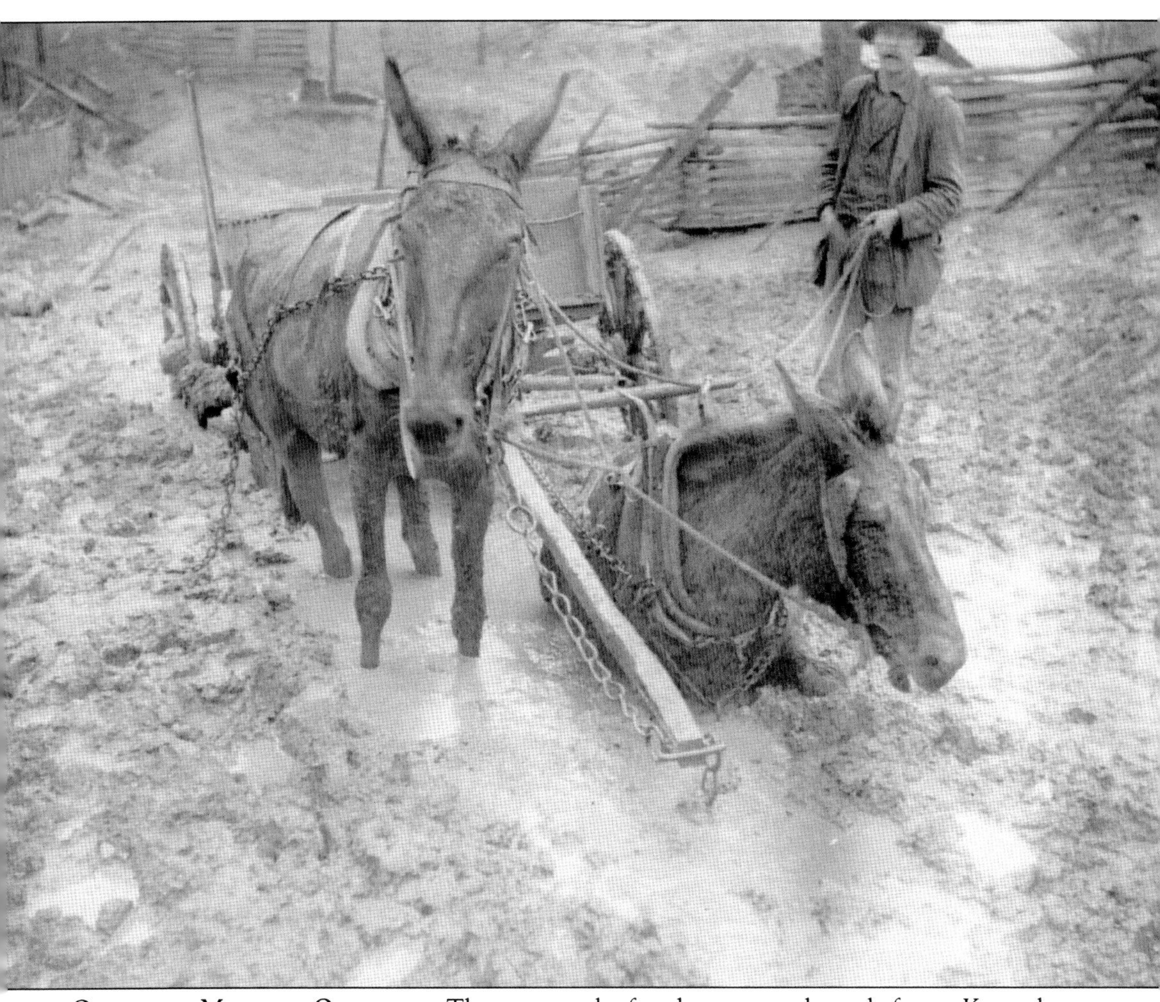

One in the Mud, the Other out. These two mules faced a common hazard of some Kentucky roads at the beginning of the 20th century. Dusty roads in summer could become quagmires of mud in the spring or frozen ponds in the winter. Many Kentucky families depended on mules, because they were cheaper to own than horses and were well adapted to small farms. Mule breeding became a specialty in Kentucky and was a major economic product for many Bluegrass-area breeders. Kentucky mules became a sought-after commodity throughout the nation and brought the highest prices at auction. Many were "requisitioned" during the Civil War, and many more were bought by the military to serve in the Spanish-American War and World War I. Mules were notorious for being stubborn and having violent tempers, but they outlived horses, adapted better to hot climates, and required less food. (Berea College Special Collections.)

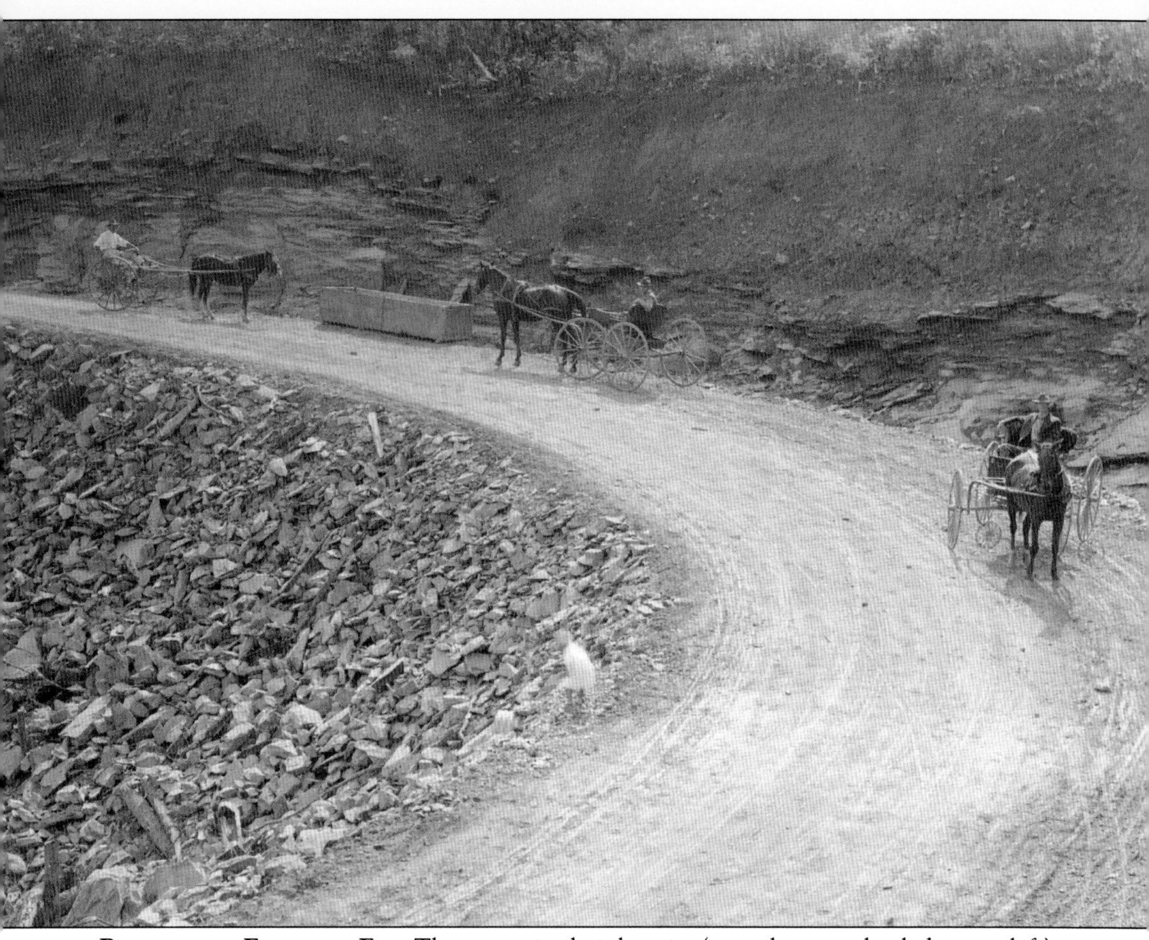

Road to the End of an Era. These men in their buggies (note the two-wheeled cart at left) are traveling on the relatively smooth, flat Dixie Highway, which was under construction between Berea and London, Kentucky, sometime between 1915 and 1919. The Dixie Highway is significant as the first highway to link the rural American South to the urban North. It ran from Michigan to South Florida. After it crossed the Ohio River, it split in two; the western route traveled through Louisville and Nashville, and the eastern route went via Lexington, Berea, and Williamsburg. The final result is better understood as a network of connected paved roads rather than one single highway. It was constructed and expanded from 1915 to 1927, when the US government took control of the system. The name Dixie Highway persists in locations along its length where the main flow of traffic has been rerouted to modern highways and the old Dixie Highway remains as a local road. Roads like this ended the horse-drawn era and created the age of the automobile. (Berea College Special Collections.)

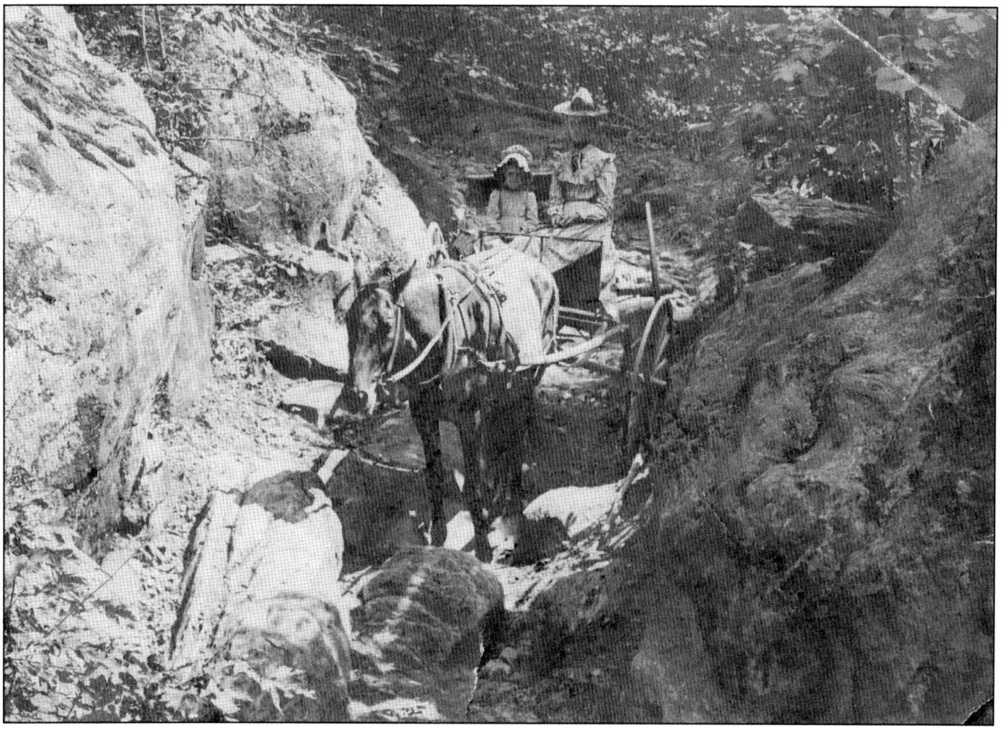

END OF THE ROAD. It is not easy to determine what this lady and little girl are thinking, but it is pretty clear that the horse is not able to go any farther. Maybe the driver made a wrong turn into this dead end and needs to back up. Or, perhaps, the photograph was staged as a humorous comment on mountain roads. (Berea College Special Collections.)

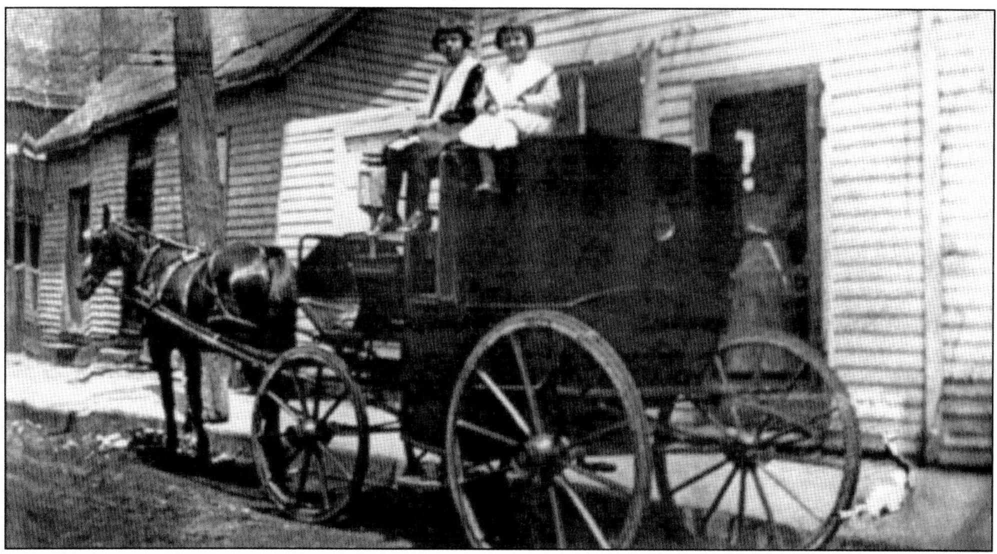

LAST HORSE-DRAWN TAXI IN PARIS. Electric interurban streetcars began running up and down High Street in Paris in 1902, and the first automobile made its appearance in the city in 1904. Thus, it was no surprise that, by 1908, Charles Coleman would be operating the last horse-drawn taxi in town. The two little girls are sitting where the driver, known as a "hack," sat while operating this handsome hansom cab. (Hopewell Museum.)

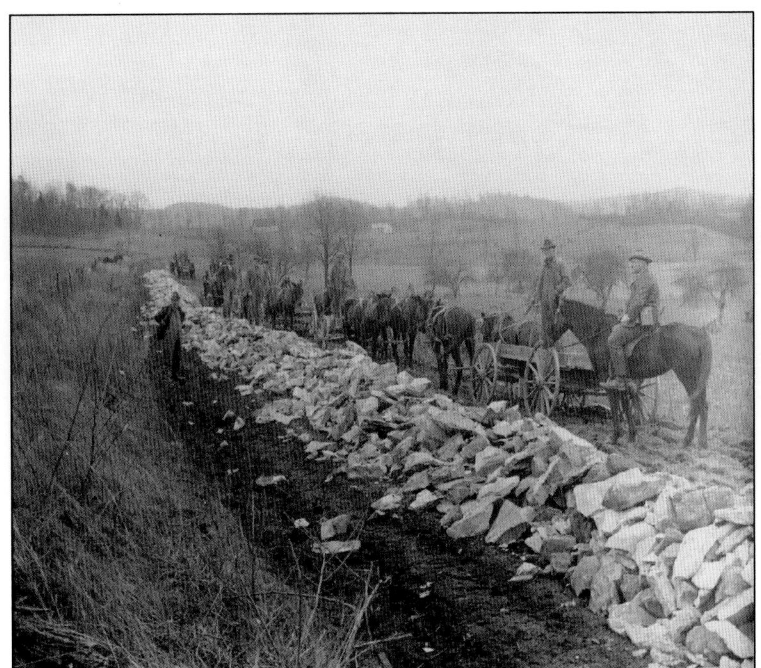

Rocky, Rocky Road. The big rocks in this 1903 photograph may not look like it, but they will provide a much smoother and mud-free ride than the plowed right-of-way beneath them. After being spread out, they were rolled and pressed into place. The well-dressed man on the far right was most likely the managing engineer of the road project. (Berea College Special Collections.)

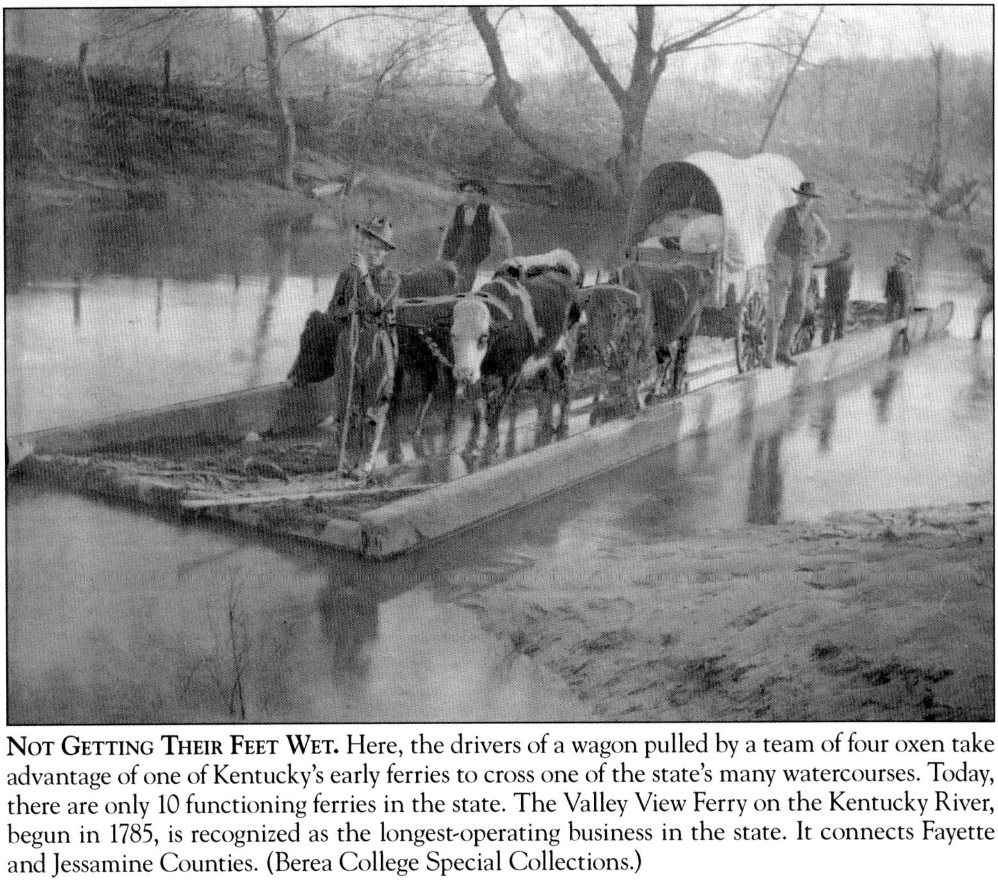

Not Getting Their Feet Wet. Here, the drivers of a wagon pulled by a team of four oxen take advantage of one of Kentucky's early ferries to cross one of the state's many watercourses. Today, there are only 10 functioning ferries in the state. The Valley View Ferry on the Kentucky River, begun in 1785, is recognized as the longest-operating business in the state. It connects Fayette and Jessamine Counties. (Berea College Special Collections.)

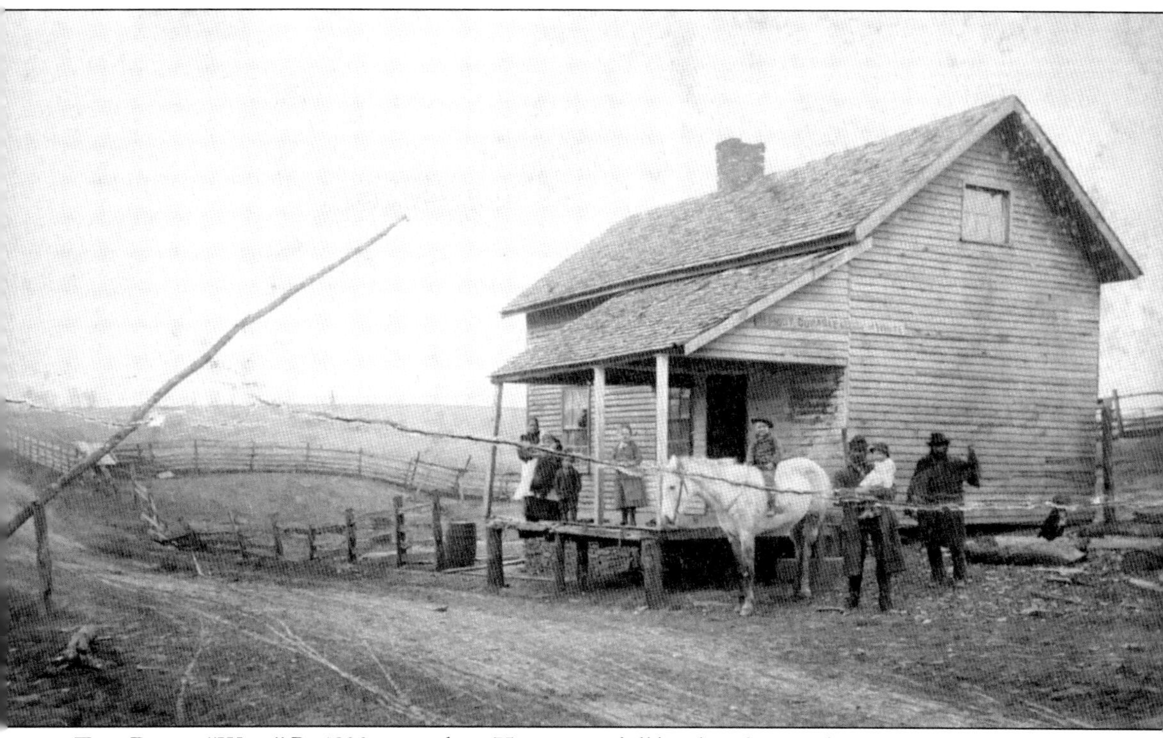

Toll Roads "War." By 1890, more than 75 percent of all hard-surface roads in Kentucky were part of the toll-road system. The first charters from the state allowing the construction and operation of toll roads were issued in 1817. Tolls could be collected every five miles, but not within a mile of a town. By 1890, about the time of this glass-plate negative of the John Chafin family near Sharpsburg in Bath County, the public outcry for "free roads" had reached a crescendo. Tollhouses were burned, gates were destroyed, and gatekeepers were threatened and beaten. Perhaps the Chafin family suffered in that way. The state's legislature was reluctant to act against tollgate attackers, being quietly sympathetic to the cause. The so-called Tollgate Wars lasted from 1890 to 1897, at which time the toll roads were either sold to the state or driven out of business by the violence. (KHS, CAO1987ph13.chafin1.)

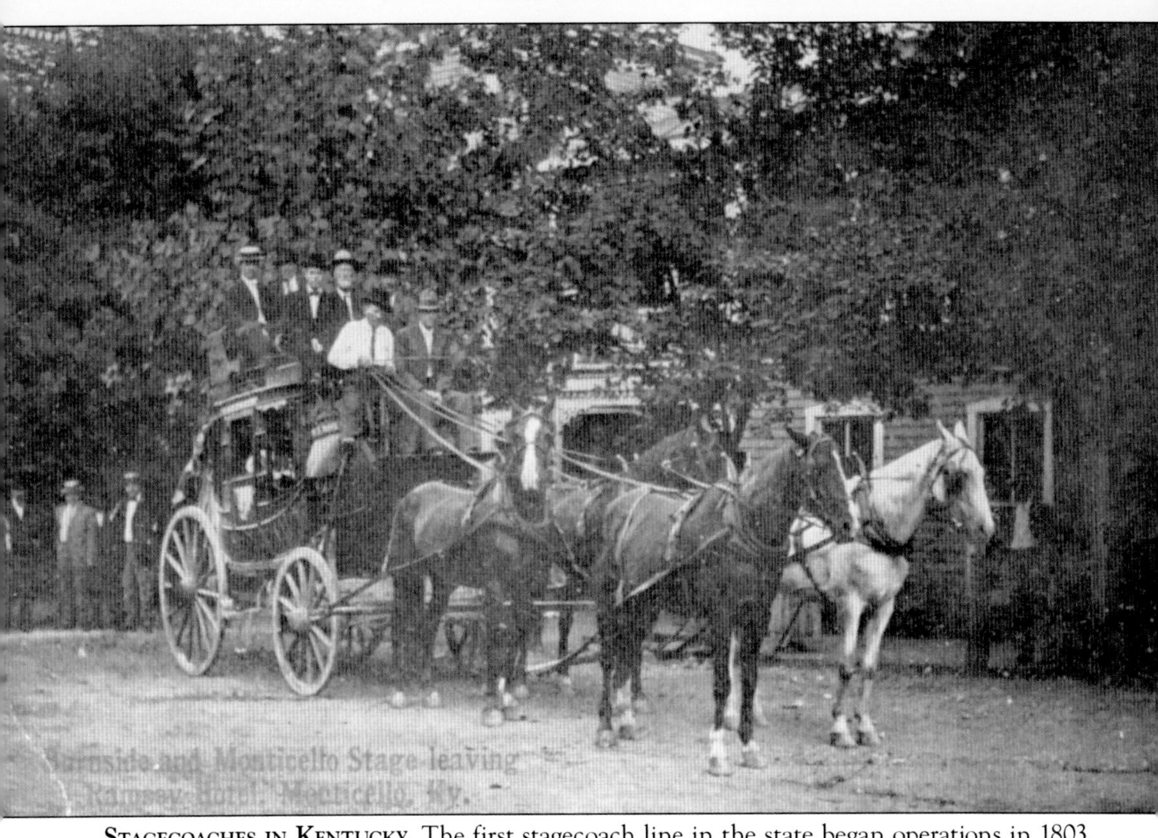

Stagecoaches in Kentucky. The first stagecoach line in the state began operations in 1803. It ran northeast from Lexington through Winchester and Mount Sterling to Olympian Springs, in Bath County, a trip of nearly 70 miles at a time when coaches traveled six to seven miles per hour. Even after railroads spread across the state, stagecoaches were very useful in connecting railroad passengers with small towns and remote resorts. This 1907 postcard shows the Burnside & Monticello Stage Line, with seven men on top of the coach and as many as eight to ten passengers inside. The following advice to stagecoach travelers was published in 1877: "If a team runs away, sit still and take your chances; if you jump, nine times out of ten you will be hurt . . . Don't smoke a strong pipe inside, especially in the morning; spit on the leeward side of the coach. If you have anything to take in a bottle, pass it around; a man who drinks by himself in such a case is lost to all human feeling." (KHS, Graphic5_Box12_392.)

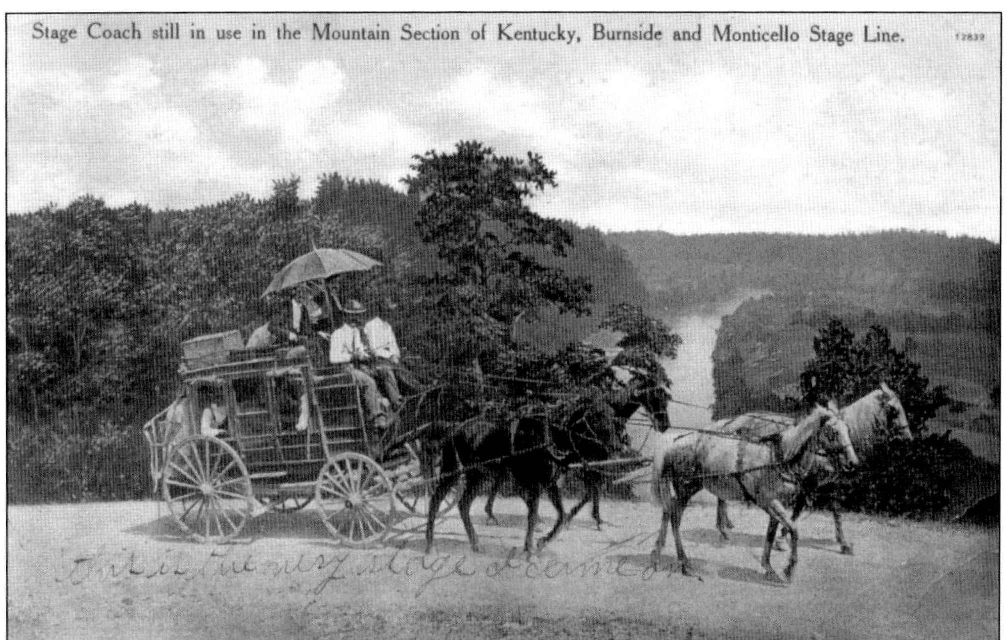

STAGECOACH IN THE MOUNTAINS. This 1909 hand-colored postcard presents a romantic view of stagecoach travel in Eastern Kentucky. From 1896 until 1915, a stagecoach ran from Monticello to Burnside. The route between the two towns made it possible for the citizens of Wayne County to connect with the railroad station in Burnside and provided improved delivery of the US mail. (KHS, Graphic5.Box1.383.1.)

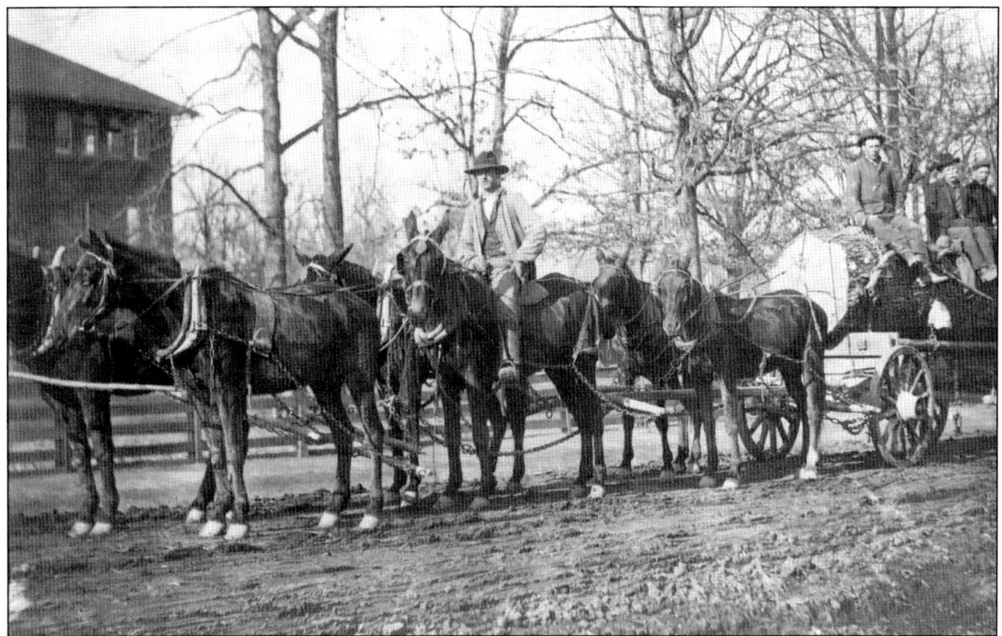

SIX MULES AND A TREE TRUNK. This six-mule hitch had a rider who calmed and encouraged the mules as they pulled a massive tree trunk through the streets of Berea in the 1890s. When it came time to haul heavy loads, mules were favored by many Kentuckians. Jacks (male donkeys) were bred to female horses to produce a mule, which was most often sterile. (Berea College Special Collections.)

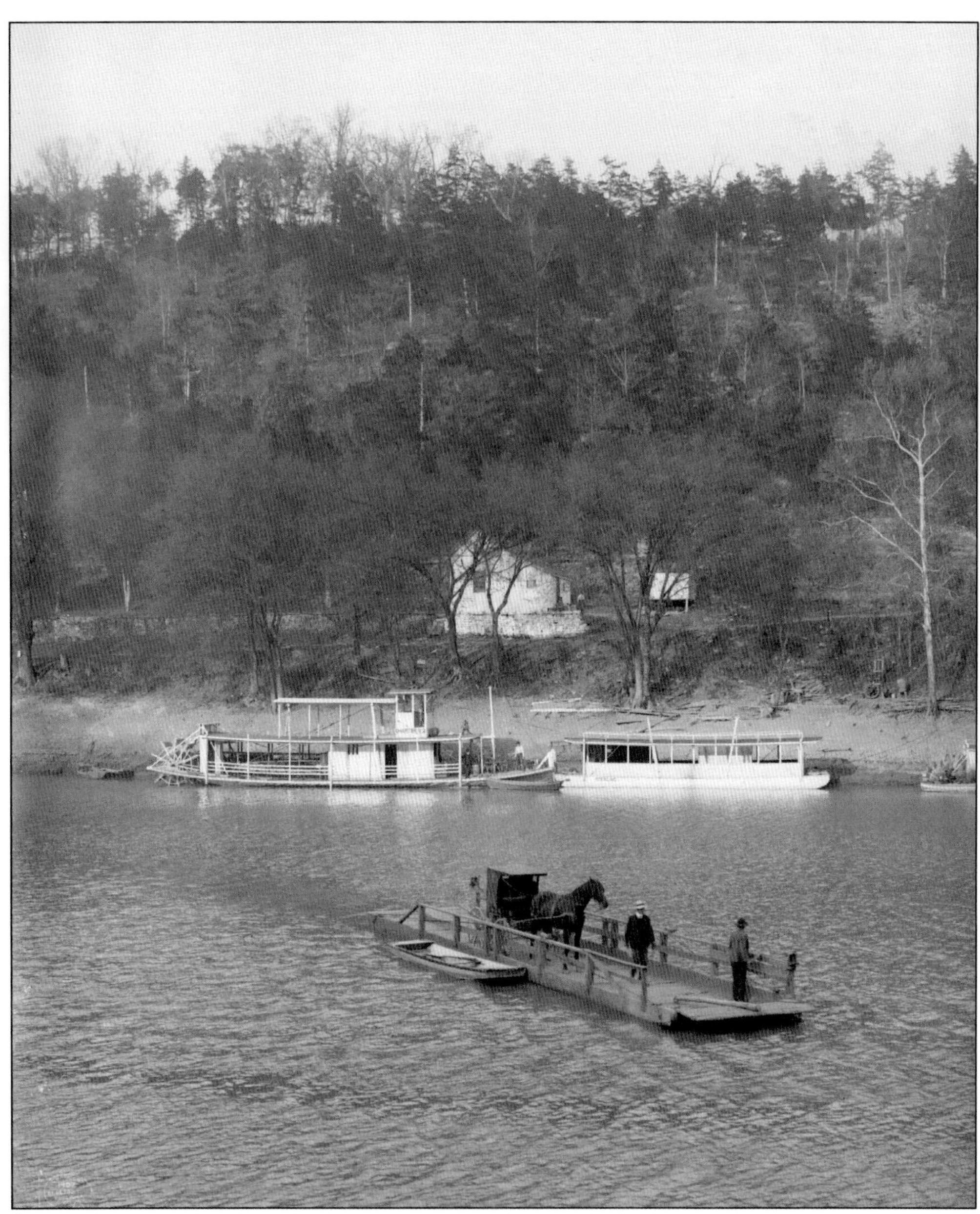

HIGH BRIDGE FERRY. John Filson's 1784 map of "Kentucke" showed four ferries in operation around Lexington. One of them crossed the Kentucky River in the area now known as High Bridge, after the soaring railroad bridge built there for the Cincinnati Southern Railroad in 1877. Before the bridge was built, it was known as the Shaker Ferry, because it was owned and operated by the nearby Shaker community of Pleasant Hill. This 1907 photograph shows a man in a white straw hat with a black "saltbox" carriage that is Shaker in nature. The ferry was guided by an underwater cable. The man at right is holding a tiller that used the current of the Kentucky River to push the ferry from one bank to the other. The cable or rope sunk when the ferry was docked, and, if the passing boats were like the ones seen in this image, they would have shallow drafts that would not foul the line. This is known as a reaction ferry, and it only worked in waters with a steady current. (LOC.)

Two

Farming with Horses and Mules

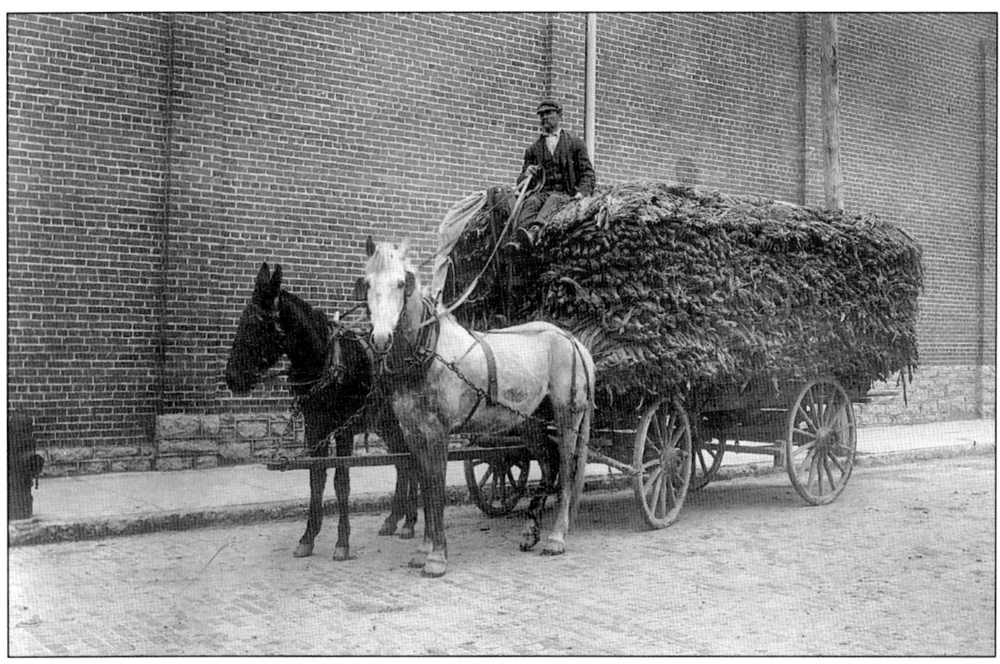

King-Sized Load of Tobacco. For decades, many farmers in Central Kentucky counted on burley tobacco as their cash crop, making a delivery to the tobacco warehouse a cause for celebration. This 1910 photograph shows Charles Henry Kuster at the Paris Tobacco Warehouse. His huge load of burley tobacco is in a wagon pulled by an unusual pair: a white horse and a mule. (Ted and Betsy Kuster.)

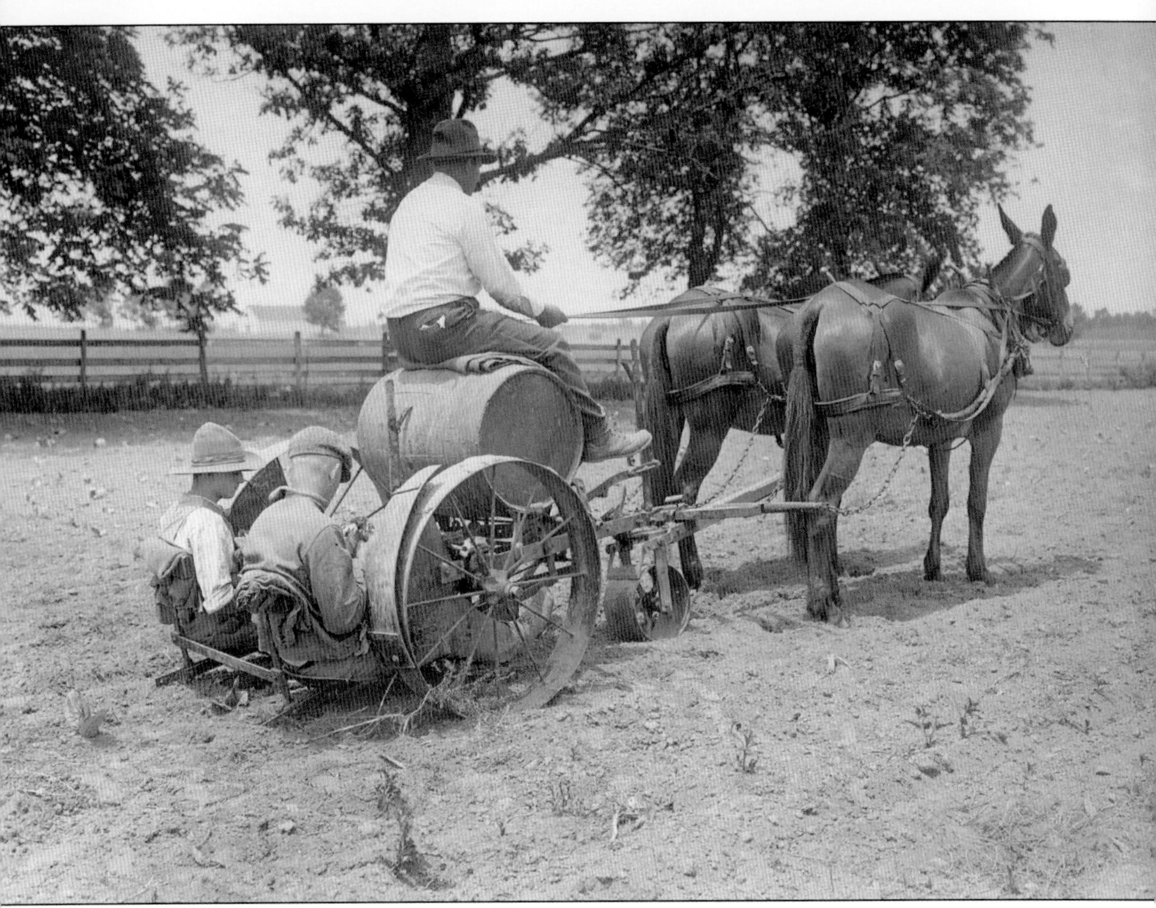

Setting Tobacco Plants. Tobacco plants have to be set out by hand, and the process has not changed much since this undated photograph was taken of a man driving a horse-drawn tobacco setter. The two boys are setting out the plants. The process is essentially the same today, except that the setter is drawn by a tractor. Farmers in the state grow three types of tobacco: burley, dark air-cured, and dark fire-cured. Each type of tobacco is used in a different type of product. Burley tobacco is by far the most prevalent crop, and is grown in 110 of Kentucky's 120 counties. The other two types of tobacco are grown mainly in Western Kentucky. Millions of pounds of tobacco are still grown each year in Kentucky, but the crops are much smaller than they were in decades past. (UK Special Collections.)

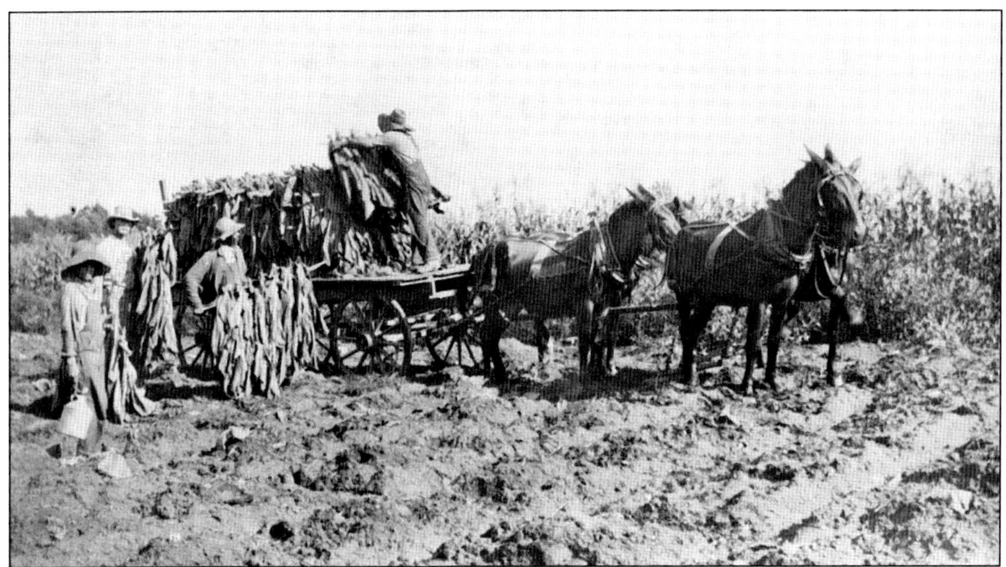

Loading Tobacco. In this 1916 photograph, three men load sticks of tobacco onto a mule-drawn wagon on a farm in Henderson County. At left, a boy is carrying what looks like refreshments for the crew. Tobacco is harvested by cutting the stalks of the plants at ground level and then impaling the stalks on a wooden stake, which is left in the field so the tobacco can begin drying. (KHS, HED.1990ph2.24HED4.)

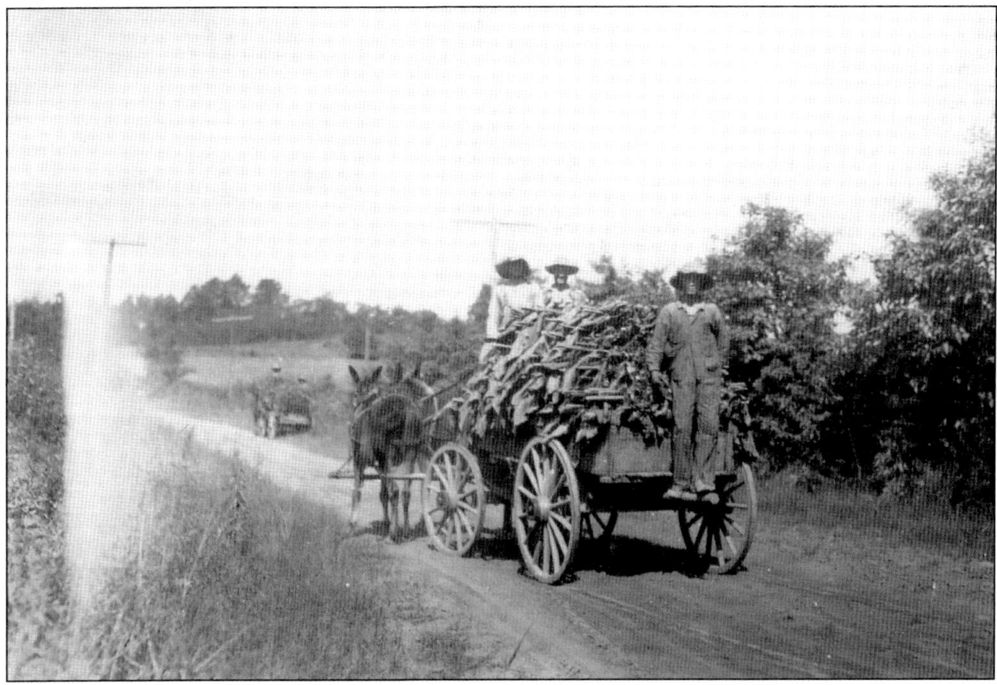

Hauling Tobacco to the Barn. The trip from the tobacco field to the barn was a slow one for these men in their mule-drawn wagon. They were photographed near Hebbardsville in 1916. Even today, heavily laden wagons drawn by tractors instead of mules or horses can back up traffic for miles on two-lane roads as they move their precious cargo from the fields to the barns each fall. (LOC.)

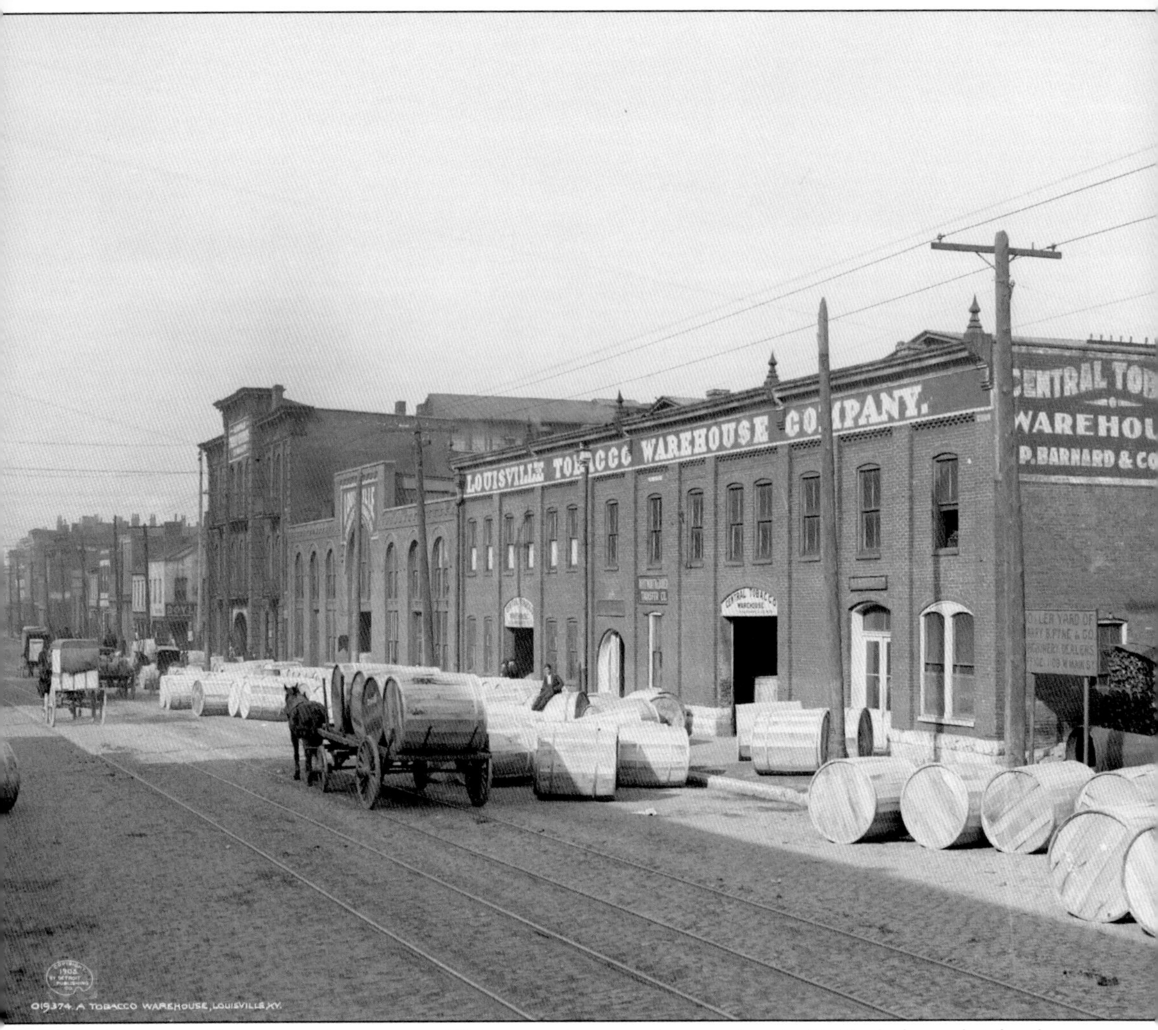

TOBACCO HOGSHEADS DELIVERED. This great photograph was taken in 1906 of a large, brick tobacco warehouse labeled "Louisville Tobacco Warehouse Company" on the front and "Central Tobacco Warehouse" on the side. Also shown are the surrounding businesses and the street, with several horse-drawn vehicles, including a wagon holding four hogsheads of tobacco not yet unloaded. There are numerous hogsheads in the street in front of the warehouse waiting to be rolled into the building and prepared for sale. Each hogshead of tobacco weighed between 900 and 1,000 pounds. Besides the two white half-moon signs marking the doorways of the Central Tobacco Warehouse, there is a sign over the doorway at center that reads "Whitworth and Dover Transfer Co." At the right end of the building is a boiler yard for another Louisville business. (LOC.)

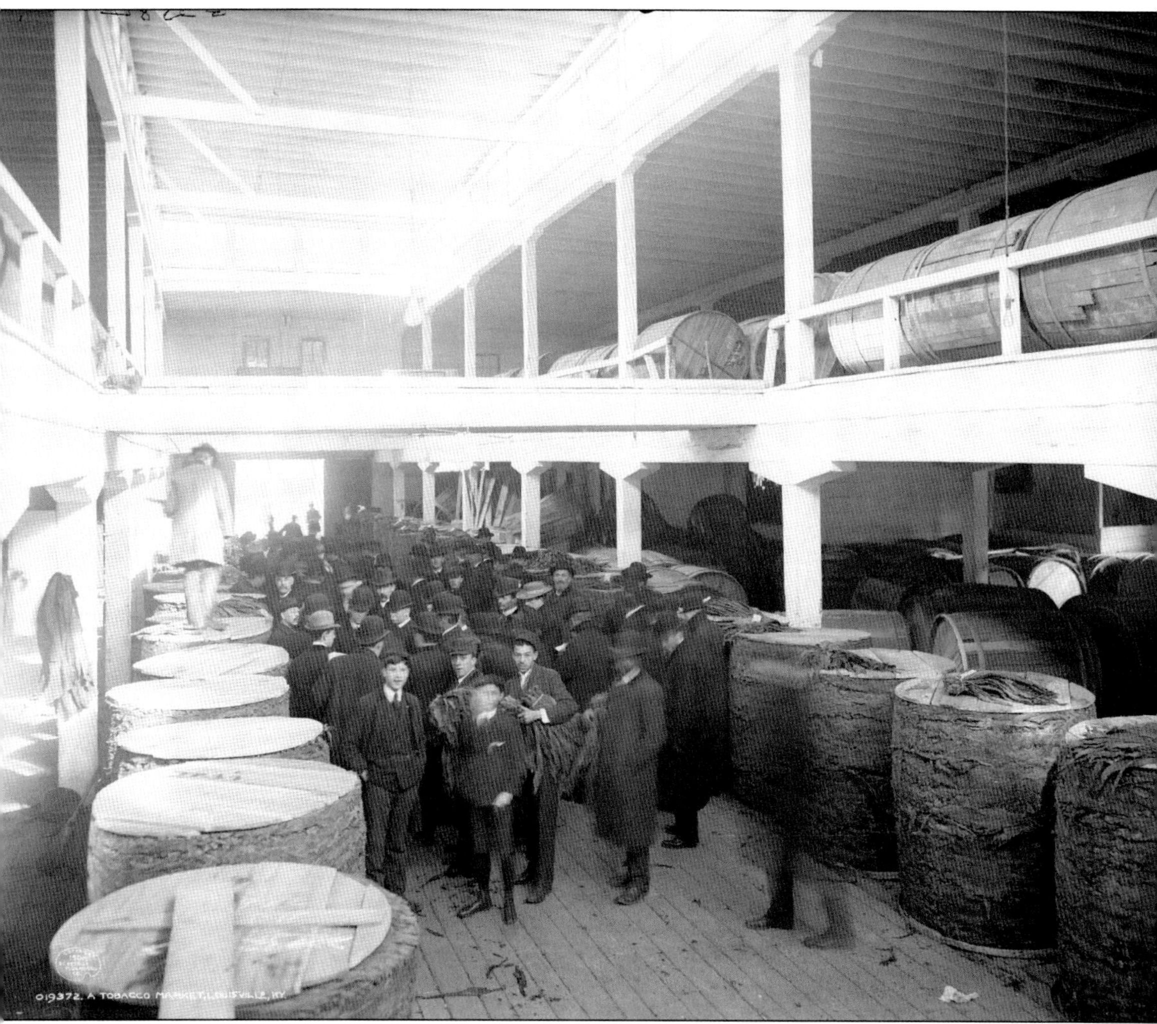

TOBACCO WAREHOUSE INTERIOR. This photograph was taken inside the Louisville/Central Tobacco Warehouse, shown on the facing page. The staves have been removed from the hogsheads of tobacco on the right side of the aisle, and a sample of the tobacco has been laid on top so that prospective buyers can inspect the quality of the product. An auctioneer walked in front of the group of buyers, selling each hogshead. As each sale was completed, a marker was placed on the hogshead indicating the buyer and the price paid per pound. Hogsheads were a good way to move the heavy loads of tobacco before the invention of the gasoline engine and the forklift, as they could be rolled onto and off of wagons using a narrow ramp and rolled into and out of warehouses. (LOC.)

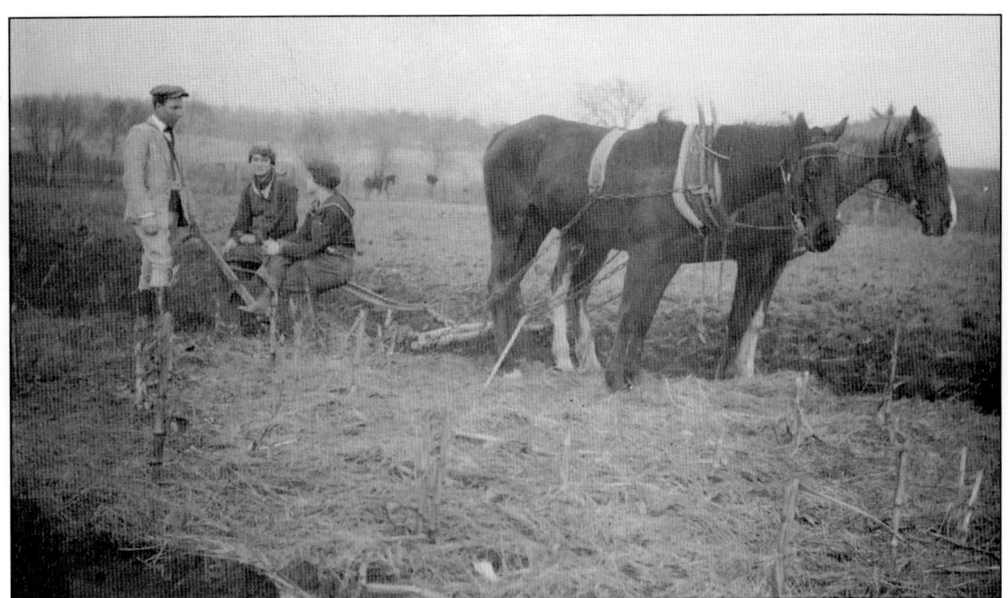

Taking a Break. Perhaps this man and the two ladies sitting on the plow were taking turns guiding the plow to break up the sod in springtime. The man, however, is not really dressed for the work. Or, perhaps, the person who was guiding the plow, pulled by a team of horses, was the one who snapped this undated photograph. (UK Special Collections.)

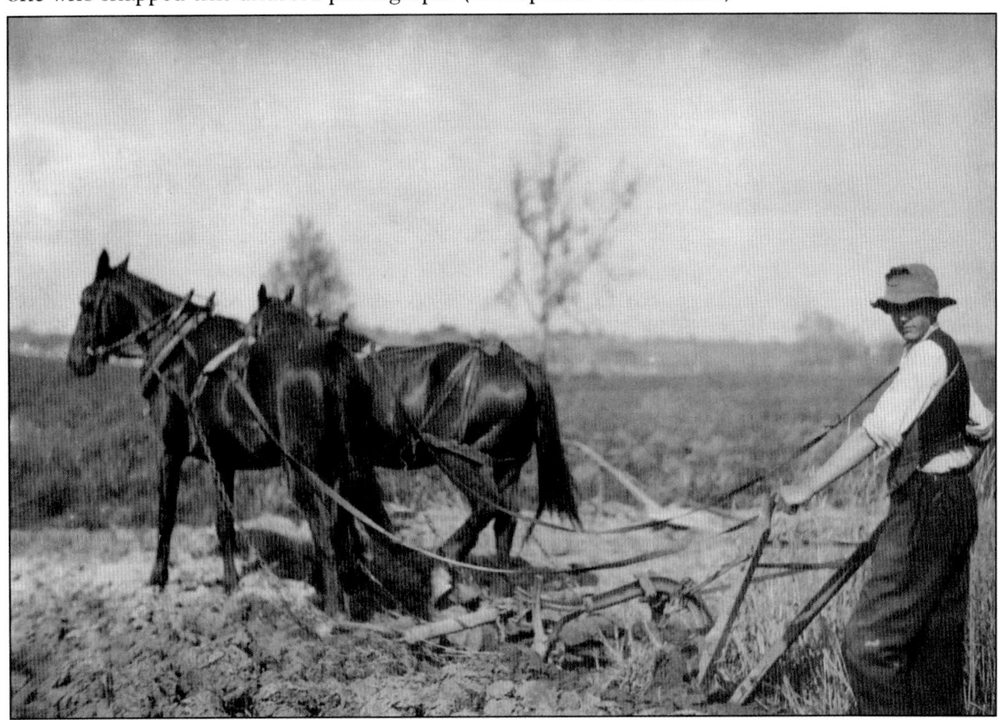

Tilling the Soil. Lummie Durkett is seen near Elizabethtown in May 1916 in one of a series of photographs showing youngsters working. Durkett was using a team of two horses to pull the plow and break up the soil in early spring. Children often worked on their family's farm, sometimes to the detriment of their education, as many farm chores did not fall into the school schedule. (LOC.)

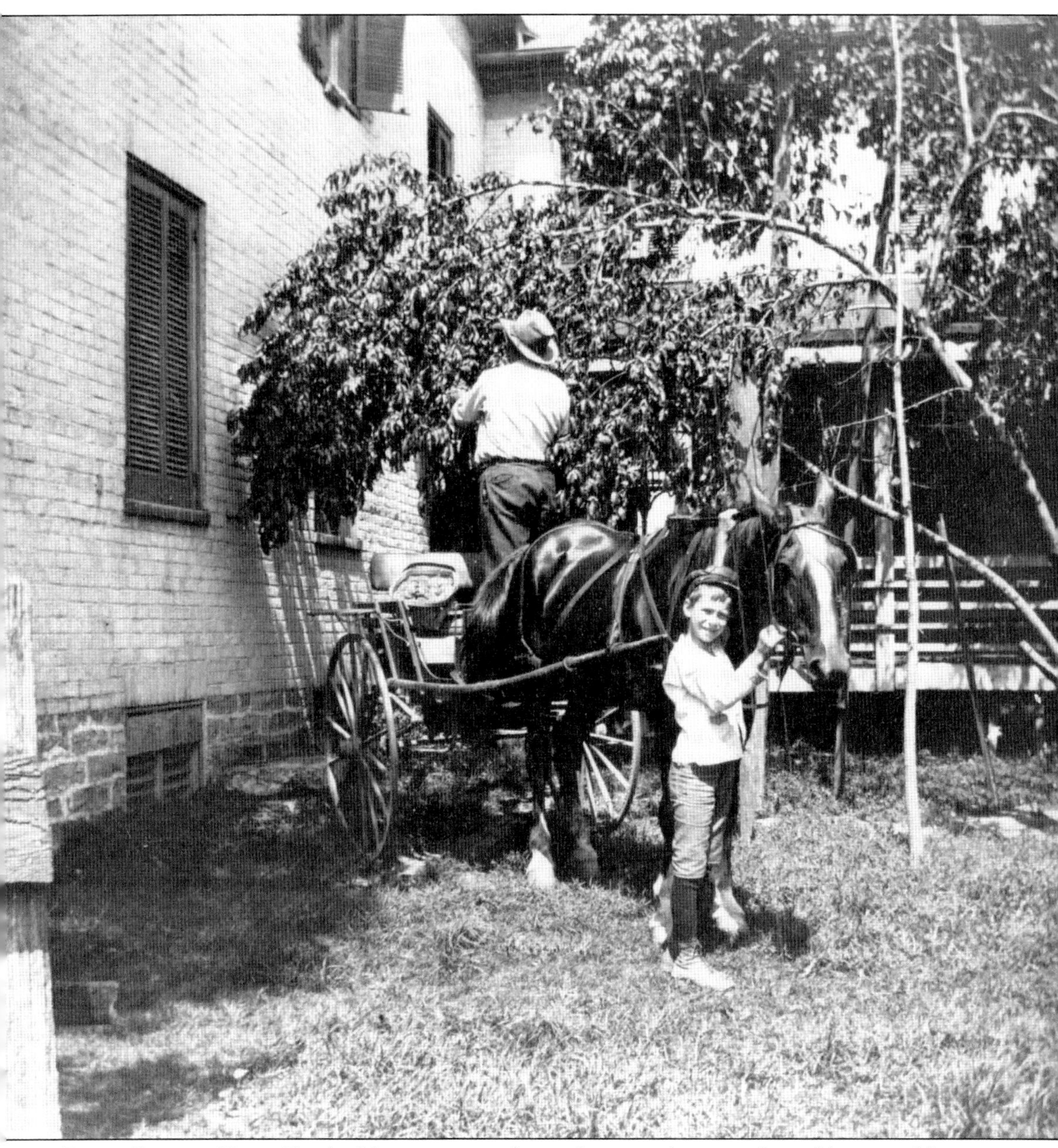

Peach-Picking Trio. Charles Hunsinger stands in a buggy picking peaches, ably assisted by a young boy identified only as Claude and a very calm-looking horse. Claude is holding the horse's head to make sure the buggy does not move while Hunsinger harvests his peaches, probably behind his home, which is brick with wooden shutters and a porch. This 1908 photograph was taken in Jefferson County, near Louisville, which is outside the optimum peach-growing area of the state. Peaches can be grown in Kentucky, but because of the unpredictable winters, the most consistent crops are produced in the western end of the state and along its southern border with Tennessee. Hunsinger's peaches may have ended up as the main ingredient in peach cobblers or peach preserves. (KHS, JFA.1990ph2.10JEFA29.)

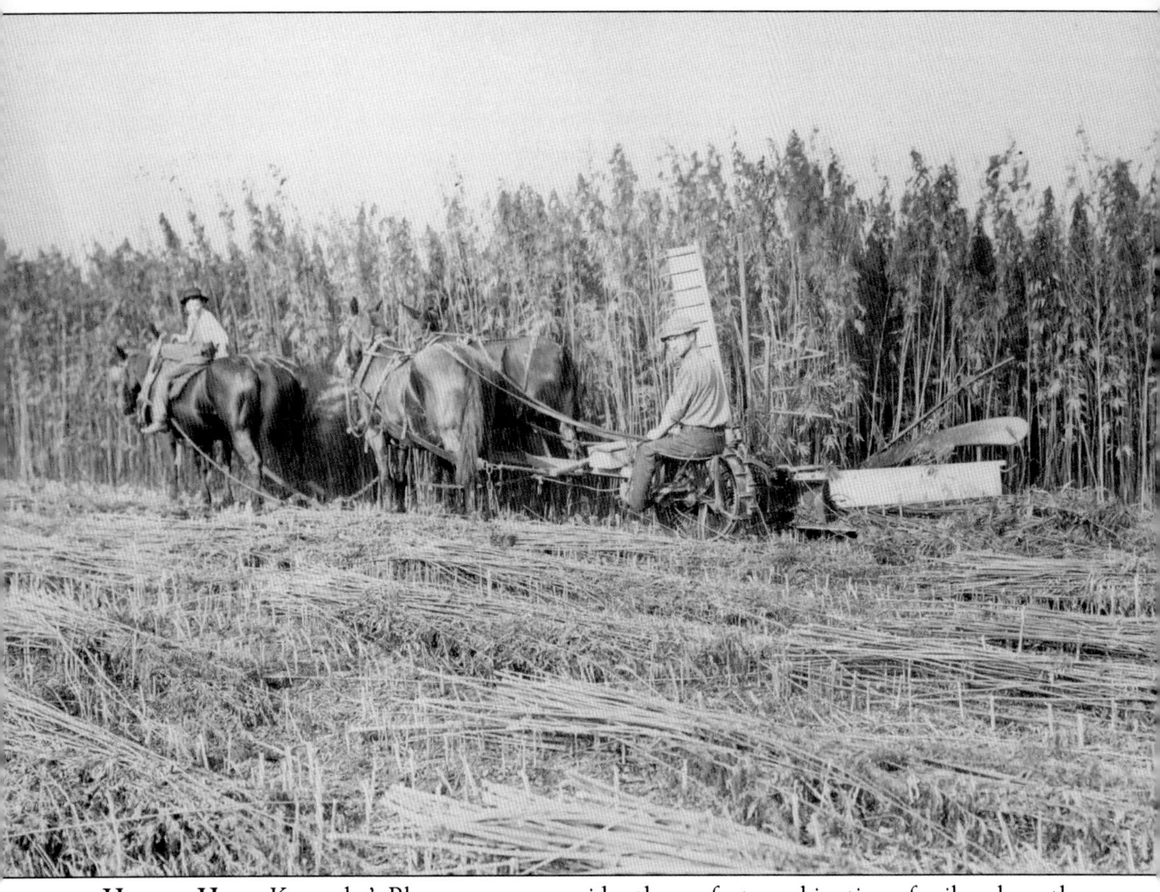

Hewing Hemp. Kentucky's Bluegrass area provides the perfect combination of soil and weather conditions for growing hemp. This was pointed out in a 1942 short film titled *Hemp for Victory* produced by the United States Department of Agriculture to entice farmers to grow hemp, as overseas sources for the crop had been cut off because of World War II. The film explained: "American hemp must meet the needs of our Army and Navy as well as of our industry. In 1942, patriotic farmers at the government's request planted 36,000 acres of seed hemp, an increase of several thousand percent." After more than 65 years of being unable to grow hemp in Kentucky because of its physical similarities with marijuana, there is a movement afoot to allow some monitored growers to once again raise the crop. This 1905 photograph shows a man and a boy harvesting hemp using a mule-drawn self-rake. A self-rake is a combined reaper and mower. (KHS, 1987PH10.12.)

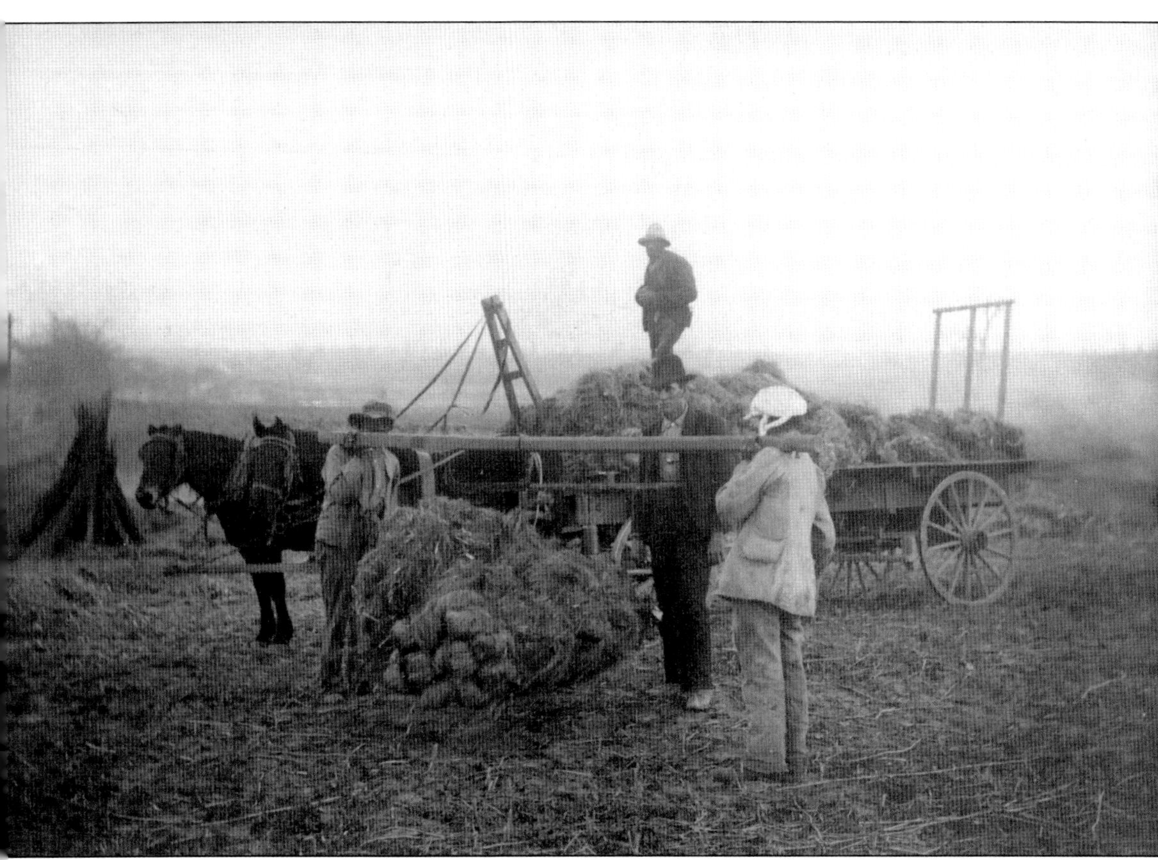

Carting Hemp from the Field. The hemp was cut and placed in shocks, one of which can be seen in the background of this photograph. The product was then allowed to "rett," or begin to break down, before it was gathered and taken to be further processed in horse- or mule-drawn wagons. In this 1905 photograph, the hemp has been bundled and is ready to be loaded into the wagon for transport. Hemp's long history can be summed up in this quote from the 1942 film *Hemp for Victory*: "For thousands of years, this plant had been grown for cordage and cloth in China and elsewhere in the East. For centuries prior to about 1850, all the ships that sailed the western seas were rigged with hempen rope and sails. For the sailor, no less than the hangman, hemp was indispensable." (KHS, 1987PH10.24.)

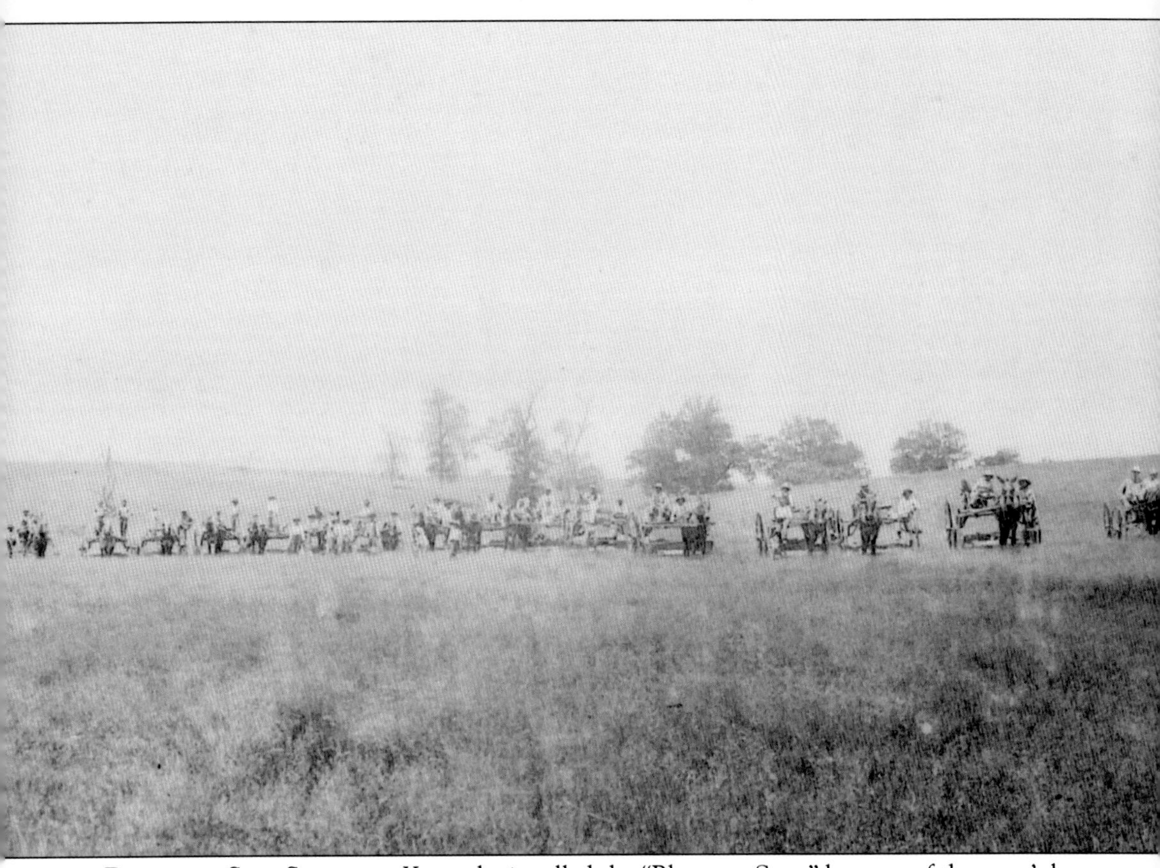

Bluegrass Seed Stripping. Kentucky is called the "Bluegrass State" because of the grass's long history in the state. According to the *Kentucky Encyclopedia*, after cattle owned by the early European settlers polished off the native cane that was a major feature in the early Kentucky landscape, it was replaced by bluegrass seeds imported from Europe. This photograph, taken in Bourbon County, shows men using horse- and mule-drawn box bluegrass seed strippers. There are two men in each of the box strippers, one to drive the horse or mule and the other to draw the seed heads from the steel comb along the front of the box to the back of the box. (Hopewell Museum.)

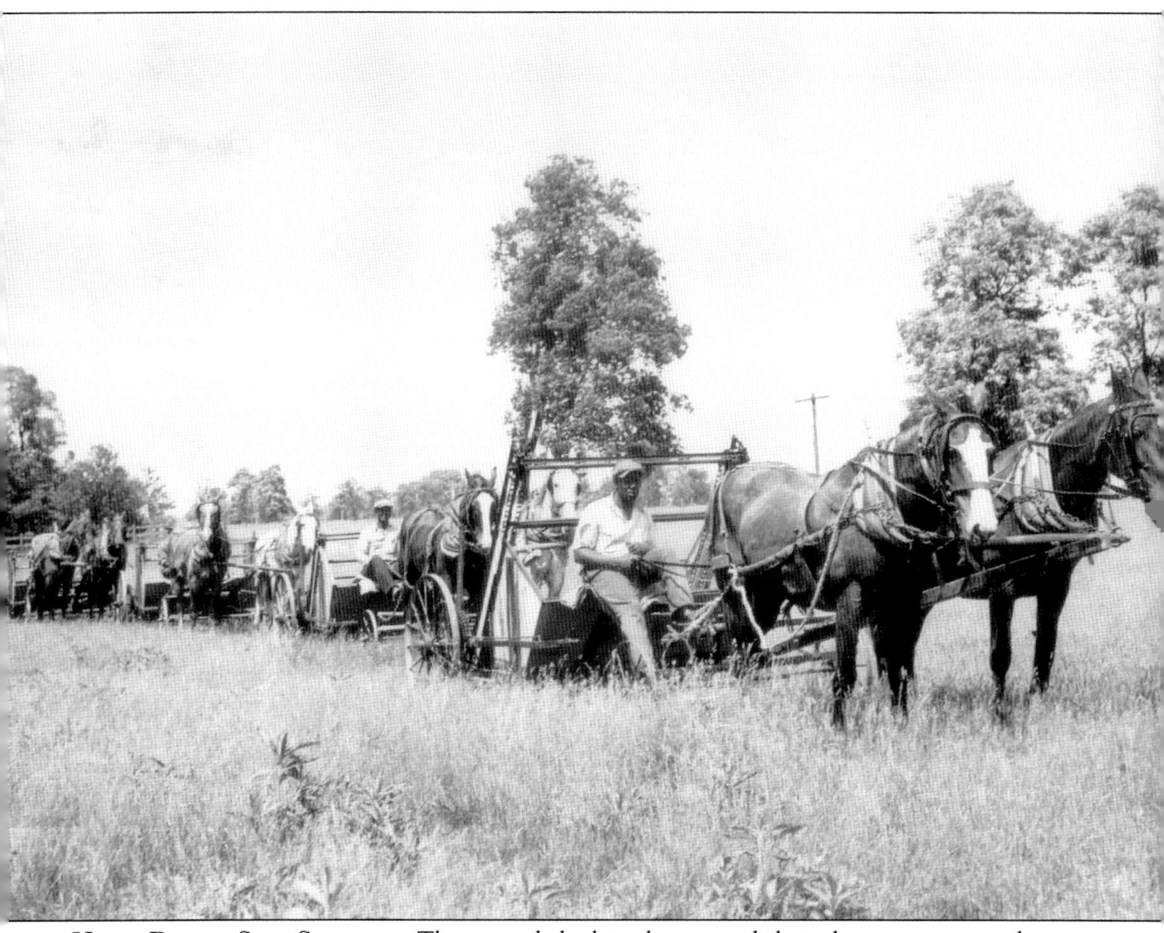

Horse-Drawn Seed Strippers. These sturdy-looking horses and their drivers appear ready to get to work at their task of stripping the valuable seeds from the bluegrass plants in this undated photograph. Bluegrass served as a prime grazing grass for livestock and yielded a cash crop if the seeds were harvested. The harvested bluegrass seeds were an important crop in the state through the 1940s, so it was almost always accomplished using seed strippers drawn by either horses or mules. The seeds had to be dried and processed before they could be bagged and sold. (UK Special Collections.)

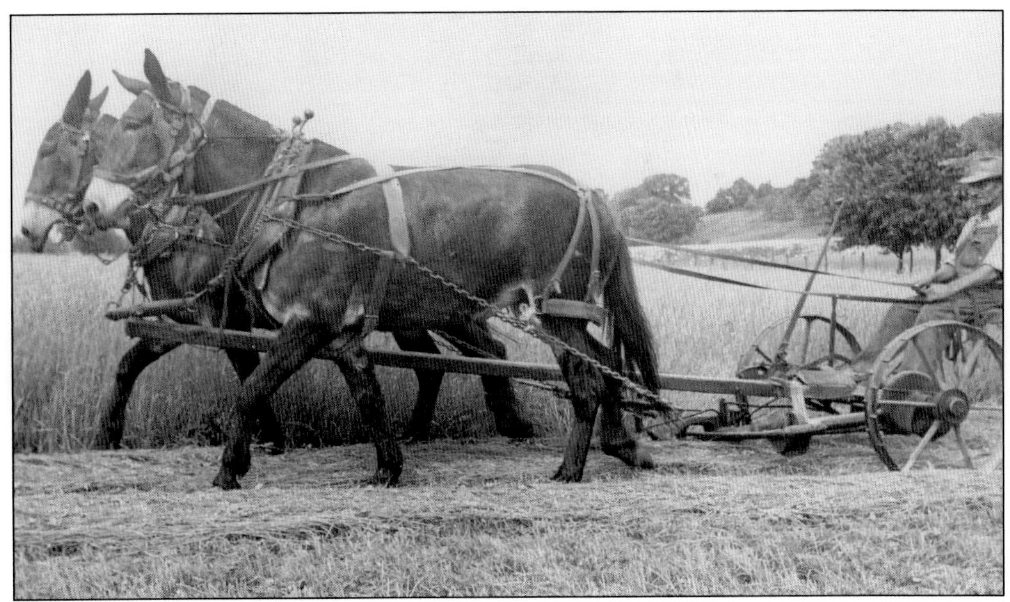

Rudy and Pearl at Work. Mules and horses not only helped farmers plant, cultivate, and harvest their crops more quickly and efficiently than when it was done by hand, but they also added personality to the farmer's life. In oral histories stored at the Kentucky Historical Society, people reminisce about their draft animals, all with names and distinct personalities. (Berea College Special Collections.)

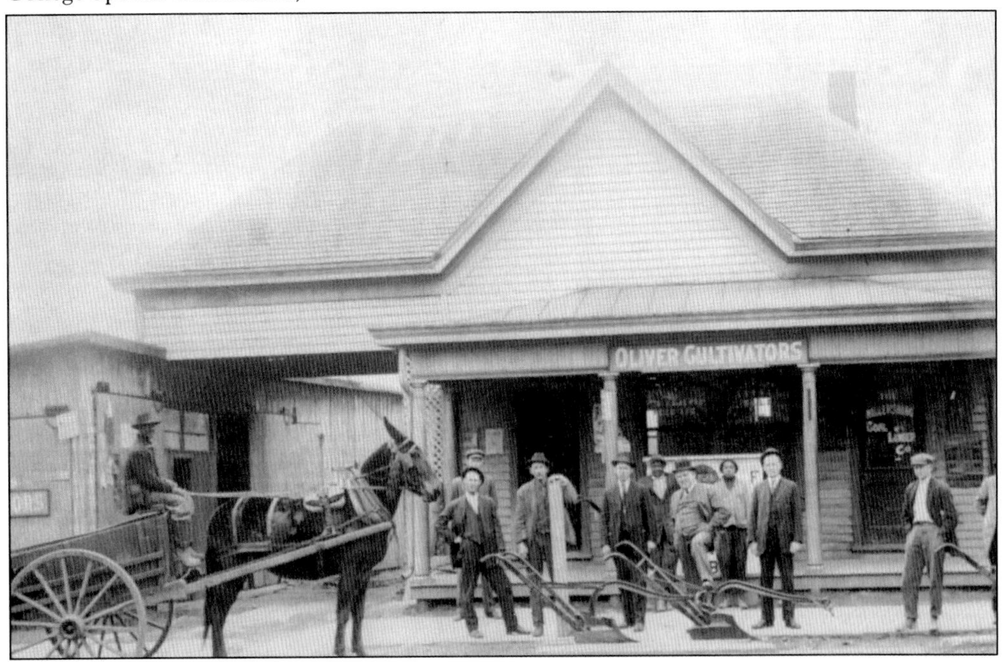

Oliver Cultivators. This photograph was taken in front of the Millersburg Coal & Lumber Company building. The wagon driver is identified as "Mule," and the man in the center of the photograph, standing behind the plow wearing a dark suit, is Will Butler, co-owner of the company. Oliver Cultivators, advertised on a sign above the doorway, were produced by the Oliver Chilled Plow Works in Indiana. (Hopewell Museum.)

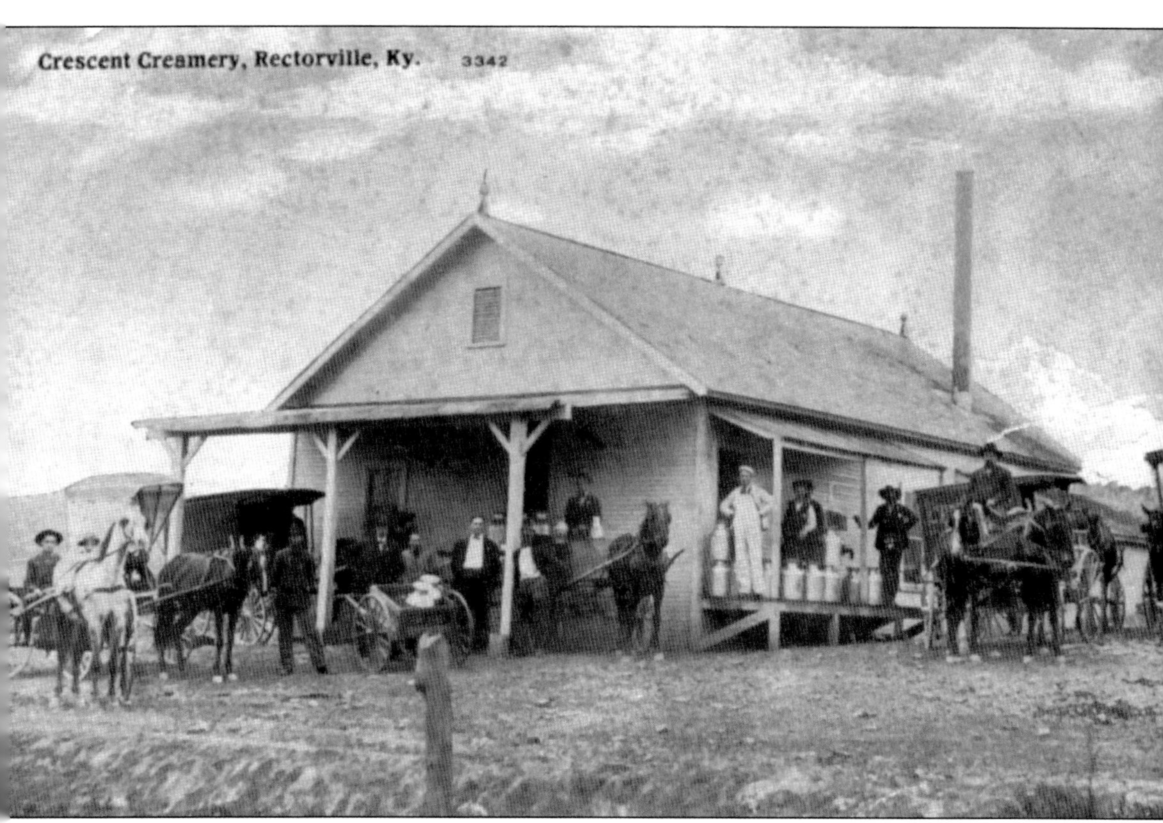

The Crescent Creamery. As can be seen in this 1907 photograph of the Crescent Creamery in Rectorville, which is in Mason County, creameries were often busy places. Streams of farmers in horse-drawn buggies and wagons brought raw milk in big silver milk cans to the creamery to be processed. Each farmer had his name on the milk cans belonging to his farm, which were cleaned and returned so they could be filled again. The creamery's finished products were loaded onto delivery wagons to be taken to stores and homes. There are at least five horse-drawn vehicles in this photograph, including a large creamery delivery wagon pulled by a team of horses at right. Improvements in cream separation techniques and refrigeration allowed creamery businesses across the country to produce a wider variety of products, including ice cream and lots of types of cheeses. (KHS, Graphics5_Box 15_272.)

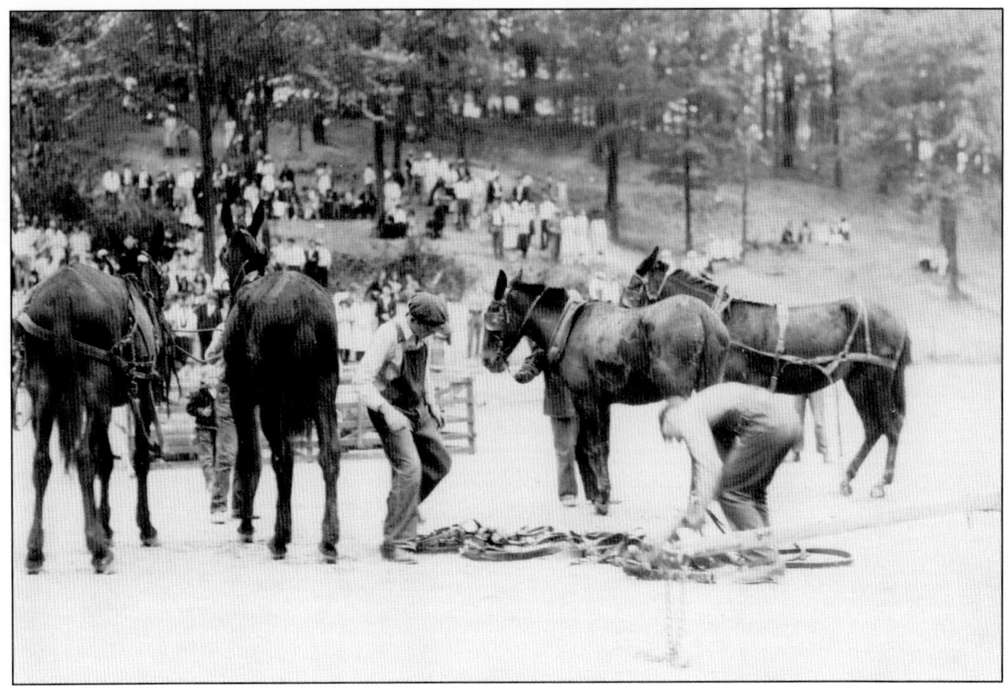

Student Demonstration. At the 1898 Farm Fair in Berea, students demonstrate how to harness mules. A mule is the product of breeding a horse and a donkey. They are said to inherit their sturdy, agile body from the horse and their tolerant temperament and ability to carry heavy loads from the donkey. The phrase "stubborn as a mule" perhaps indicates that their temperament is not always so tolerant. (Berea College Special Collections.)

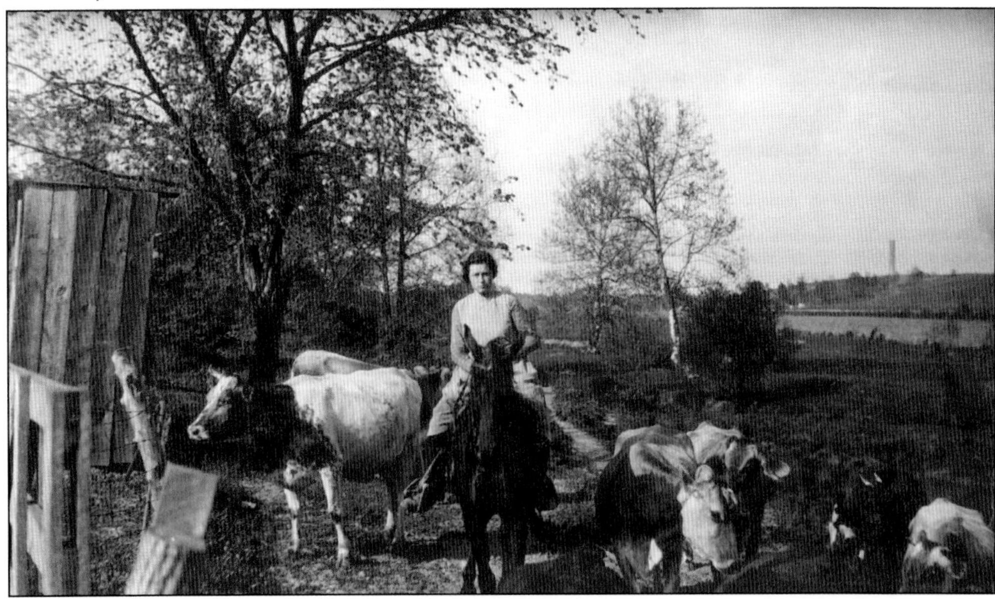

Girl Herding Cattle. A young girl on horseback herds dairy cattle to the barn to be milked. This photograph was taken in May 1916 at a dairy farm near Elizabethtown. Milk and milk products, like butter and cheese, were consumed by the family who owned the farm. They often sold the excess to generate much-needed cash. (LOC.)

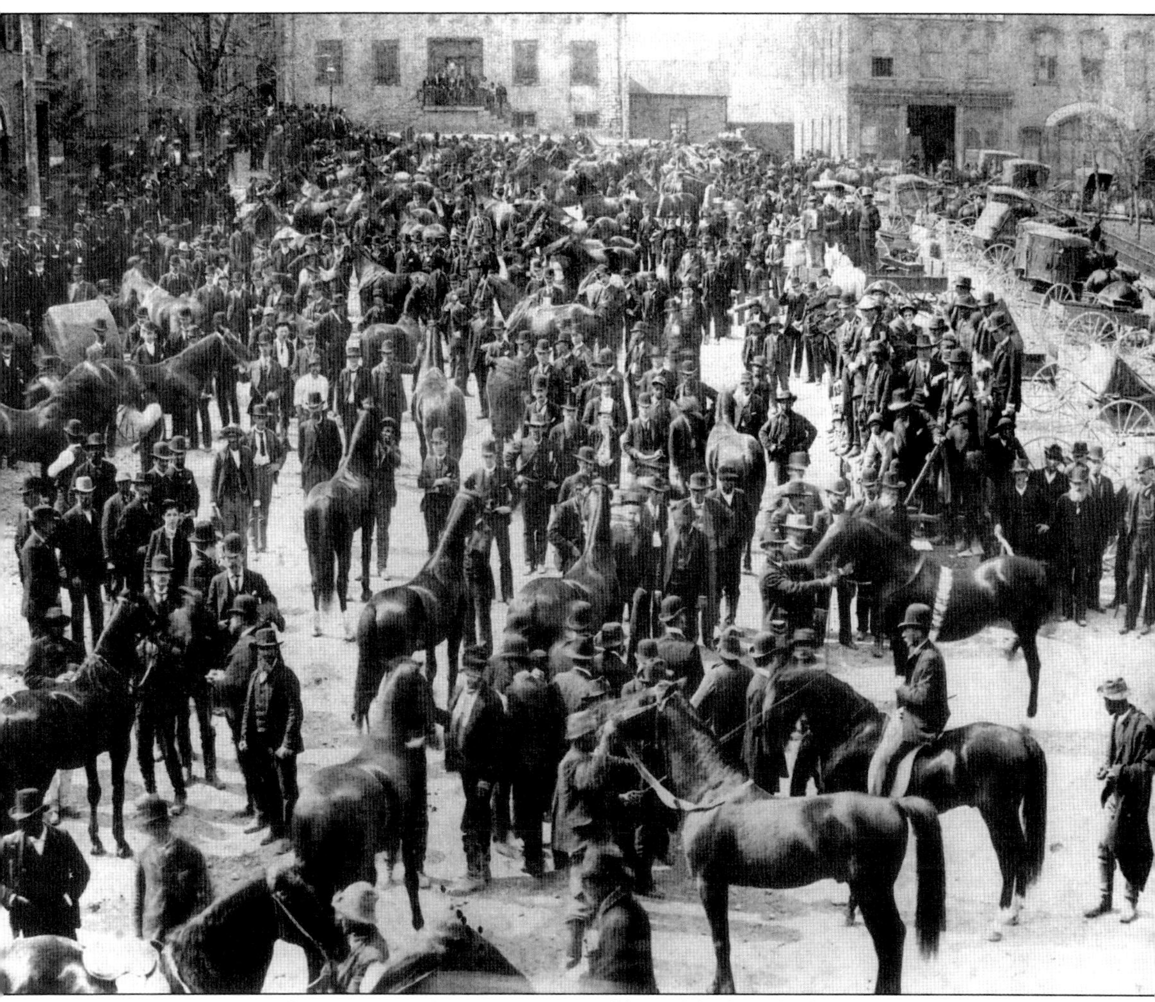

"Stallion Day" on Courthouse Square. Men and boys, black and white, flocked to "stallion day" on Broadway, which runs along one side of the Bourbon County Courthouse in Paris. In fact, there are so many men, boys, and horses in this photograph, probably taken in the 1870s, that one would expect some blurring from movement. Instead, all the people and animals are frozen perfectly in time. Long before the multimillion-dollar equine auctions at Keeneland and Fasig-Tipton in Kentucky, horsemen bought and sold horses and breeding rights at gatherings like this around the state. Even as early as 1800, Kentucky was recognized for the quality of the horses bred in the state, and Bourbon County horse breeders have long been acknowledged as some of the foremost producers of Thoroughbred, standardbred, and saddlebred horses in the world. (Hopewell Museum.)

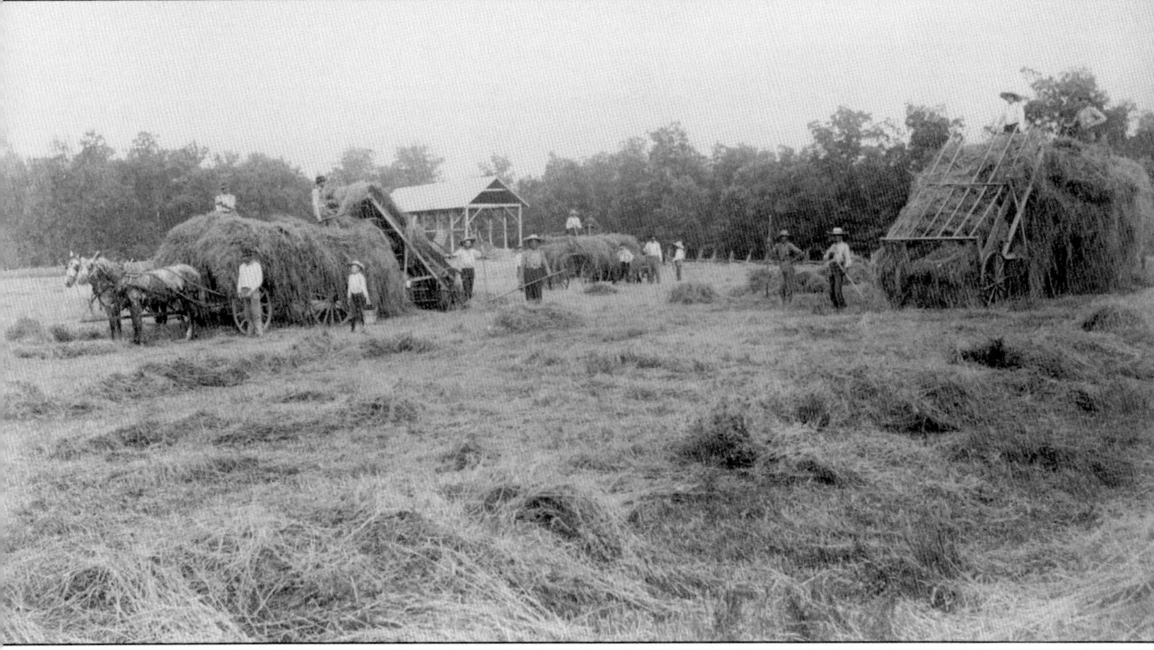

MAKING HAY. Sunshine is critical to good-quality hay, as cut hay is left in the field for a period of time before it is collected. Rain during that vulnerable period can adversely affect the quality of the crop. Hay is fed to animals when they are unable to graze, such as in the winter or when they live in an urban area. This photograph was taken in Hopkins County in 1892. Although the horse- or mule-drawn hay rake had been invented by that time, it looks like this crew is raking the hay by hand. Other photographs in this series show the wagons, piled high with hay, being drawn by horses up to a huge hay shed with a roof but no sides, where the cargos are unloaded. The shed can be seen in the left background. (KHS, 1987ph28.2.3.)

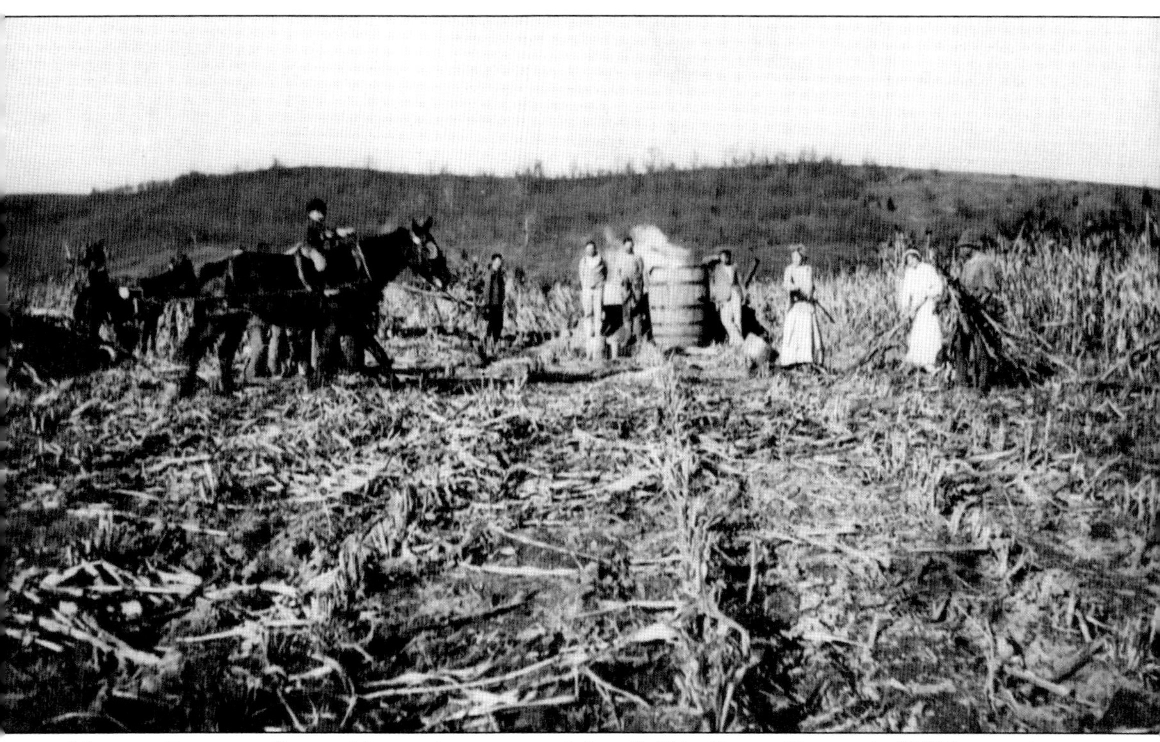

MAKING SORGHUM SYRUP. Men and women work in a field in Boone County in 1917, harvesting sorghum cane and making sorghum syrup using a mule-driven sorghum mill. Sweet sorghum syrup, sometimes called sorghum molasses, is famous in Kentucky for making hot buttered biscuits taste even better. Production of the syrup, which is very labor-intensive, declined after World War I due to a shortage of farm help. According to the University of Kentucky Cooperative Extension Service, in 1899, the first year of statistics on sorghum syrup production, 1,277,206 gallons of syrup were produced. Sorghum syrup is still made in the state today, but the amount is only a tiny percentage of the amount produced in 1899. (KHS, BNE.1990ph2.4BNE28.)

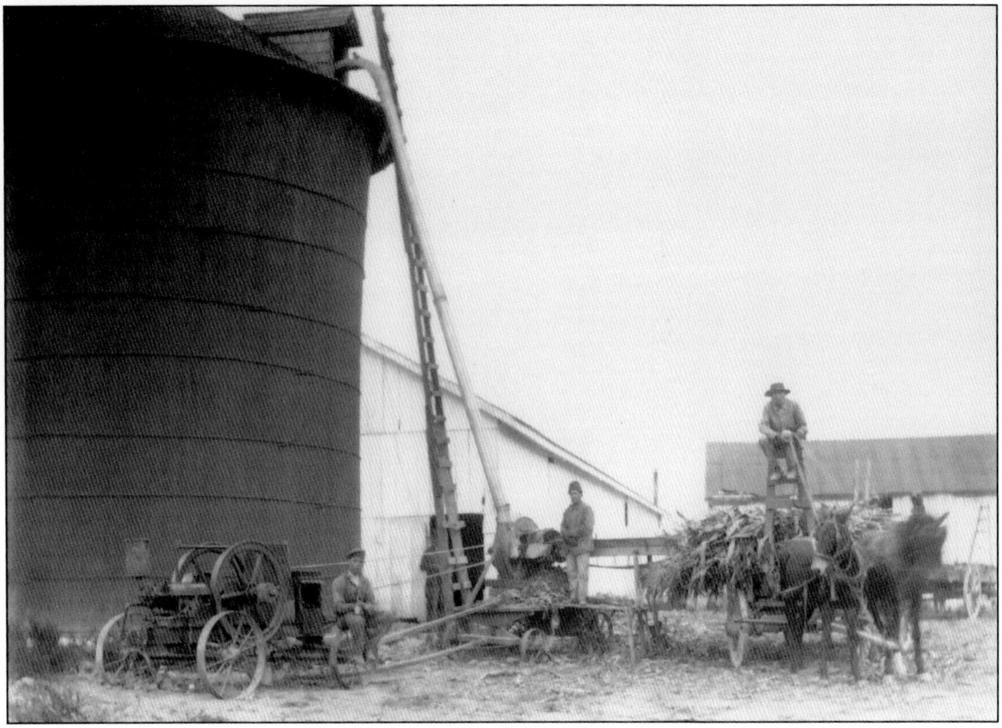

LOADING CORN. A wagon pulled by a team of mules is loaded with newly harvested corn. The corn is being separated from the stalks and then blown up through the tube into a wooden silo. This photograph, probably from the 1920s, shows a time when machines powered by steam were beginning to replace the traditional horse- and mule-drawn equipment. (Authors' collection.)

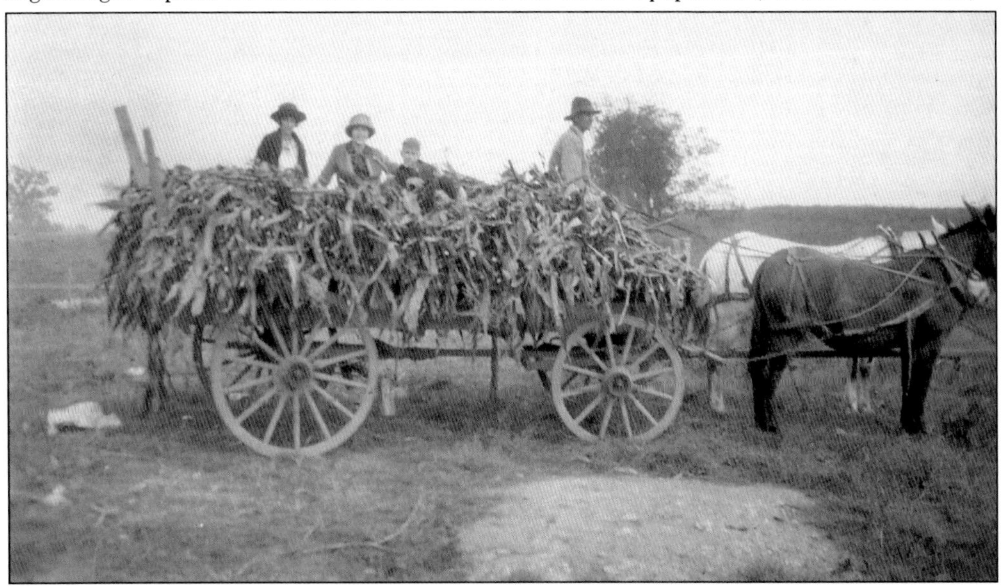

HAULING FODDER. These two young women and a boy are seated in a wagon filled with fodder ready to be taken to the barn. Fodder was stored until winter and then chopped up and used as feed for horses, mules, and cattle, as well as for bedding. This undated photograph was taken in Bourbon County. (Ted and Betsy Kuster.)

Three

In the City

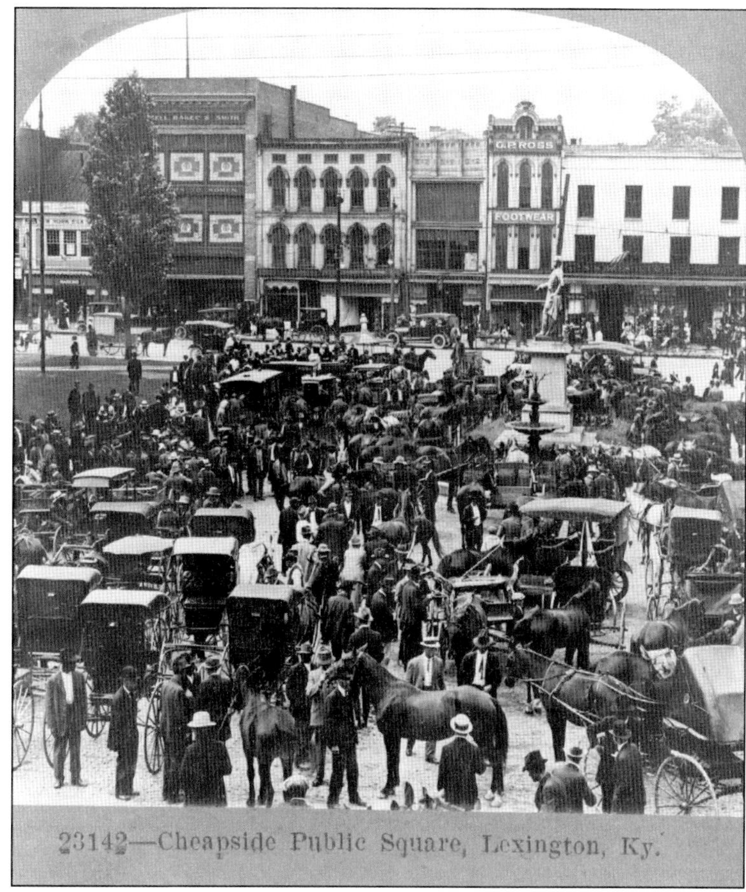

Cheapside Square. By 1920, horses were beginning to share Lexington streets with automobiles and motorized trolleys. But, as this photograph shows, the selling and swapping of horses that went on at the Cheapside Public Square, next to the Fayette County Courthouse, still drew a lot of interest. Such public events eventually disappeared from the centers of towns, as did the horses themselves. (LOC.)

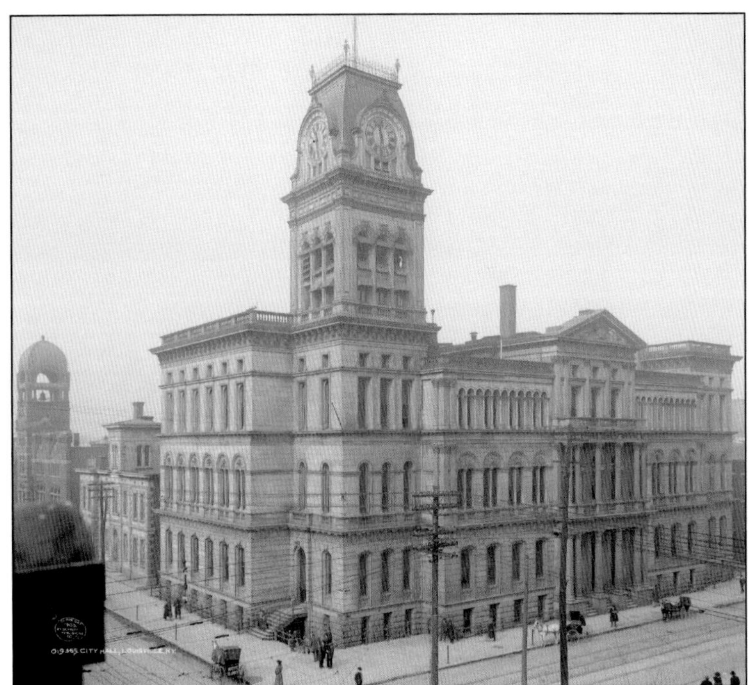

LOUISVILLE'S CITY HALL. After the Civil War, Louisville began its climb as the state's fastest-growing and most progressive city. Its leaders wanted a city hall that reflected the town's new stature, so they had this impressive edifice built of Indiana white limestone. The building, which is still in use today, was completed in 1873. This photograph was taken in 1906, when horses still dominated the city streets. (LOC.)

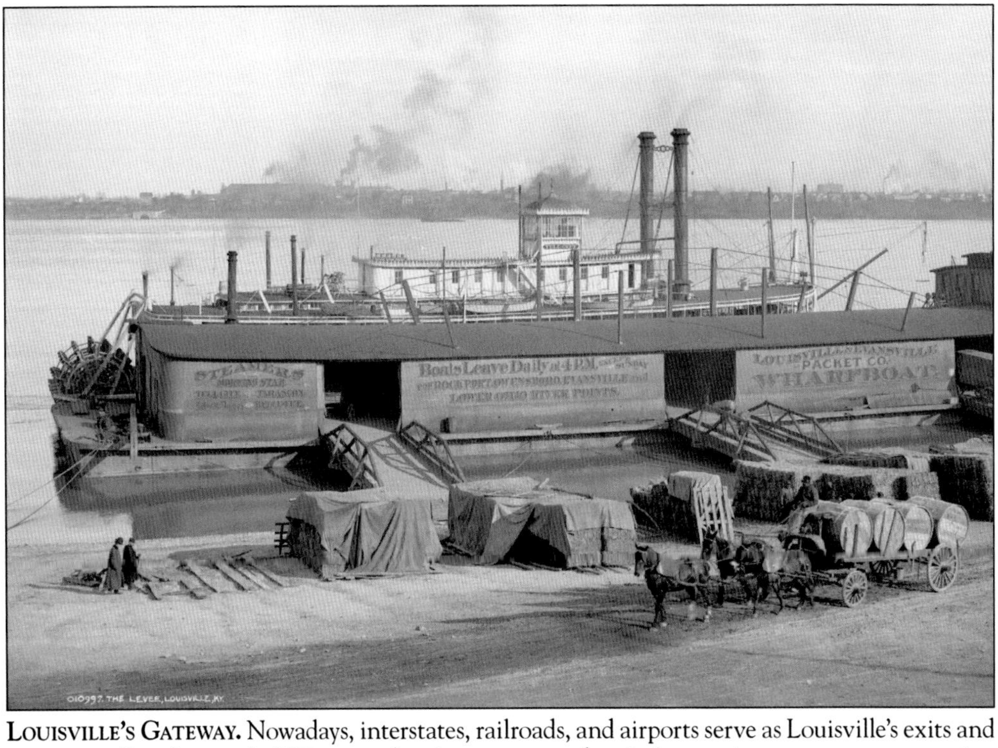

LOUISVILLE'S GATEWAY. Nowadays, interstates, railroads, and airports serve as Louisville's exits and entrances. But, for nearly 200 years, the river port was the city's most important transportation link. This 1900 photograph shows a three-horse rig, or troika, pulling a wagon loaded with huge hogsheads of what is probably tobacco. The stern-wheeler moored behind the Louisville & Evansville Packet Company's floating wharf is possibly the *Georgia Lee*. (LOC.)

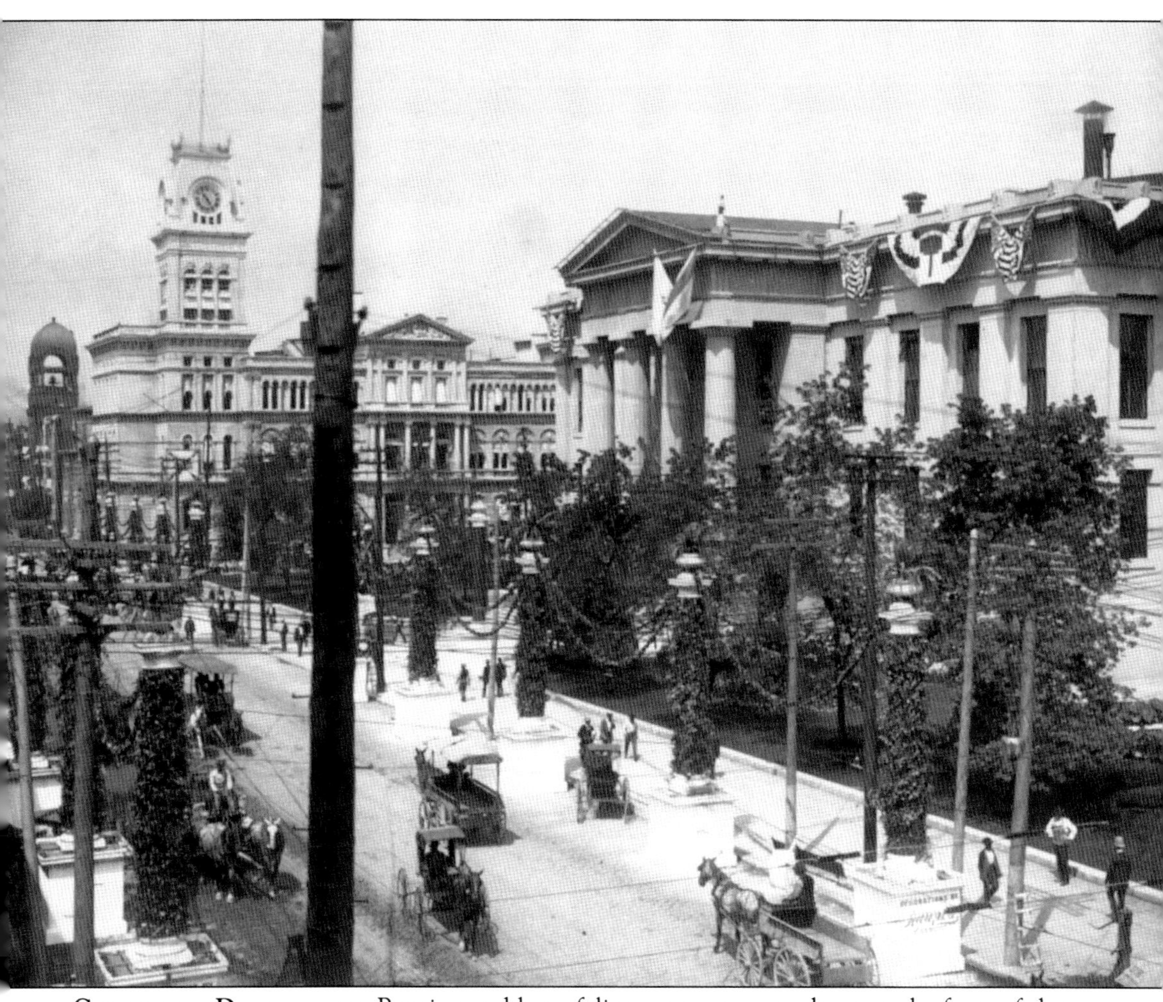

CENTENNIAL DECORATIONS. Bunting and huge foliage arrangements decorate the front of the Jefferson County Courthouse in honor of the nation's centennial. The buggies and tradesmen's wagons on West Jefferson Street are not as numerous as one would expect for a weekday, so it is likely a weekend, probably a Saturday. Construction on the courthouse was begun in 1837, but local government did not move in until 1842. When it was originally built, it was hoped that it would become Kentucky's statehouse, but Frankfort was able to fend off all attempts to move the state capital. The horses in this photograph seem to be plodding along at a sedate walk, which was the usual speed for city streets. However, there were some exceptions. Speed limits, set by municipal laws, were very hard to enforce, since there was no effective way to measure illegal speed. Prosecutions for "furious driving" were occasionally made when horses were found to be frothing at the mouth. (LOC.)

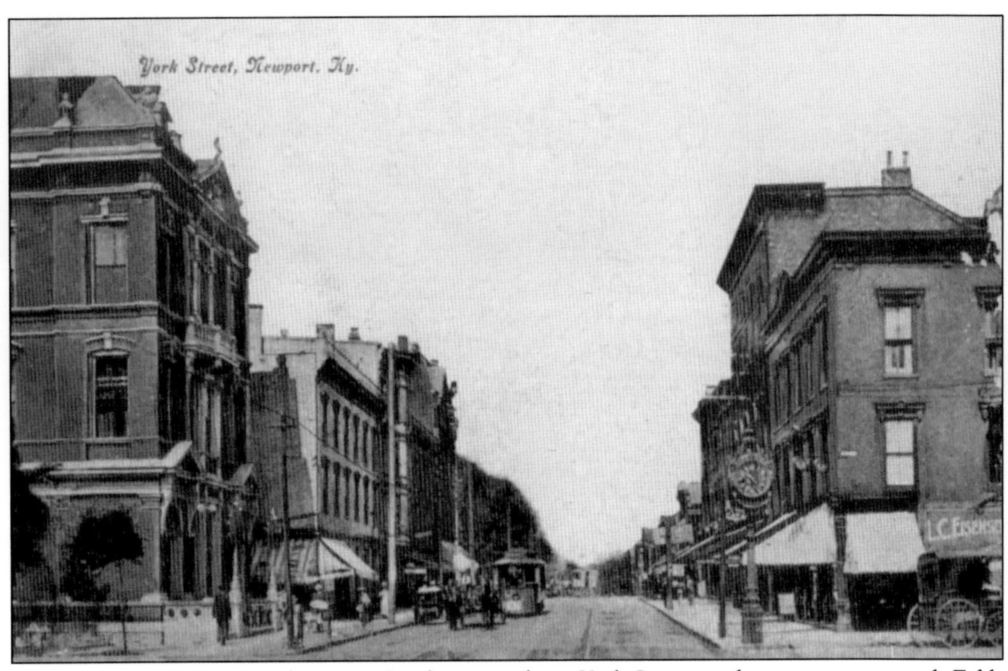

An Infamous Street in Newport. Looking north on York Street at the intersection with Fifth Street in 1923, there is no hint that this thoroughfare would become one of the most infamous streets in Kentucky's famous "Sin City." During Prohibition and especially after World War II, gambling and organized crime thrived in Newport. But, beginning in the 1970s, the city cleaned itself up, and it is once again a successful "family" town. (KHS, CAM.1990ph2.a9CAM1.)

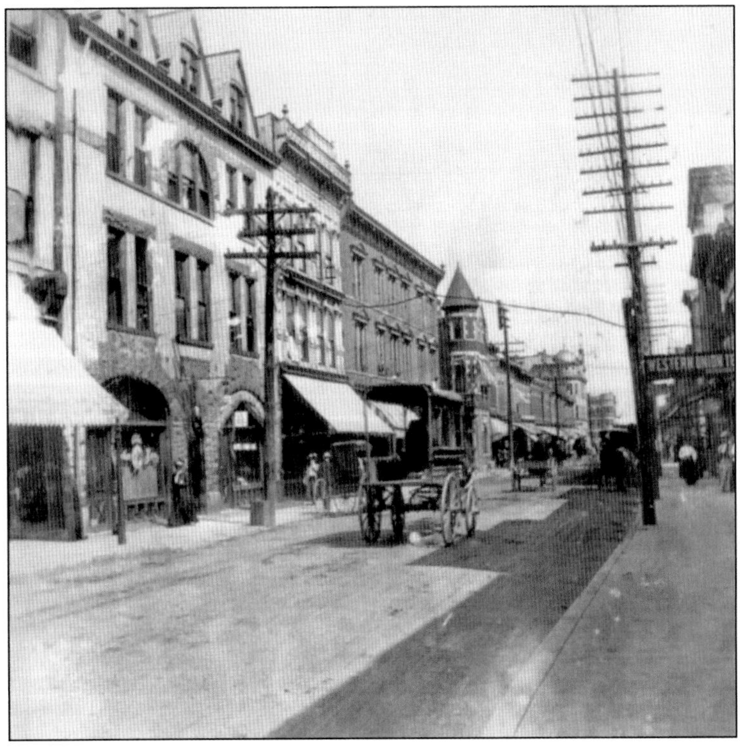

Main Street in Paris. The town of Paris was established in 1789, and its main street was laid out soon after. That is probably why it is so narrow by modern standards. In 1909, when this photograph was taken, the population was about 5,800. Many fine Victorian buildings had been erected, like the Fordham Hotel, to the left of the slow-moving delivery wagon. (Hopewell Museum.)

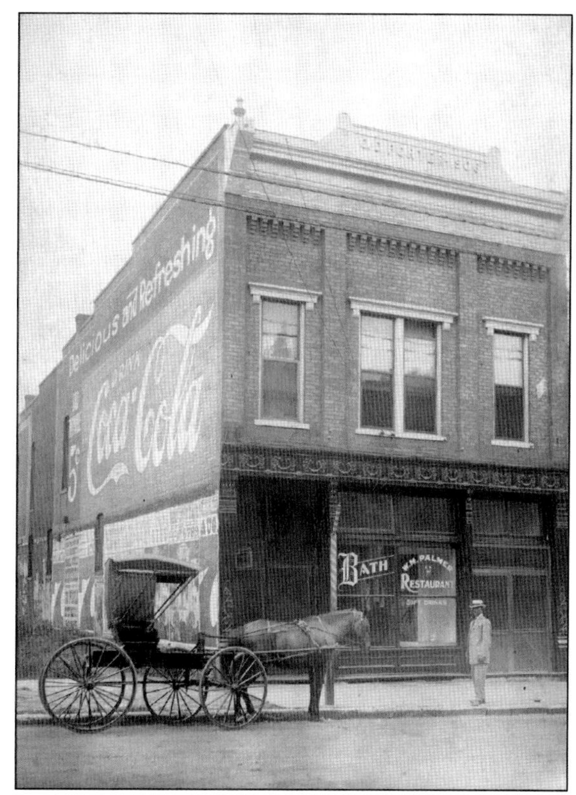

Physician and Leader. The O.D. Porter Building in Bowling Green was built in 1906 for African American physician Otho D. Porter. Born in Logan County in 1864, Porter established his medical practice in Bowling Green and was president of the National Medical Association and the Kentucky Medical Society of Negro Physicians and Dentists. Dr. Porter is pictured with a quality carriage and a fine horse, important parts of a doctor's practice. (WKU Special Collections.)

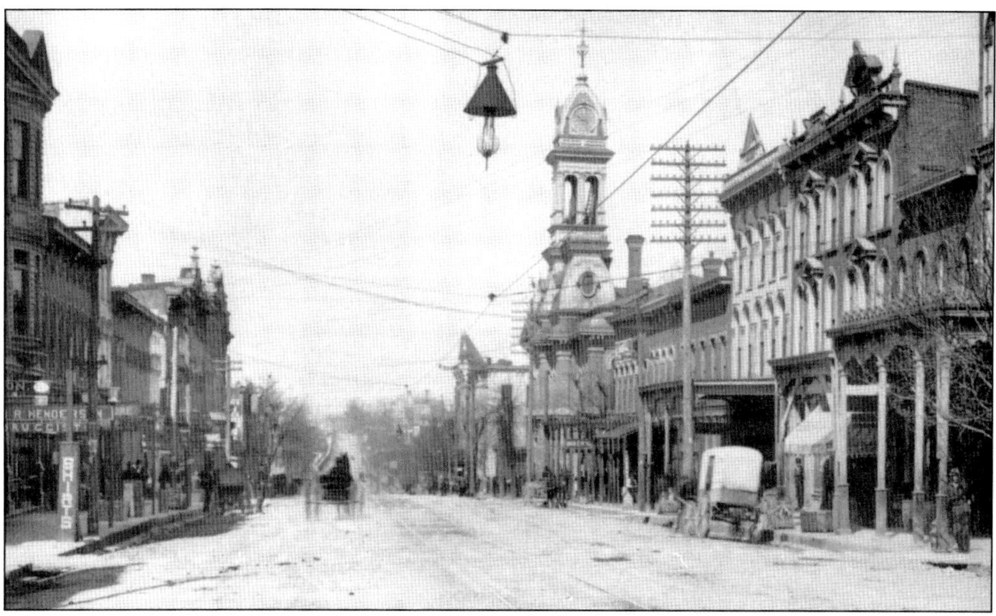

Main Street, Georgetown. This late-1890s or early-1900s photograph is looking west on Main Street in Georgetown. The tower of the Scott County Courthouse, built in 1877, can be seen on the right side of the street. The wide, dirt street has trolley tracks running down the middle and an early electric streetlamp hanging overhead. The usual array of wagons and buggies is also present. (UK Special Collections.)

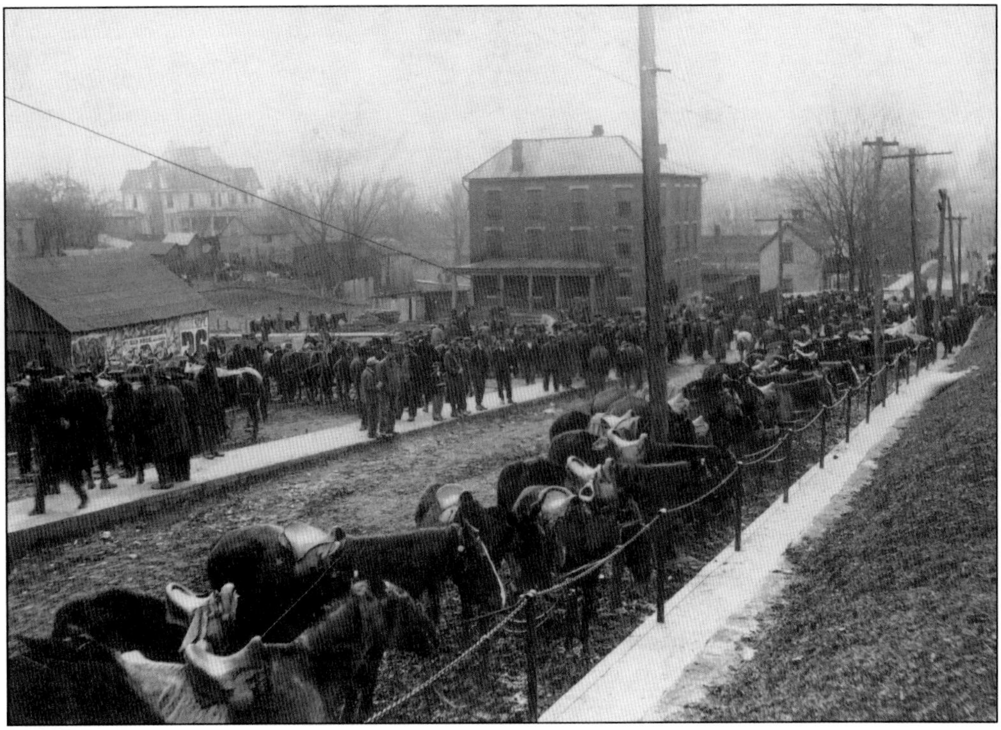

LAUREL COUNTY COURT DAY. The long row of saddled horses hitched to a fence on Jockey Street in London is a sign that it is Court Day. The occasion originated in the early 1800s, when the Kentucky General Assembly decreed that each county should meet monthly to hold court and decide on business. It became the highlight of the month for many of the county's residents. This photograph shows a 1918 Court Day. (KHS, 1999PH10.24.)

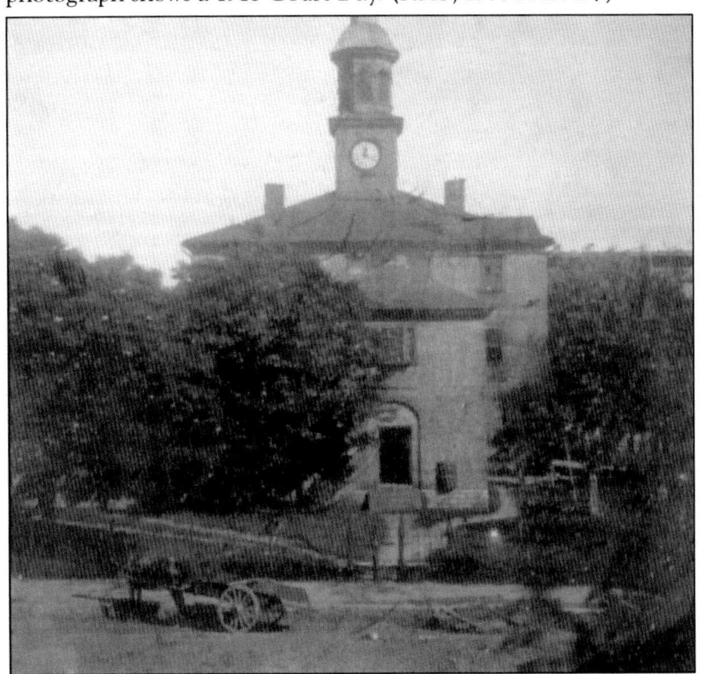

LEXINGTON COURTHOUSE. This very early bromide photograph, possibly from the 1880s, shows the brick Fayette County Courthouse's back entrance, as seen from Short Street. The building burned down in 1897, and many records were destroyed. The carriage and the dirt street are typical of the day. (UK Special Collections.)

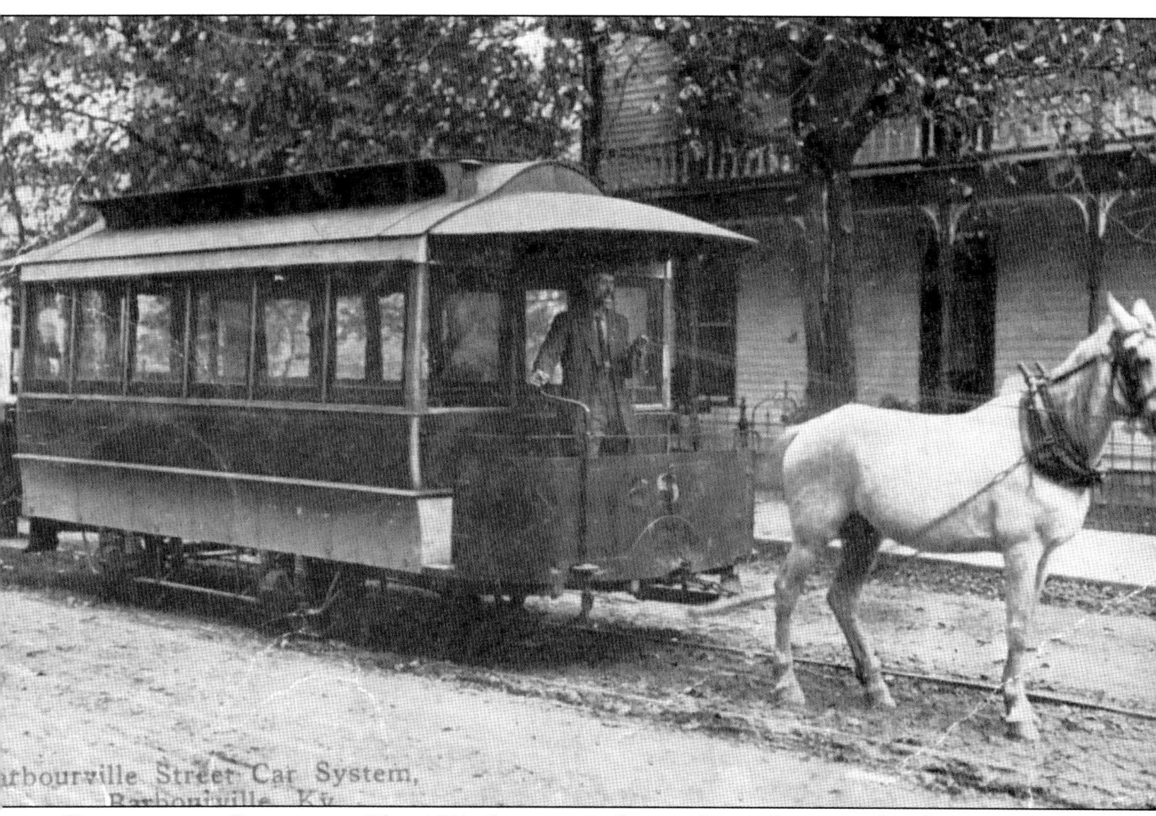

BARBOURVILLE STREETCAR. This 1914 photograph shows a horse-drawn enclosed streetcar in Barbourville. The driver has the reins in his left hand and the crank that applies the brakes in his right. Most streetcar images of the time show a two-horse rig. Note the recessed tracks in the street. The streetcars traveled at six to eight miles per hour and were considered safer than other types of "mass transit," including the new and sometimes undependable automobile. Barbourville, in Knox County, is reported to have been one of the last towns in America to discontinue horse-drawn streetcars, in 1919. Covington was the first Kentucky town to have mule- or horse-drawn service, beginning in 1867. Other Kentucky towns reported to have horse-drawn streetcars include Bowling Green, Georgetown, Henderson, Lexington, Louisville, Middlesboro, Owensboro, and Paducah. In 1890, near the height of horse-drawn streetcar use, the US Census recorded 37,434 streetcar workers in the entire country. (KHS, Graphic 5_Box 1_400.1.)

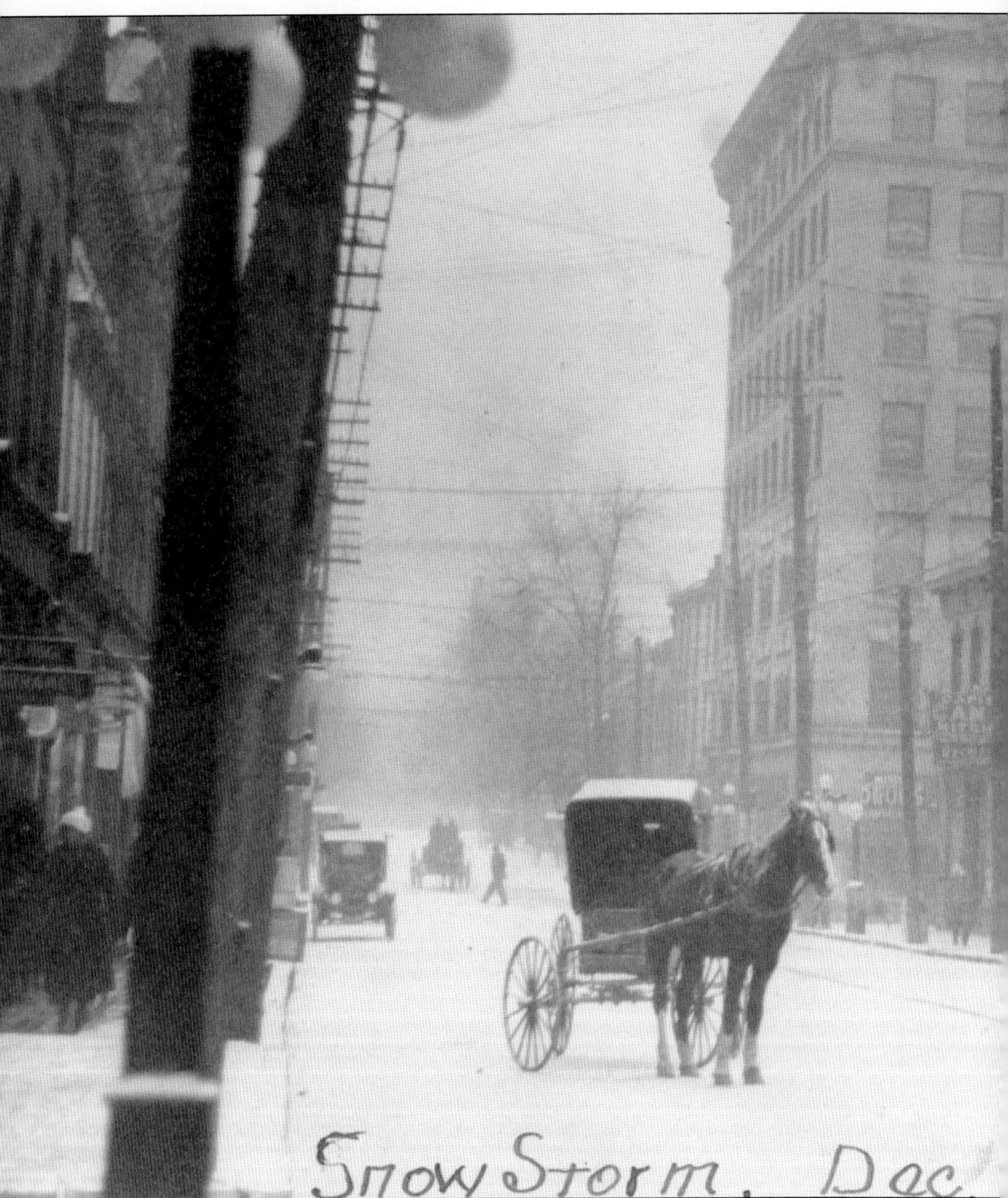

Frankfort Snow Storm. Although considered a Southern state, snow is not unheard of in Kentucky, as seen here on December 12, 1914. Among the establishments in this view of West Main Street in Frankfort are Capital Candy, Ebner Drugs, and the Manhattan Restaurant, all of which are now gone. The seven-story McClure Building was described as "Frankfort's first skyscraper" when it was built in 1907. Hopefully, the horses pulling the carriages were all shod with ice caulks. Some delivery vehicles were equipped with bobsled runners fitted with hubs that

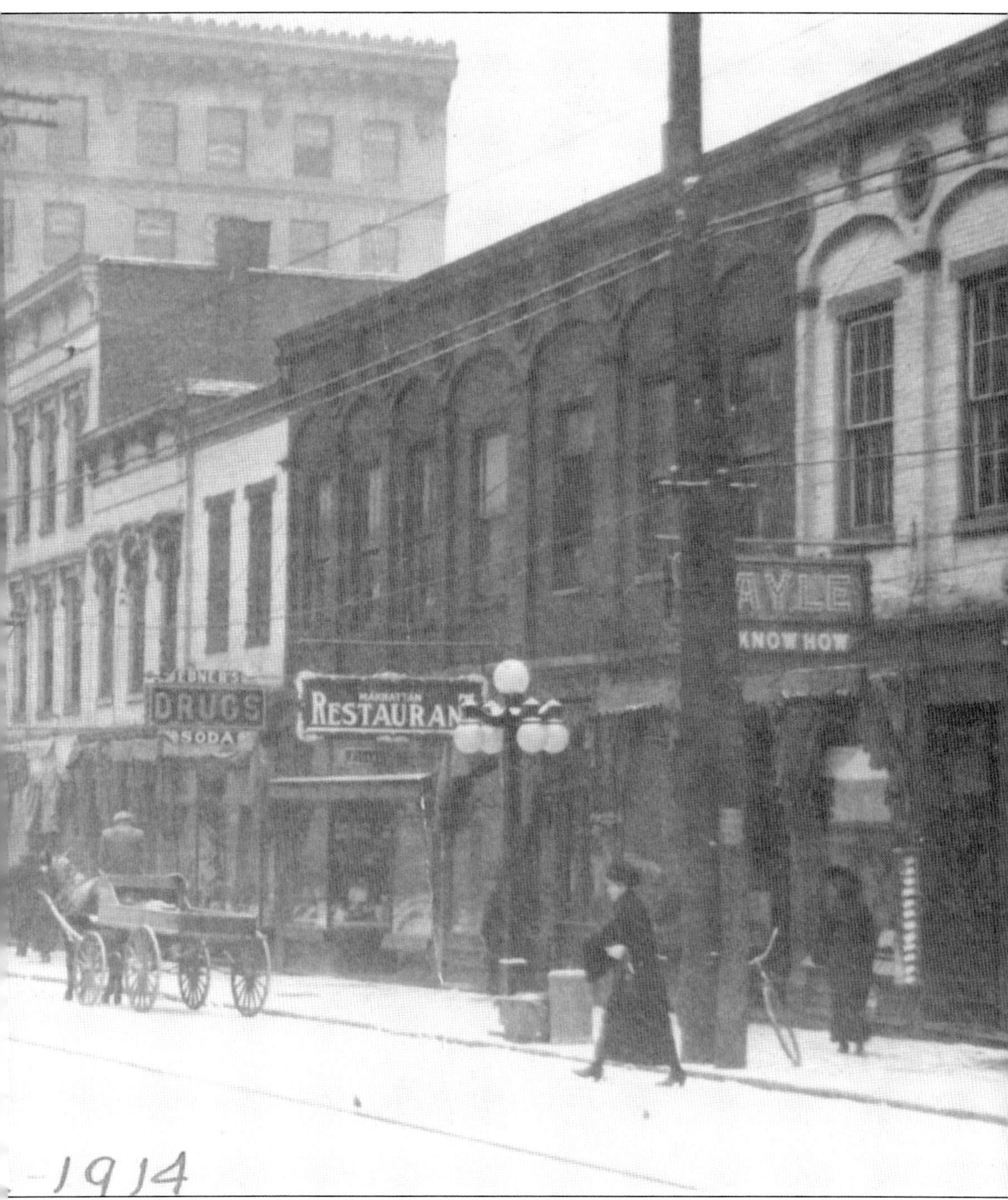

simplified the task of equipping a vehicle for winter use. Farther north, where snow covered the roads much more thickly and stayed for longer periods, large horse-drawn rollers were employed to pack down the snow. Salting, sanding, or scraping the streets was unthinkable. Northern cities had snow wardens, whose job it was to see that roads and streets had no bare spots where the wind had blown away the packed snow. Such spots were covered with snow again and then packed firm with a roller. (Capital City Museum.)

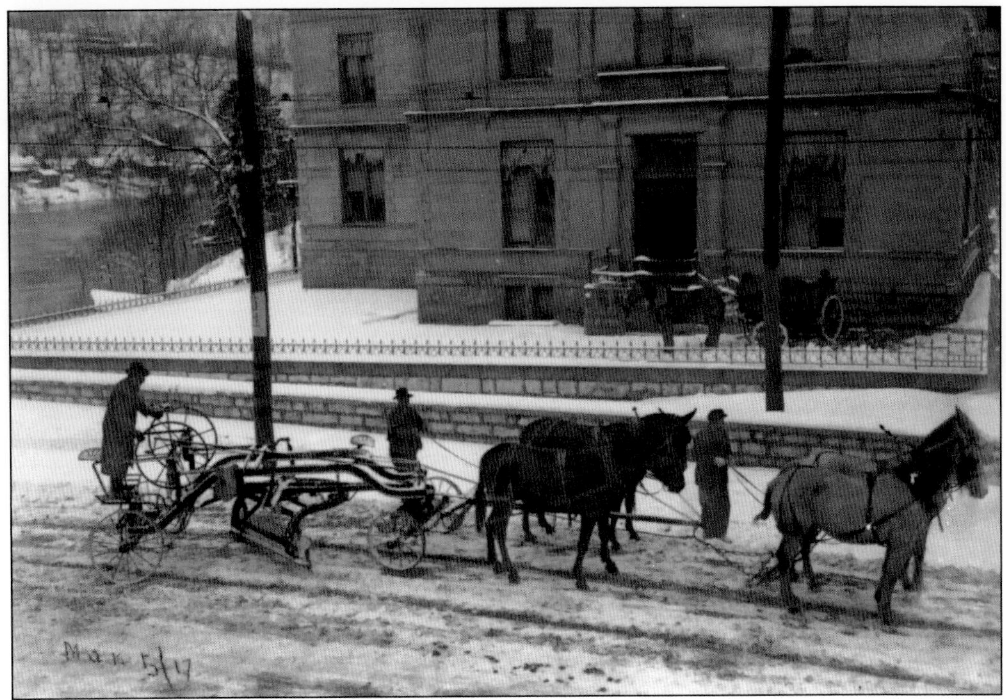

Horse-Drawn Snow Scraper. Here, four large draft horses pull a snow scraper through the streets of Frankfort in 1917. The man walking alongside the rig holds the reins for each two-horse team. The man riding on the scraper (left) used the wheels and levers not to direct the horses but to lower and adjust the angle of the scraper. (Capital City Museum.)

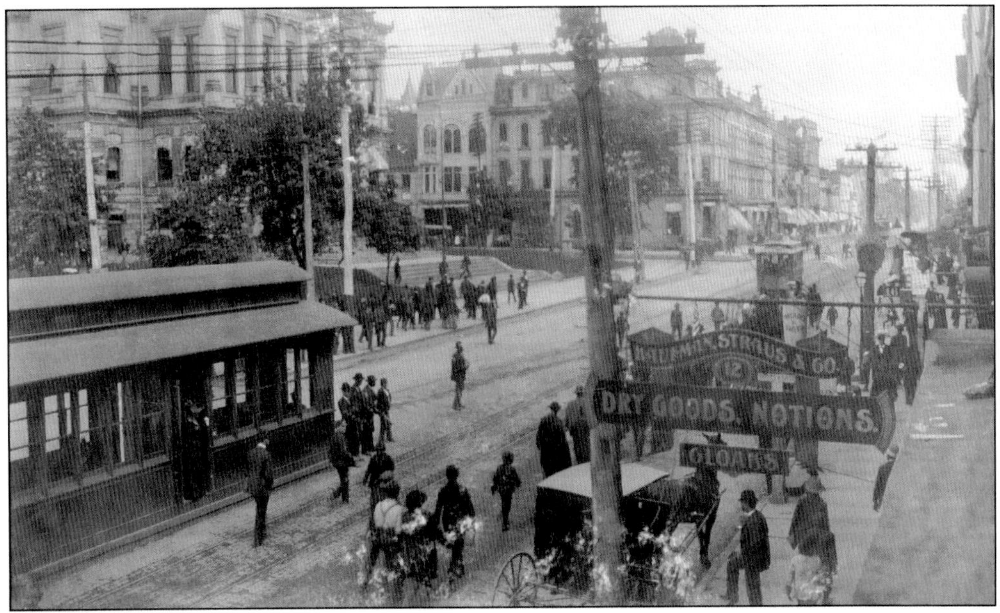

Main Street, Lexington. This photograph, likely dating to the late 1890s, shows activity in front of the relatively new Fayette County Courthouse, built in the Romanesque style. The electric streetcar was introduced to Lexington in 1890. Note the streetcar station in the middle of the street and the woman peering out from the ladies' waiting room. (UK Special Collections.)

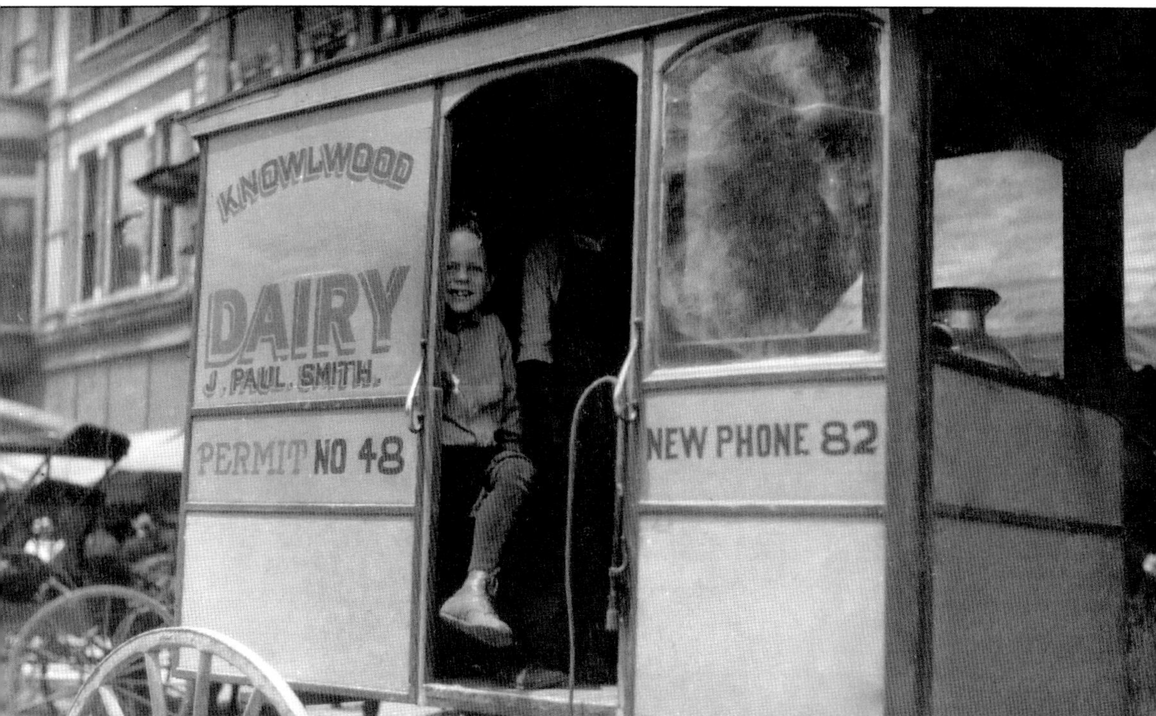

Fresh Milk Delivered. One of the last horse-drawn conveyances to disappear from towns and cities was the dairy delivery wagon. It is said that the horses were so familiar with their route that they would stop on their own at each house, wait as the milkman ran up to deliver the order, and then start up as soon as the driver reentered the wagon. Gas and tire rationing during World War II brought some horse-drawn milk wagons out of retirement for a short time. (LOC.)

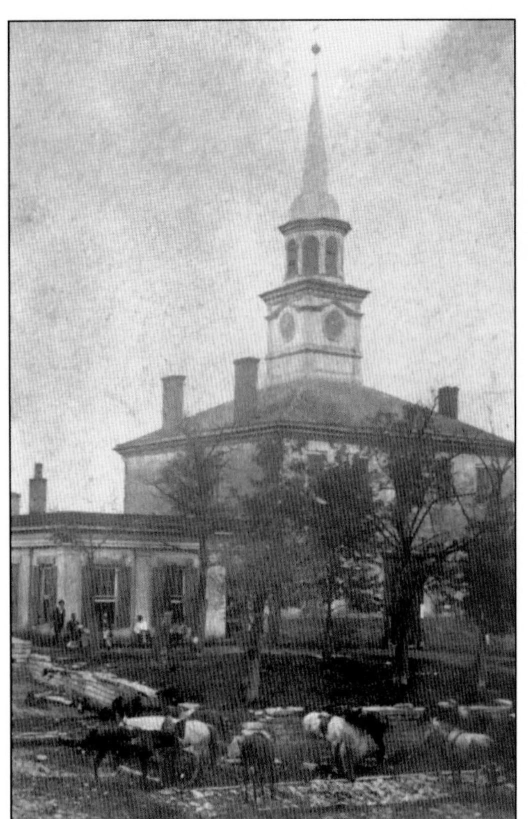

Bourbon County Courthouse. Saddled horses and carriages surround the courthouse, suggesting either an interesting trial or a tax deadline day. In February 1797, the fiscal court ordered that a new courthouse "be built to rival the great stone temple to justice in Lexington." Completed in 1799, this courthouse burned down in 1872. A larger and grander building soon replaced it. (Hopewell Museum.)

Time of Transition. This photograph, taken in the late 1920s or early 1930s, shows the transition in Versailles from horse and carriage to automobile. Shown here is the front of Citizens National Bank and a partial view of the Woodford County Courthouse (far right). The sign above the second-story window advertises Roxa Kola. A young African American man is standing on the awning above the restaurant entrance. (UK Special Collections.)

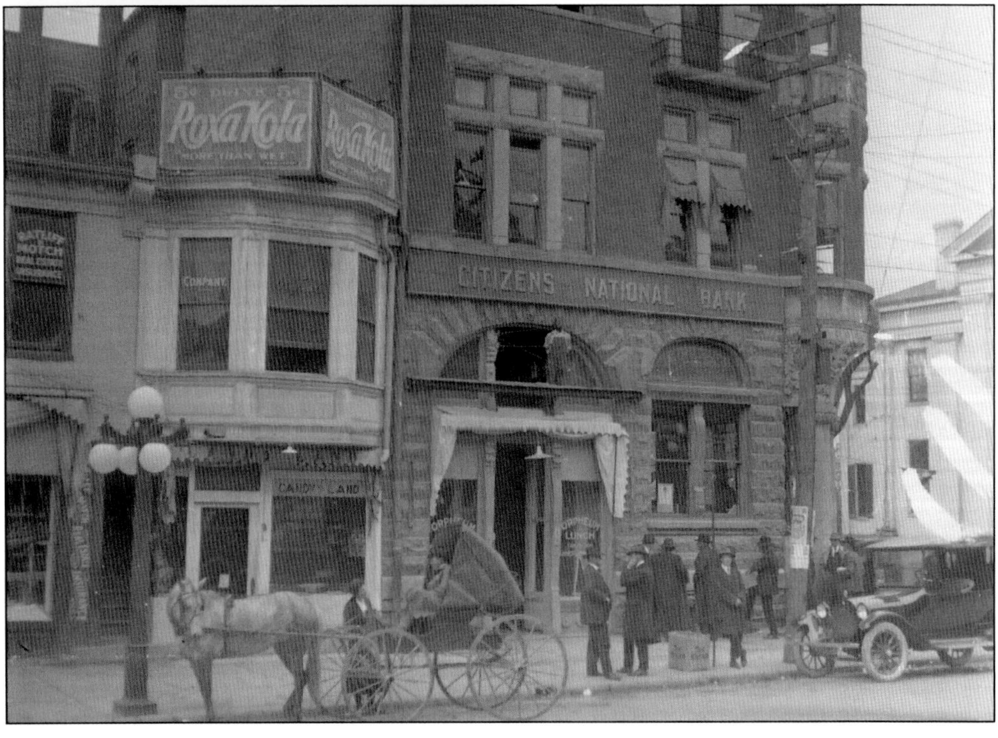

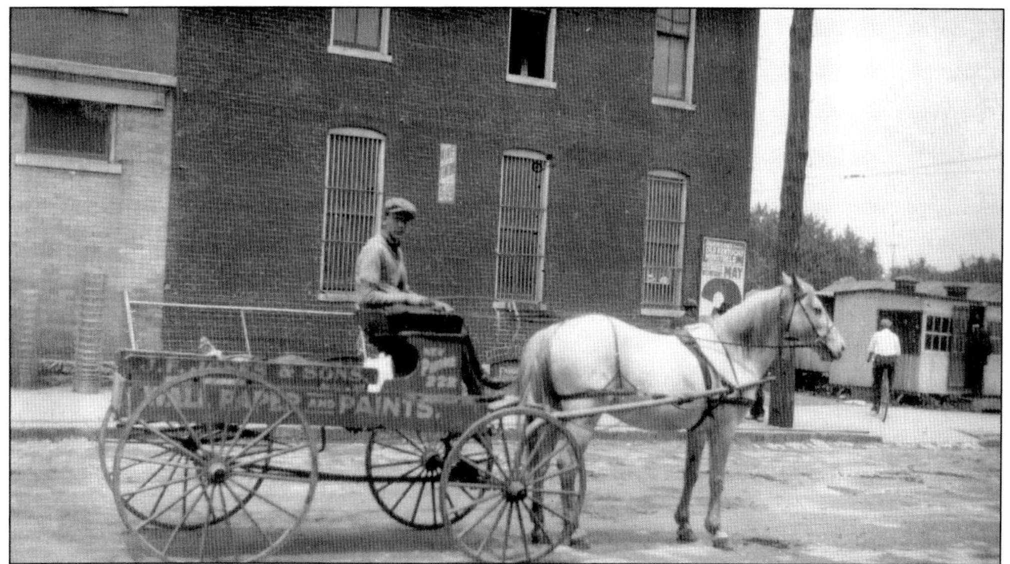

PAINT STORE DELIVERY. A young man delivers wallpaper and paint for the Bowling Green firm of J.F. Jones & Sons in 1916. The poster behind the horse advertises Robinson's Famous Old Kentucky Minstrels. The show was presented "under canvas," which meant in a large tent. This particular minstrel show once starred Milt G. Barlow, an actor from Harrison County who became famous for developing the character "Ole Black Joe." (LOC.)

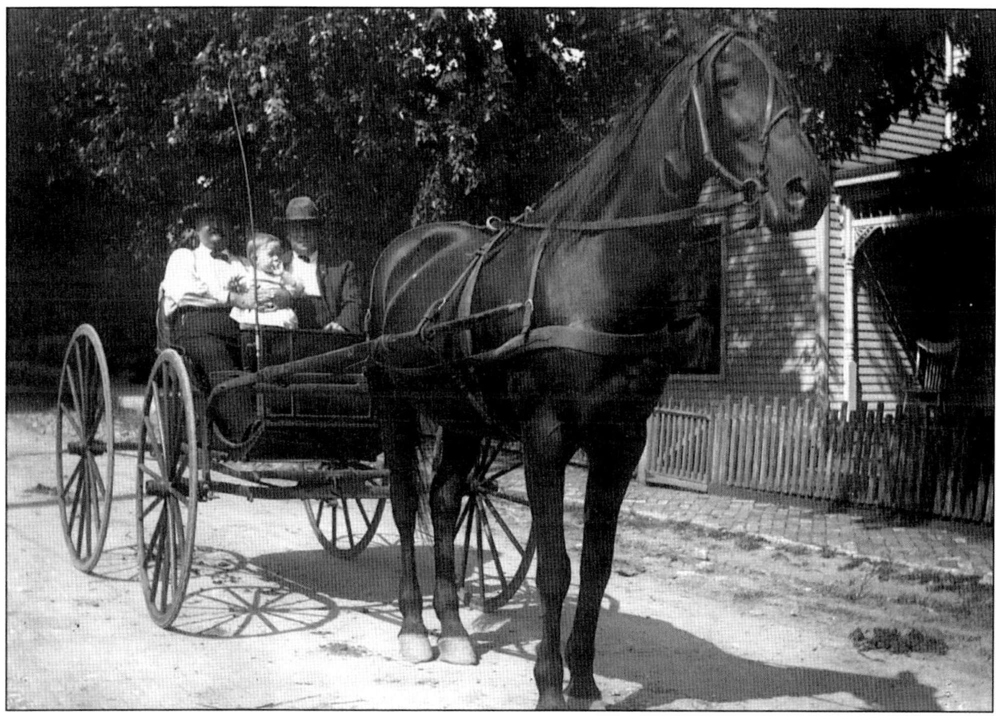

FAMILY OF COUNTY CLERKS. In 1905 in Paris, three generations of the Paton family pose in a carriage. The trio held the elected position of Bourbon County clerk for a total of 66 years. Ed D. Paton (left) served from 1895 to 1906; Pearce Paton (right) served from 1906 to 1942; and little Ed Drane Paton served from 1948 to 1967. The horse is identified as Queen. (Betty Witt.)

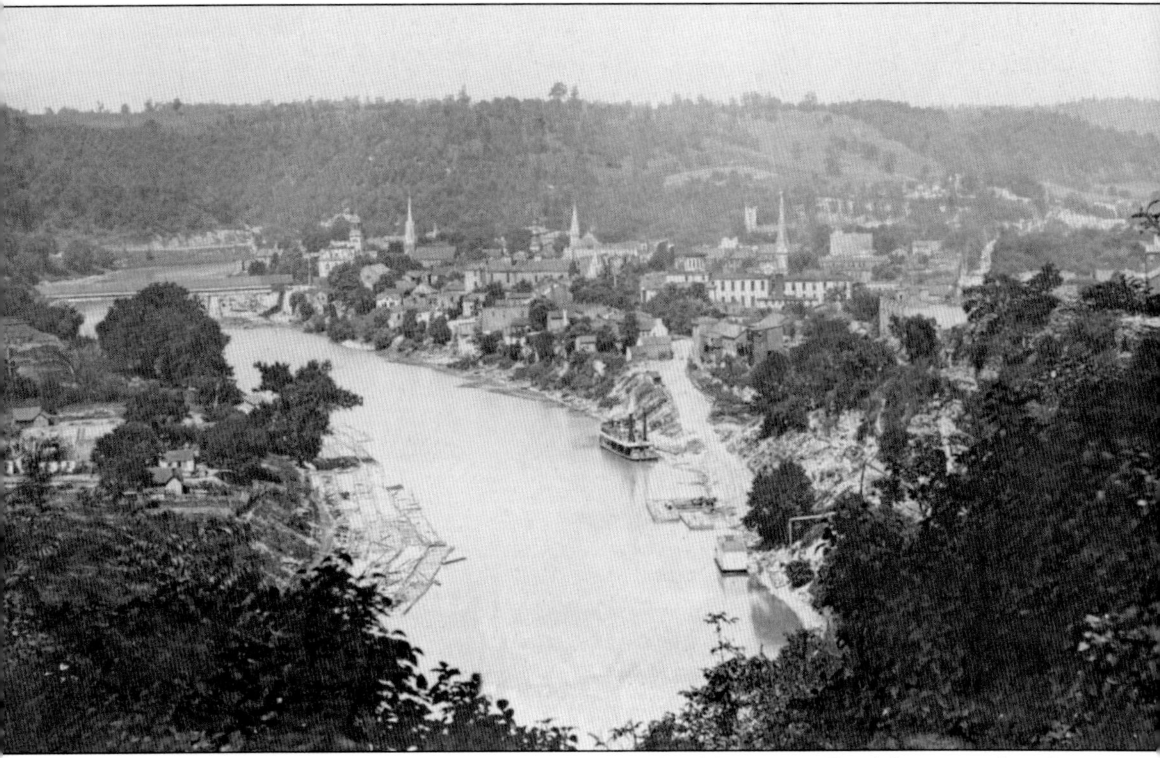

FRANKFORT ON THE RIVER. This stunning photograph of downtown Frankfort was taken from Boone's Bluff, the site of the Frankfort Cemetery, in the 1880s or early 1890s. The covered bridge in the distance on the river was built in 1843 and was replaced by the current "Singing Bridge" in 1893. In 1862, Confederate troops, who had captured Frankfort a few days before, threatened to burn the bridge to cover their retreat before a larger Union force. They spared it after residents agreed to disable it by tearing up the floorboards. At lower center, workmen can be seen unloading items from a barge onto a wagon. The four horses will then haul it up the steep road into town. The rafts of logs pulled up on the left side of the river were floated down from Eastern Kentucky. The rafts consisted mainly of heavy, dense oak and poplar logs, which were not very buoyant. They contained just enough hickory logs to keep the raft afloat. (Capital City Museum.)

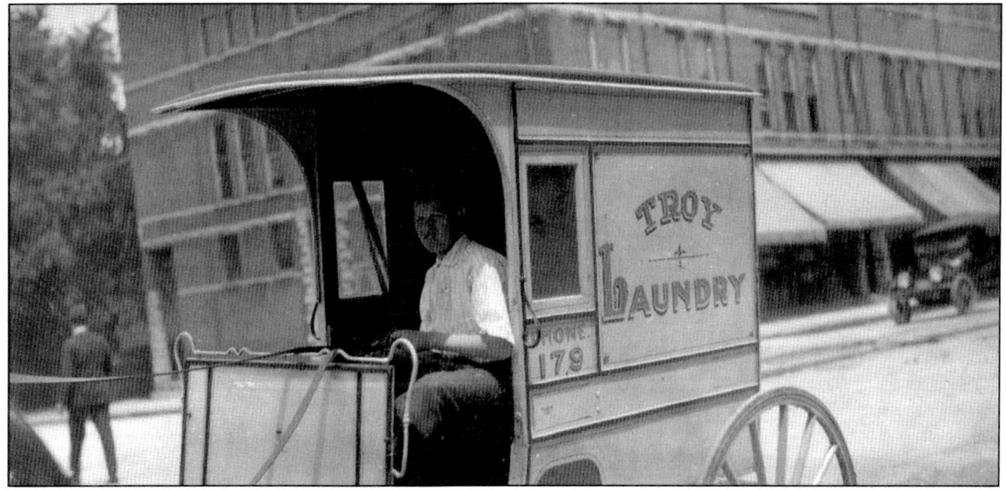

Laundry Delivery. In 1916, there was no wash-and-wear or permanent press, but there was Troy Laundry in Bowling Green. Men in delivery wagons came to customers' houses, picked up dirty clothes, and returned them clean and pressed. Patrons dialed "179" on their telephones or asked the operator to connect them to the laundry. Customers could also send a Troy Laundry postcard for next-day service. (LOC.)

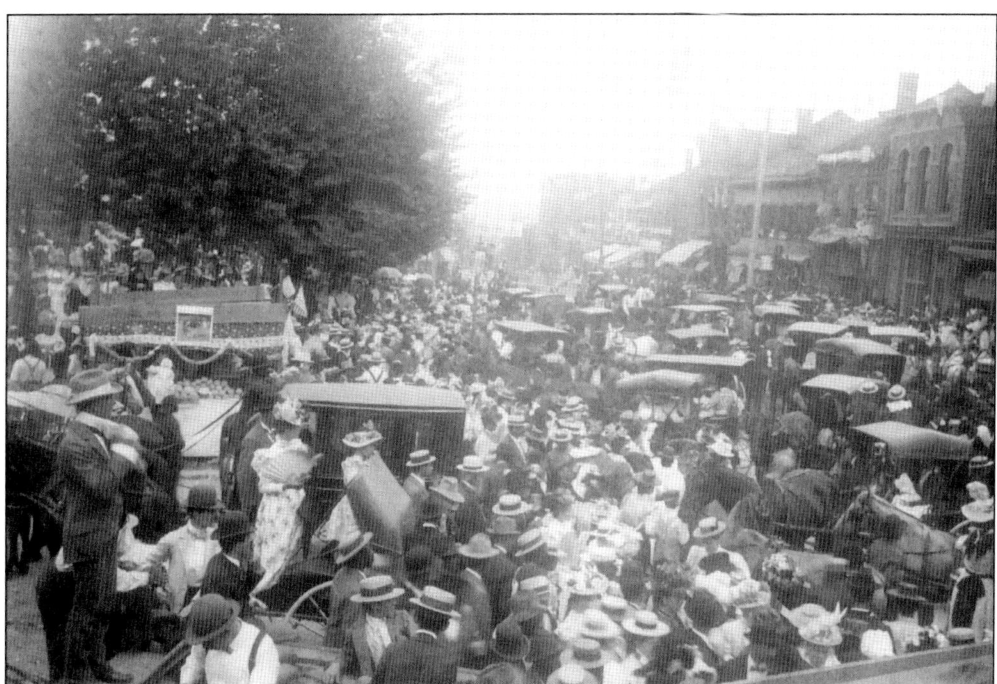

Carriages, Horses, and Hats. A large crowd celebrates the nation's victory in the Spanish-American War. They are gathered in August 1899 in the courthouse square in Paris. The men in their straw boaters, the women in elaborate chapeaus, and the many horses and carriages all evoke Kentucky's horse-drawn era. One can only imagine the traffic jam that ensued at the conclusion of the gathering. (Hopewell Museum.)

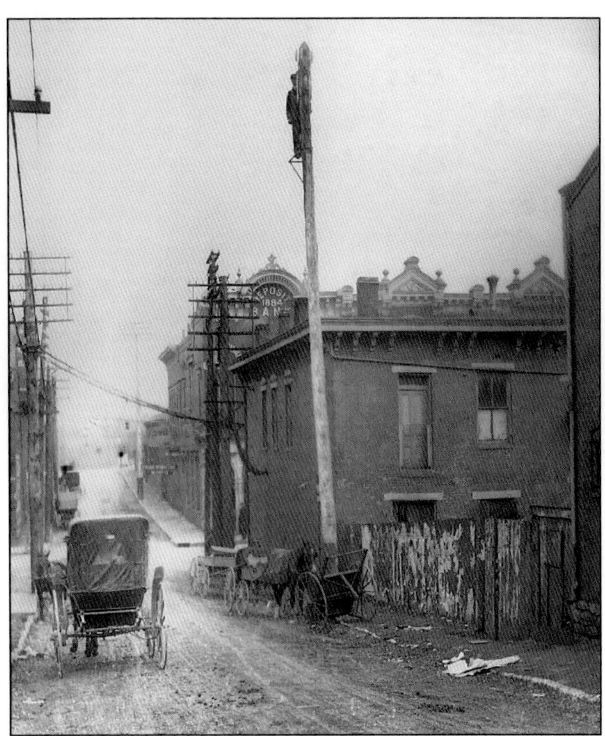

Back Street View. This photograph, taken in Paris in the late 1890s, shows an unpaved side street with several carriages parked on the left, waiting for occupants. The handcart and work wagon probably belong to the lineman standing at the top of the pole, most likely working on the telegraph. He was kind enough to place a wrap on his horse on what seems to have been a cold, wet day. (Authors' collection.)

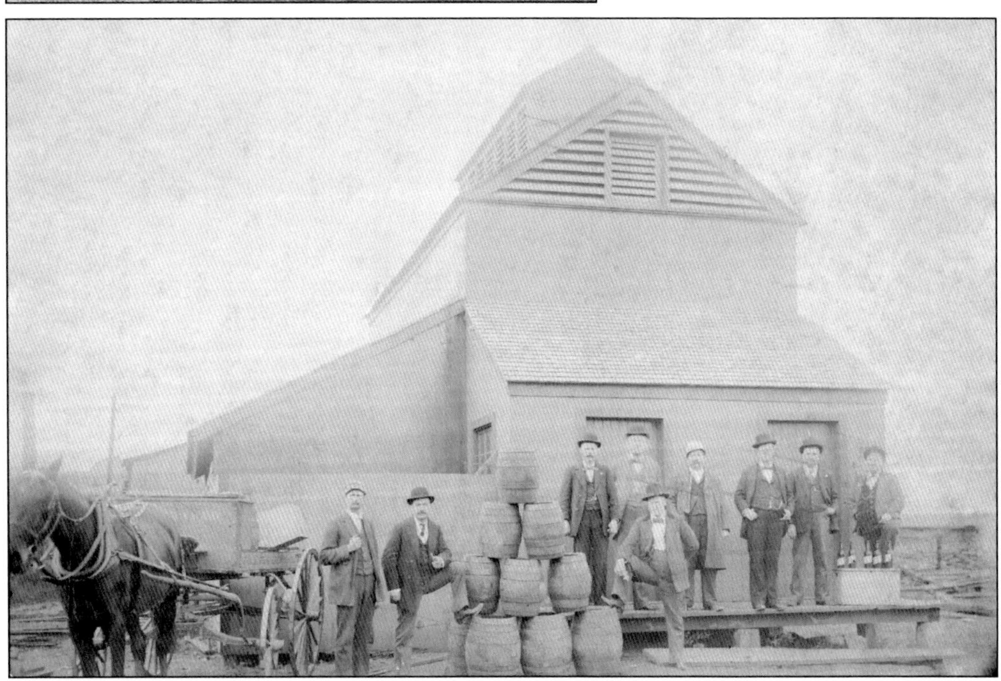

Well-Dressed Millers. Photographs such as this one make working with historical materials so much fun. It is labeled "Stephen's Mill, Broadway–Bowling Green." However, upon closer inspection, the gentlemen seem too well dressed to be working millers, and the building does not look like a mill. The barrels resemble beer barrels, and the beer bottles indicate that this is probably a brewery. Or, it is one heck of a party. (WKU Special Collections.)

Four

Fascinating Faces

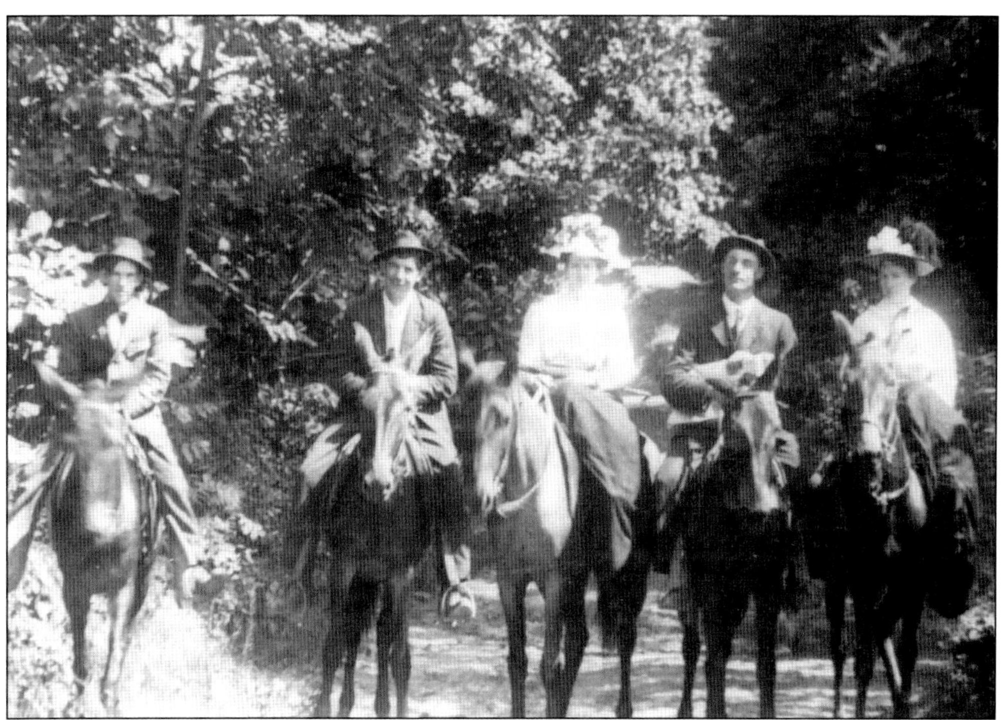

Wedding Belles. This 1908 photograph of the wedding of John and Virgie Walker was taken near Deer Creek in Carter County. The bride (center) and her attendant are both wearing lovely hats and riding sidesaddle. The bride is seated on a horse, while the rest of the party are riding mules. The groom (second from right) is holding something bulky in his arms. (KHS, BOD.1990ph2.8BOD31.)

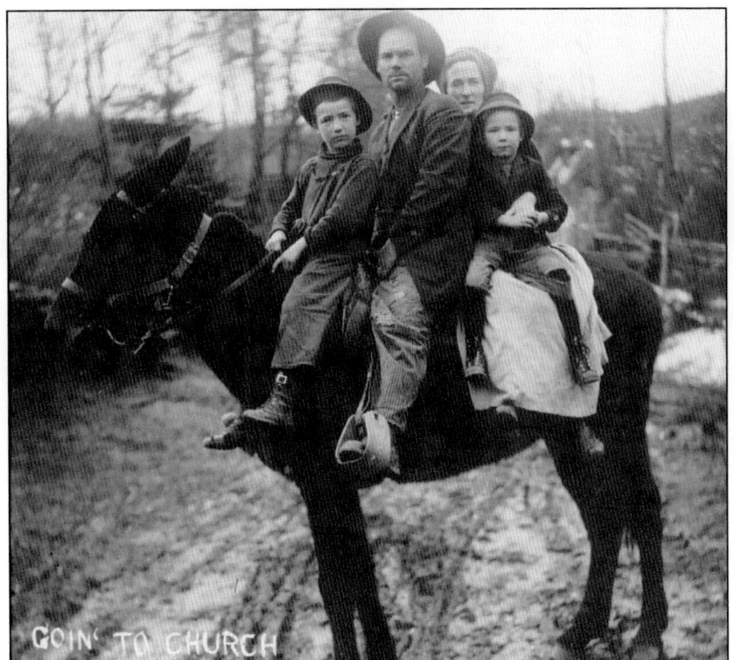

Family Going to Church. Instead of loading up the station wagon, families piled on the family mule for a trip to church during Kentucky's horse-drawn era. Hopefully, the trip to church was short for this family in the mountains of Eastern Kentucky. It looks like there is snow on the ground, and the weather appears to be cold in this undated photograph. (Berea College Special Collections.)

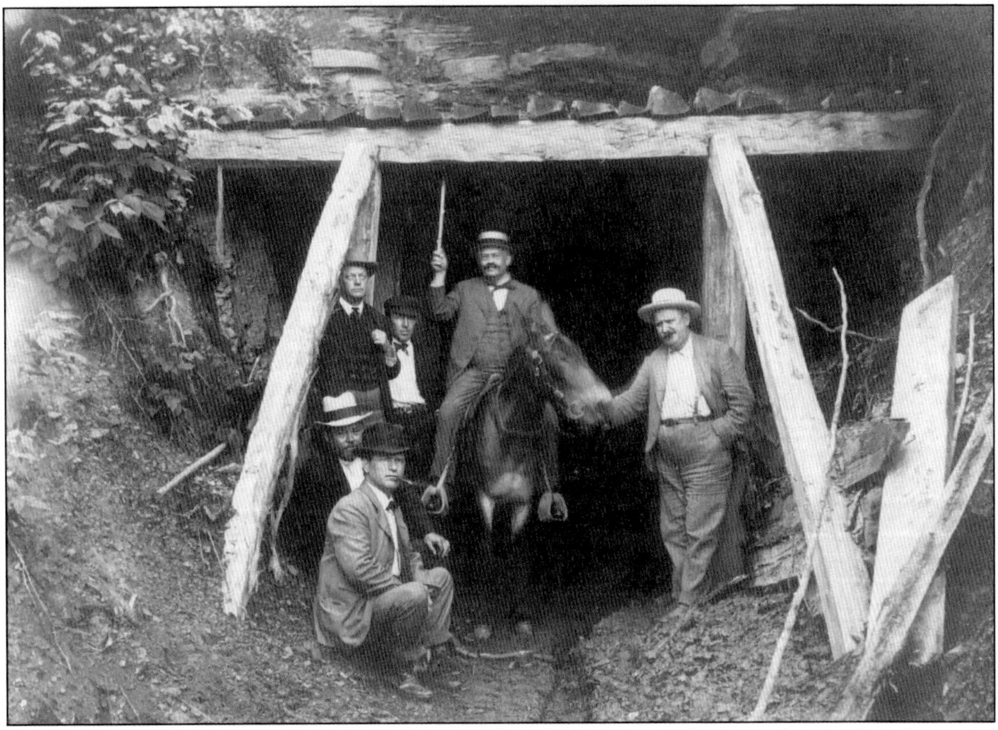

It Is That Tall. The gentleman on horseback is holding a stick up to the roof of this mine entrance, perhaps showing the height of the mine shaft. The mine was owned by Elkhorn Coal Corporation. The six men posing in front of the mine are probably coal company executives. The only other information on this undated photograph is the caption "8 feet thick," perhaps referring to the mine's vein of coal. (UK Special Collections.)

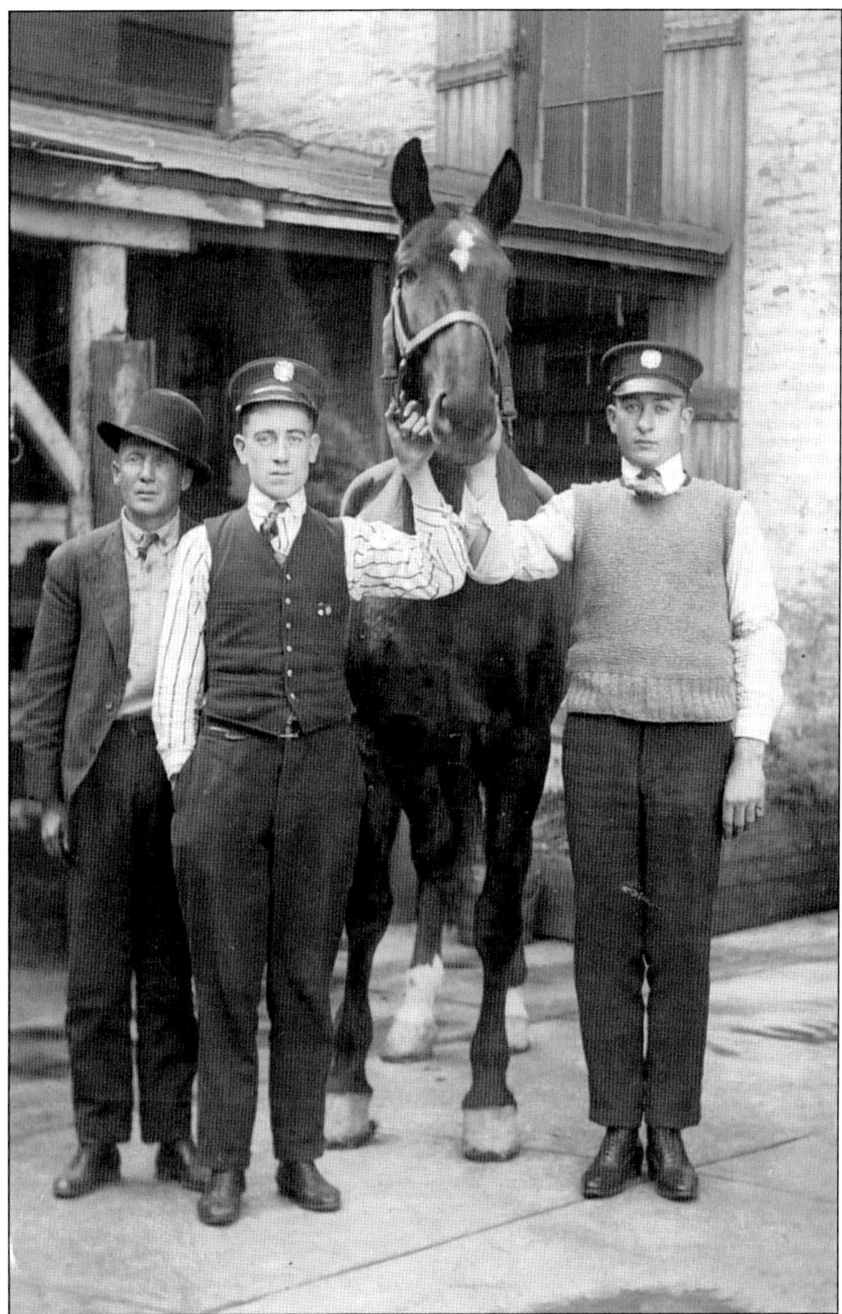

Three Men and a Horse. This undated photograph, taken in front of a livery stable in Frankfort, features four fascinating faces. The two younger men holding the horse's bridle are Frankfort firemen and could be brothers. They are neatly dressed, with matching caps centered with shiny gold badges. The man on the left looks a little less neat and is wearing a sporty, tilted hat. The fourth face in the photograph is the horse's. He looks calm and intelligent as he gazes directly at the viewer. Both of those traits were highly desirable in horses that were employed to pull fire engines, as they had to keep calm in the face of noise, confusion, and heat from the flames. (Capital City Museum.)

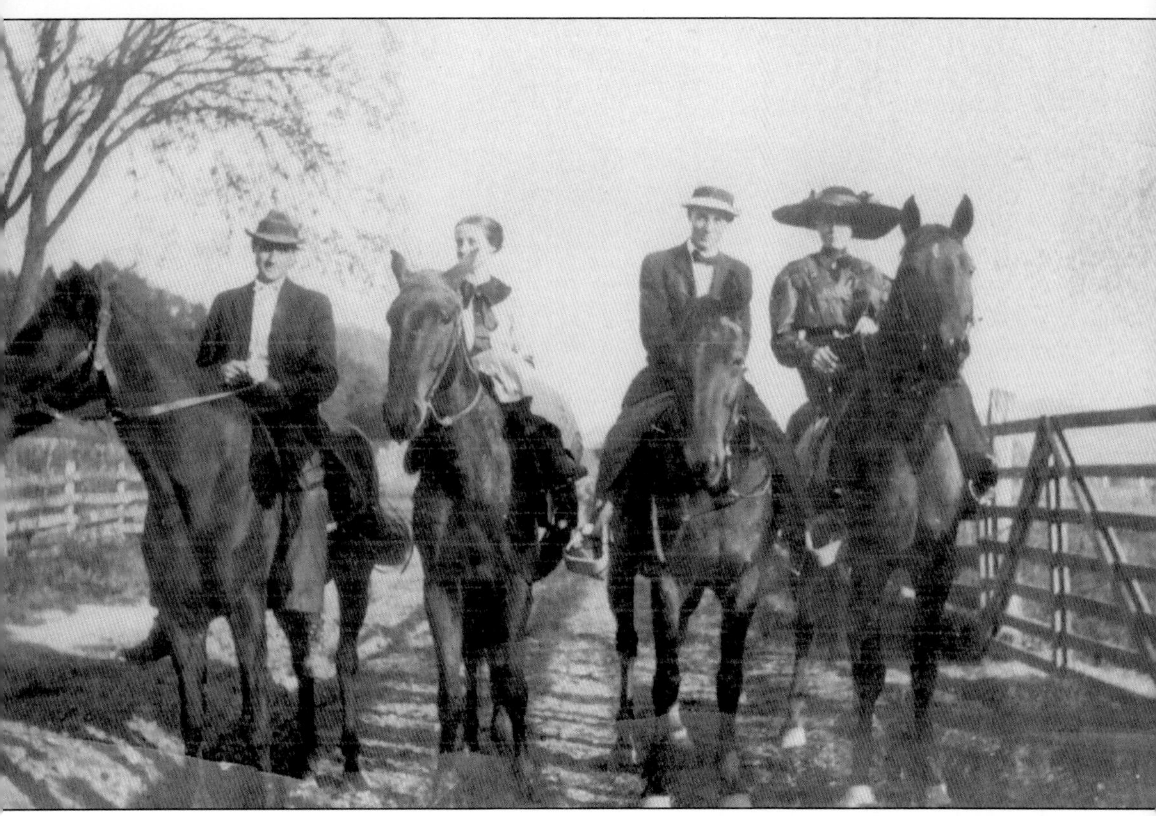

MOONLIGHT SCHOOL TEACHERS. Moonlight schools were classes held on evenings when there was enough light to see the footpaths and dirt roads, which adult students followed to the local schoolhouses for an opportunity to learn to read and write. The schools were the brainchild of a Rowan County teacher, Cora Wilson Stewart, who devised a series of textbooks and enlisted the help of volunteer teachers, like the four seen here. On the back of the photograph is written, "Moonlight School teachers out searching for pupils." The teachers visited isolated homesteads to let people know about the program. In 1911, when the program got under way in Rowan County, 1,200 adults were enrolled. By 1915, an estimated 40,000 adults had learned to read and write through this program, which was later copied by other Southern states. (UK Special Collections.)

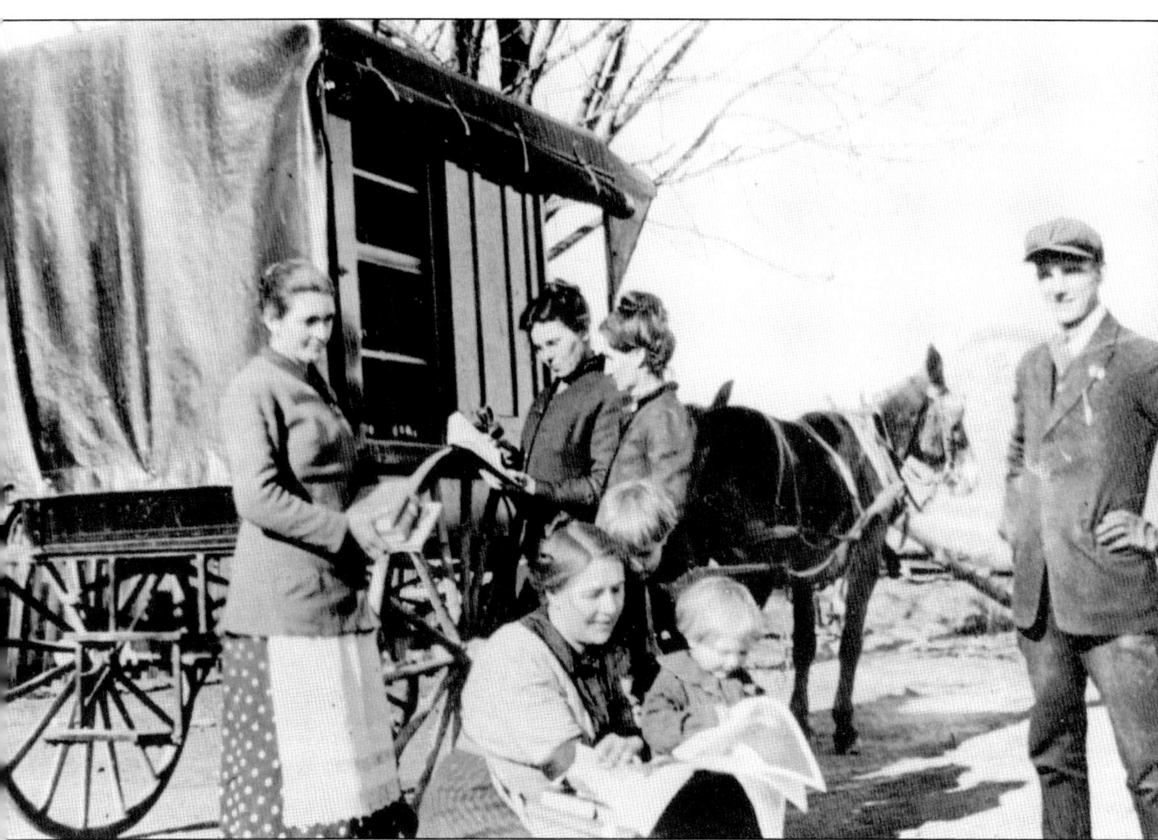

Early Bookmobile. In the 1890s, Berea College, in Madison County, began sending "traveling libraries" into the less-populated, more isolated areas of the state "by wagon, mail train, river boat and mule back," according to a news release from the school. At one point, the program had a yearly circulation of more than 60,000 books. In this undated photograph, women, children, and a young man are taking advantage of a library that came to them. Berea College was founded in 1855 by the Rev. John G. Fee. His vision was of a school that would provide an excellent education for men and women of all races—truly a remarkable idea at the time, when higher education opportunities for women and blacks were extremely limited. (Berea College Special Collections.)

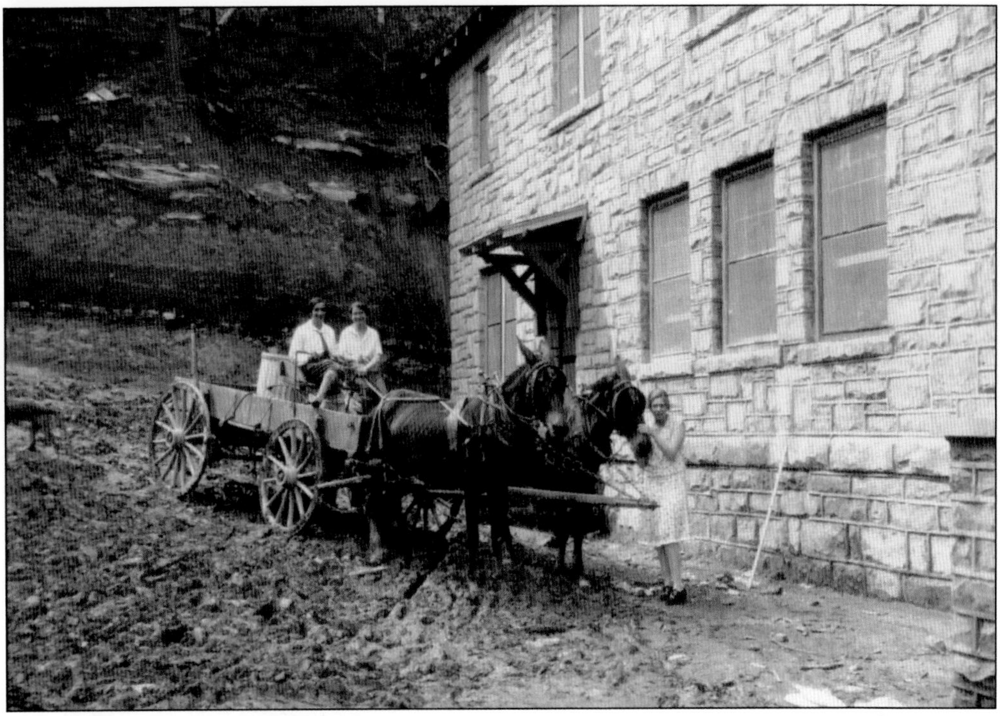

At the Hyden Hospital. This 1928 photograph shows two young women driving a wagon pulled by a team of mules and another young woman at the front of the wagon. The inscription at the bottom reads, "At the hospital at Hyden, Leslie Co., Ky." The women are probably Frontier Nursing Service nurses who worked with people living in the isolated communities in the Eastern Kentucky mountains. (Berea College Special Collections.)

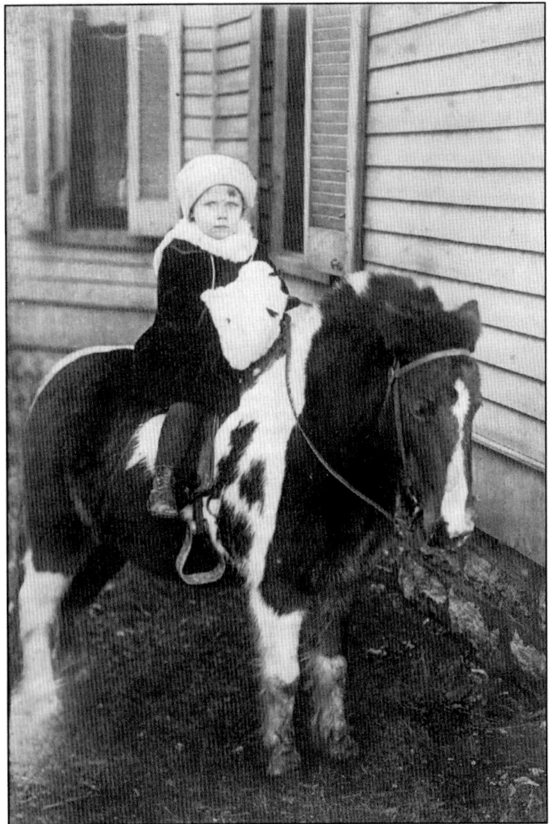

Priceless Pose on a Pony. Both four-year-old Alma Frances Bowman and her shaggy-legged pony look like they are well protected from the Bourbon County winter in this undated photograph. Posing young children on ponies or horses was commonplace during Kentucky's horse-drawn era. Pony-back photographs are still taken today at countless pony rides at school carnivals and local fairs. (Hopewell Museum.)

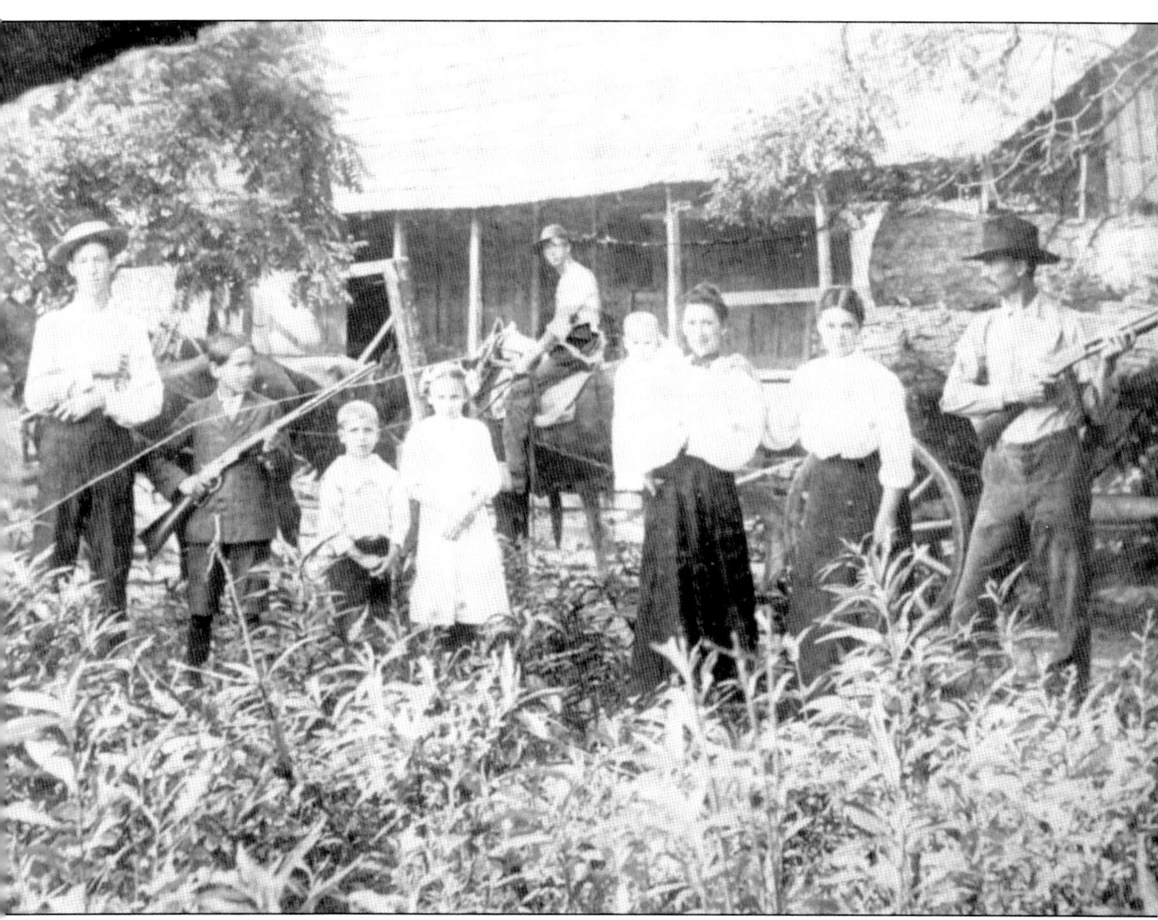

Ballard County Family. This 1904 photograph is of the family of James W. "J.W." Crews, who lived in Ballard County and made their living by logging. The horse-drawn cart at right holds several huge logs. The only person identified in the photograph is J.W. Crews, the family patriarch, who is at the far right, holding a rifle. Others pictured are, from left to right, a young man, possibly a son or son-in-law, holding a pistol; a boy holding a rifle; two younger children, probably Crews's children or grandchildren; a young man, possibly a son or son-in-law, on one of the four horses in the team; a woman holding a baby, either a daughter or daughter-in-law; and the woman next to Crews, probably his wife. (KHS, MCA.1990ph2.2MCA72.)

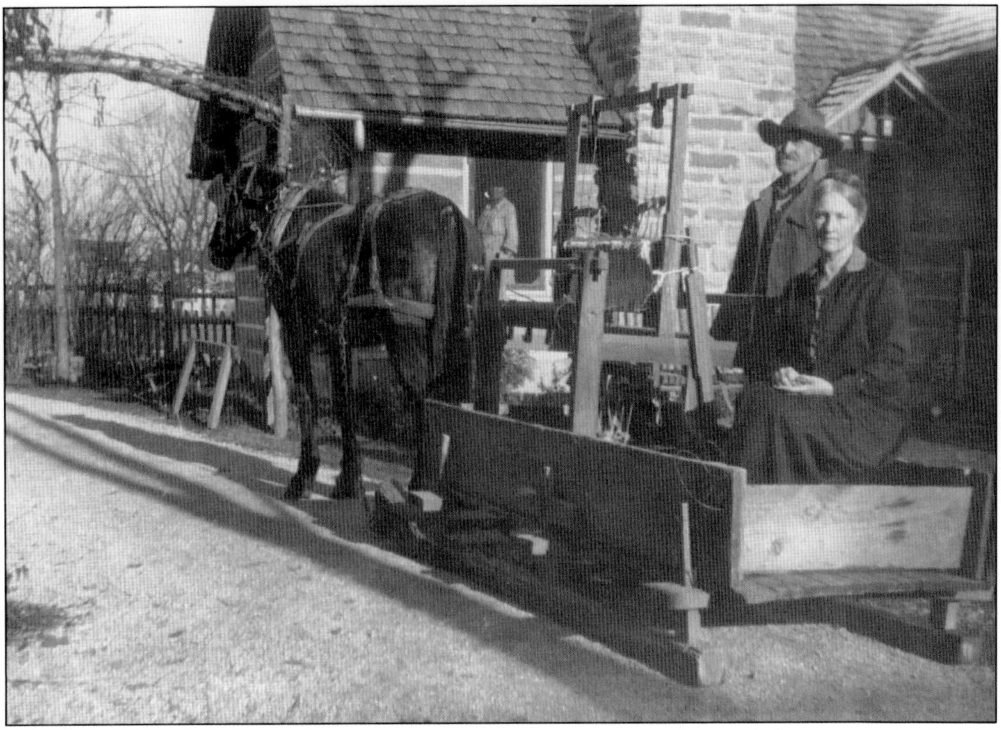

Have Loom, Will Travel. Looms are expensive items, even today, and this woman looks like she has decided not to leave hers during a trip to an unknown destination. This 1928 photograph was most likely taken in the Eastern Kentucky mountains, as this couple is using a sled instead of a wheeled vehicle to haul their unusual load. (Berea College Special Collections.)

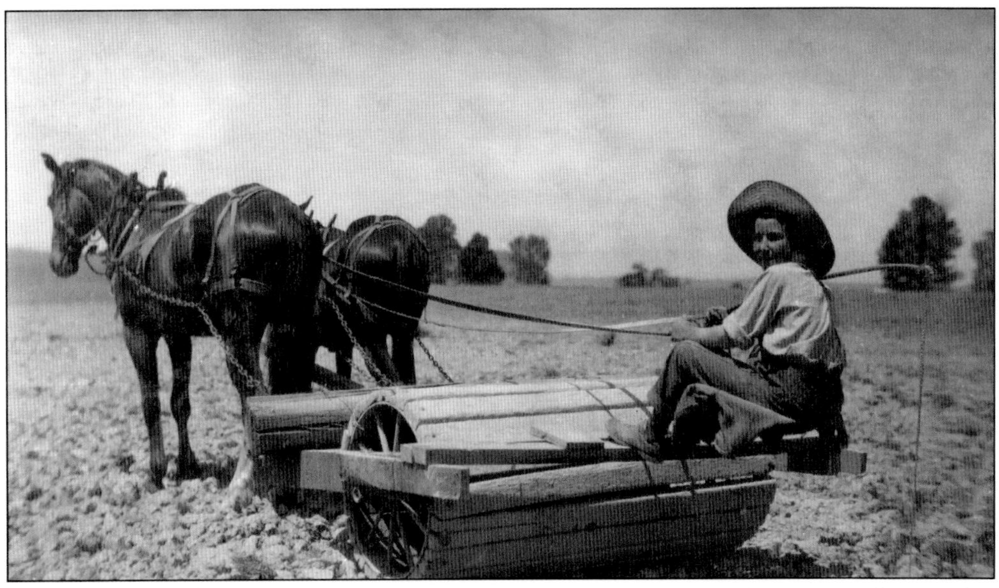

Boy Driving a Team. In May 1916, Harry Dewitt uses a team of two horses to pull a wooden roller over a newly plowed field on his father's farm, near West Point in Hardin County. Rollers were used to flatten the land and break up large clumps of soil, usually in freshly plowed fields. Flatter fields meant easier weed control and harvesting. (LOC.)

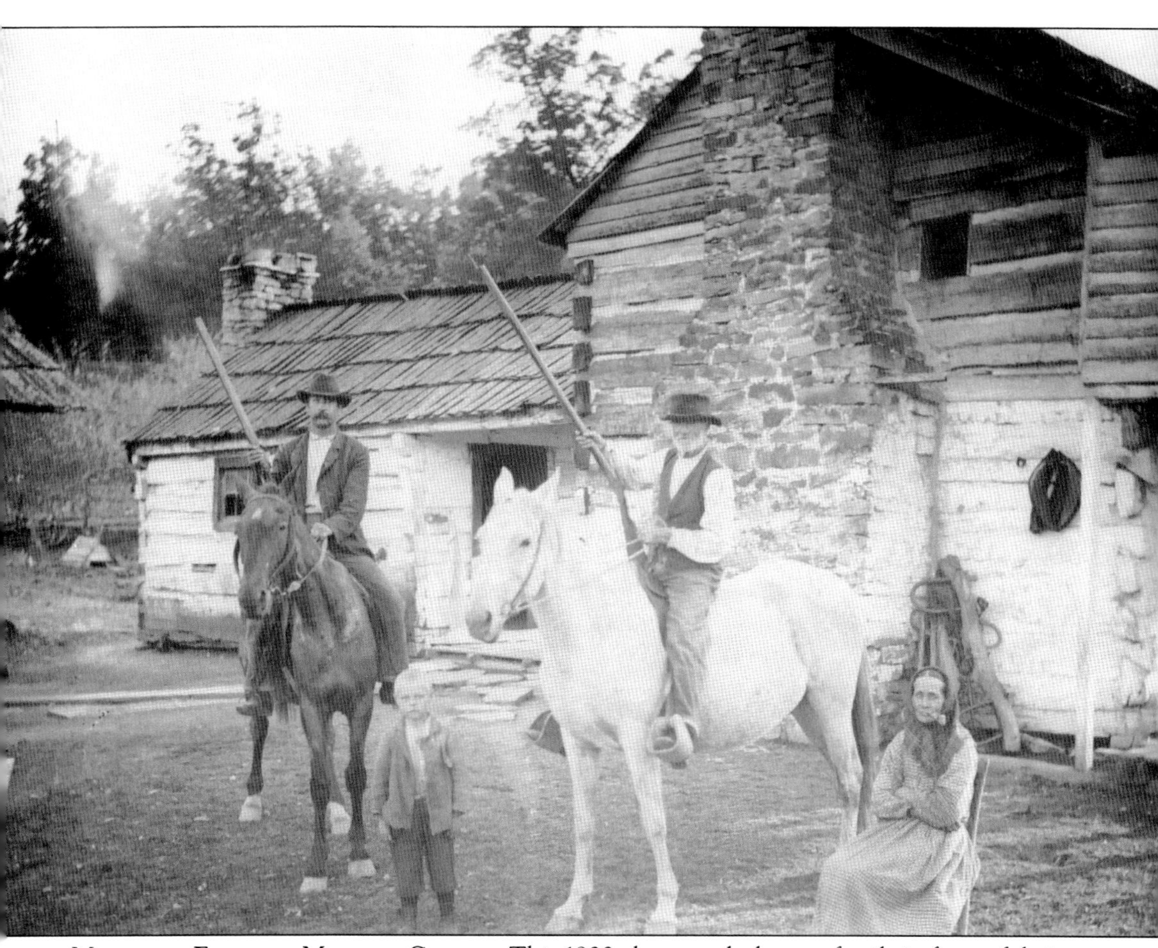

MOUNTAIN FAMILY IN MADISON COUNTY. This 1900 photograph shows a family in front of their home at the foot of West Pinnacle. The two men are mounted on handsome horses and are holding Kentucky long rifles. The man on the white horse is identified as Sam Davis. He is referred to as "the father of Isaac Davis," who is probably the younger man on the dark horse. The woman smoking a pipe in the chair is identified as Mrs. Samuel Davis, and the boy is John Davis. There is no information about where John fits in the family tree. The log home behind them is a very substantial one, with a two-story wing and two brick-and-stone fireplaces. Leaning against the cabin wall behind Mrs. Davis are wooden oxen yokes. (Berea College Special Collections.)

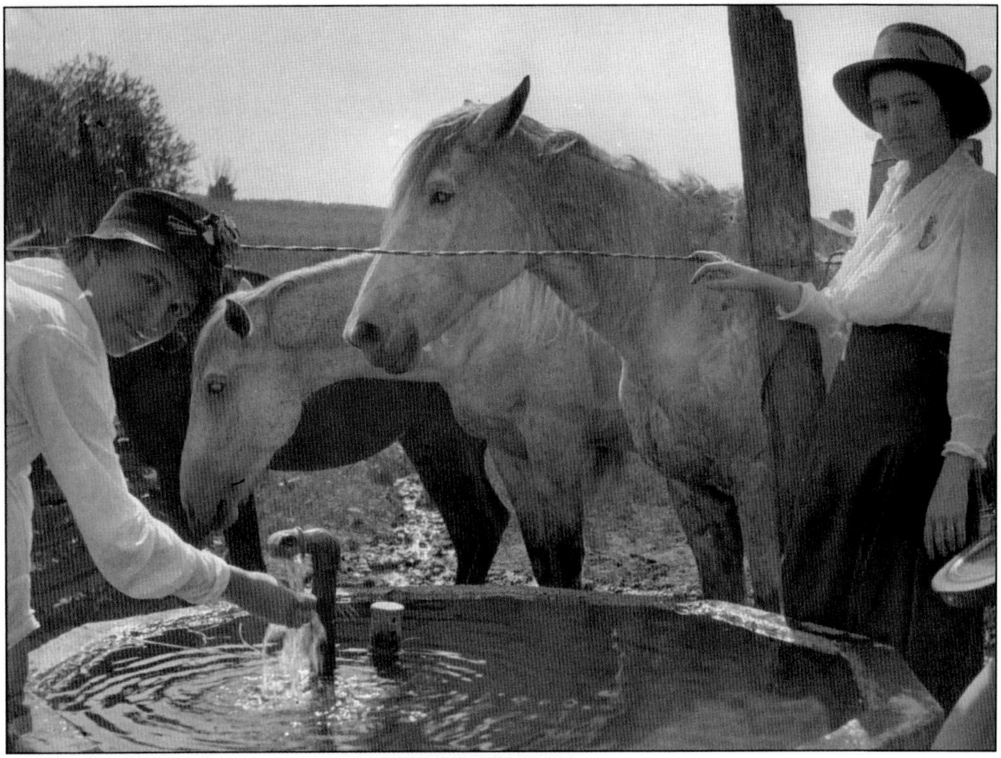

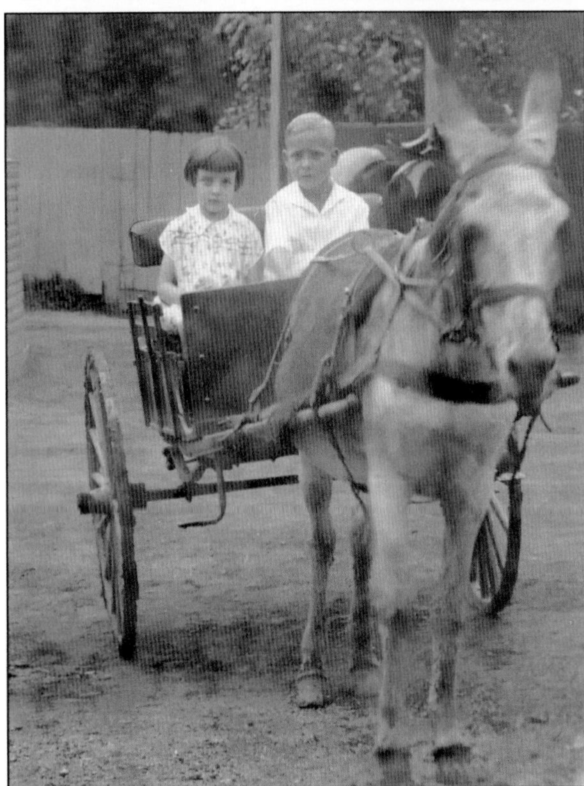

Have a Drink. Gertrude Tate Hensley and her sister Teresa Tate Newman are seen at a well in 1918. They were watering several horses near Ashland in Boyd County. One of the reasons that Kentucky is world-renowned for the horses it produces is the limestone dissolved in the water, which is said to make the horses' bones stronger. (KHS, BOD.1990ph2.1BOD5)

Out for a Ride. Kenneth Strong, holding the reins of a mule-drawn cart, is accompanied by his sister Jewell. The photograph's location is only identified as "at the zoo." The zoo in question was possibly the Cincinnati Zoo, as it was founded in 1875 and is the second-oldest zoo in America. Its original animal collection was very small, but it has grown by leaps and bounds. (Hopewell Museum.)

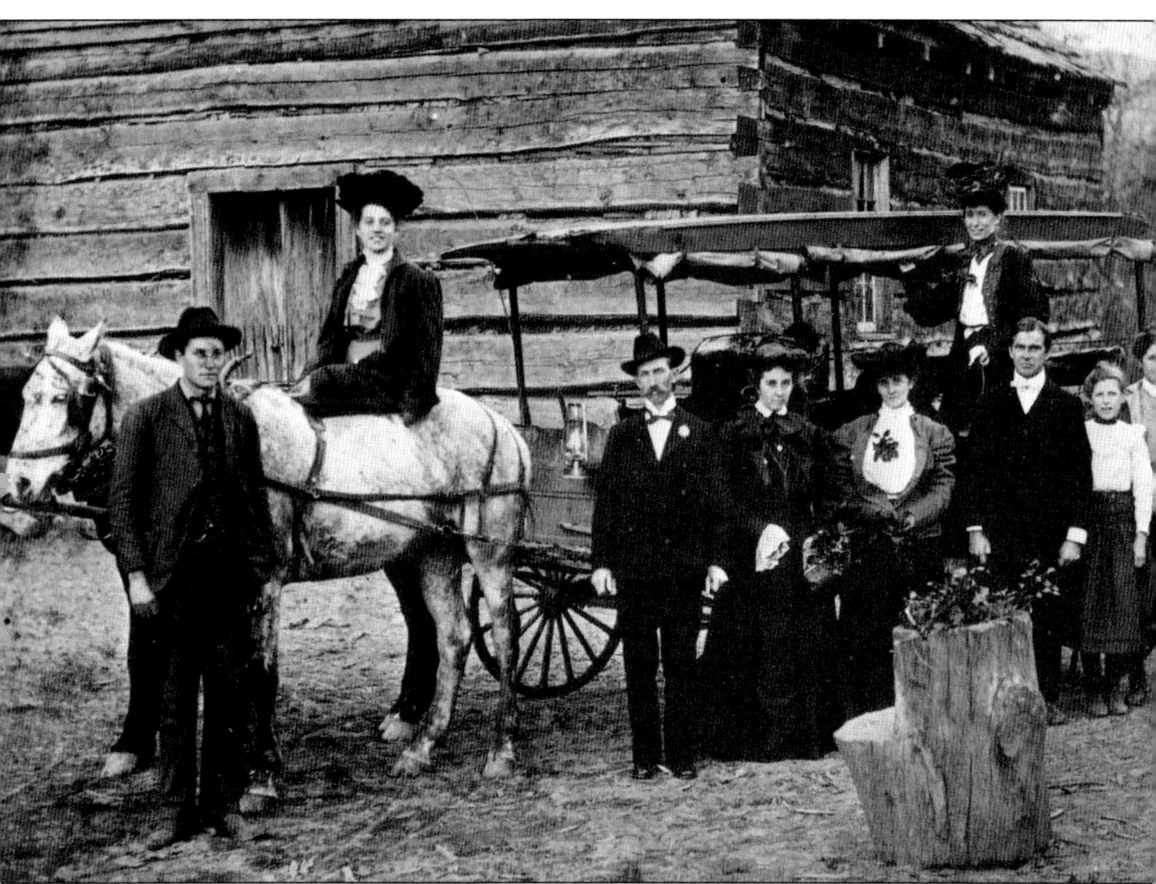

Early Church Bus. This group of churchgoers was photographed with their horse-drawn bus in 1910. The six women and three men are all neatly dressed and are standing on or near the vehicle, which was pulled by a team of horses and featured canvas sides that could be rolled up, as they are in this photograph. The sides could be rolled down when the weather was cold or rainy. It probably had benches along each side so that the passengers could sit facing each other. The lantern in the front would have provided light if darkness fell before everyone reached home. Churchgoing was an important religious and social opportunity for the people in the mountainous regions of Eastern Kentucky, who were often isolated by geography and bad roads. (Berea College Special Collections.)

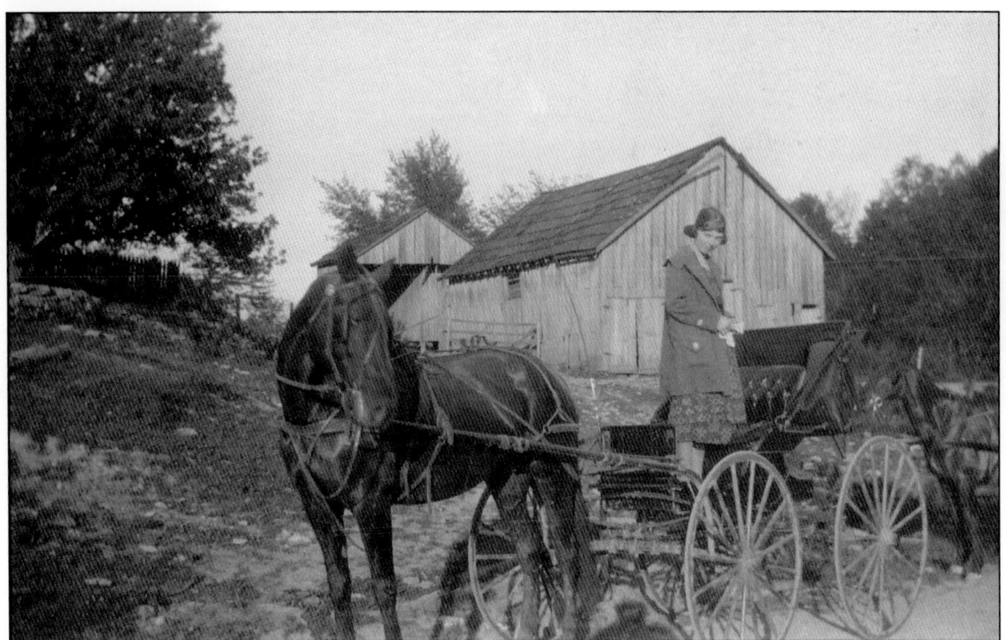

A Stand-Up Girl. Mary Waldman stands in a horse-drawn buggy near Frankfort in this undated photograph. Buggies were light, open vehicles with four wheels. Many, like this one, had convertible tops that could be raised to shield the driver from rain or too much sun. Since this was a relatively light load, the horse is harnessed using a breast-collar, not a horse collar. (Capital City Museum.)

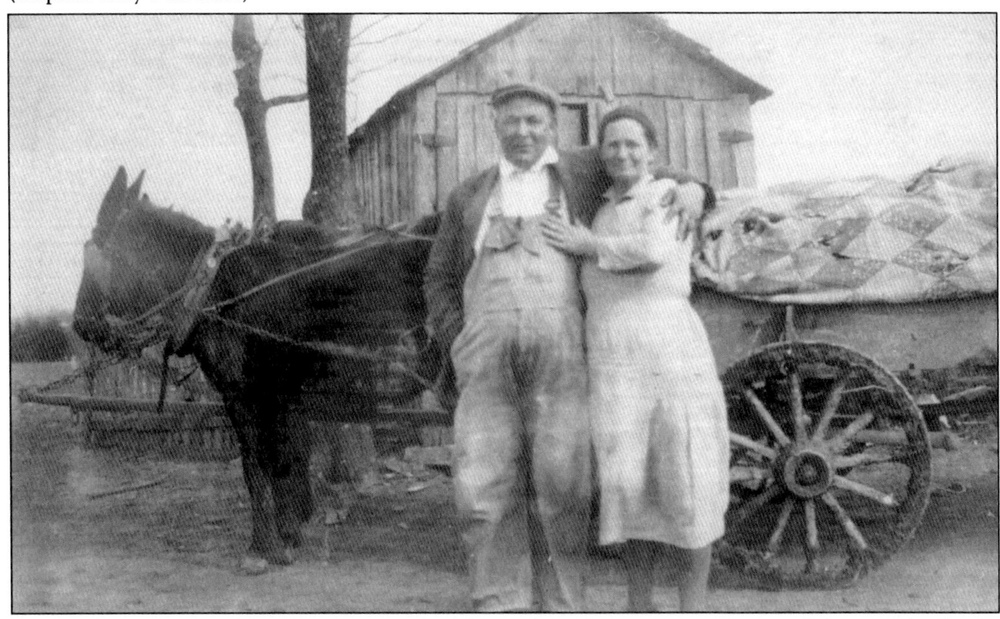

Lovely Farm Couple. W.W. Winters and his wife, Clare, pose in front of their mule-drawn wagon on their farm near Eddyville, in Lyon County, in the early 1930s. Their wagon is loaded with tobacco that they were taking to Hopkinsville to sell. The load is covered with an old quilt. Mules were a fixture on small farms throughout the state, partly because they required less food than horses. (KHS, JFI.1990ph2.a6JEFI1.)

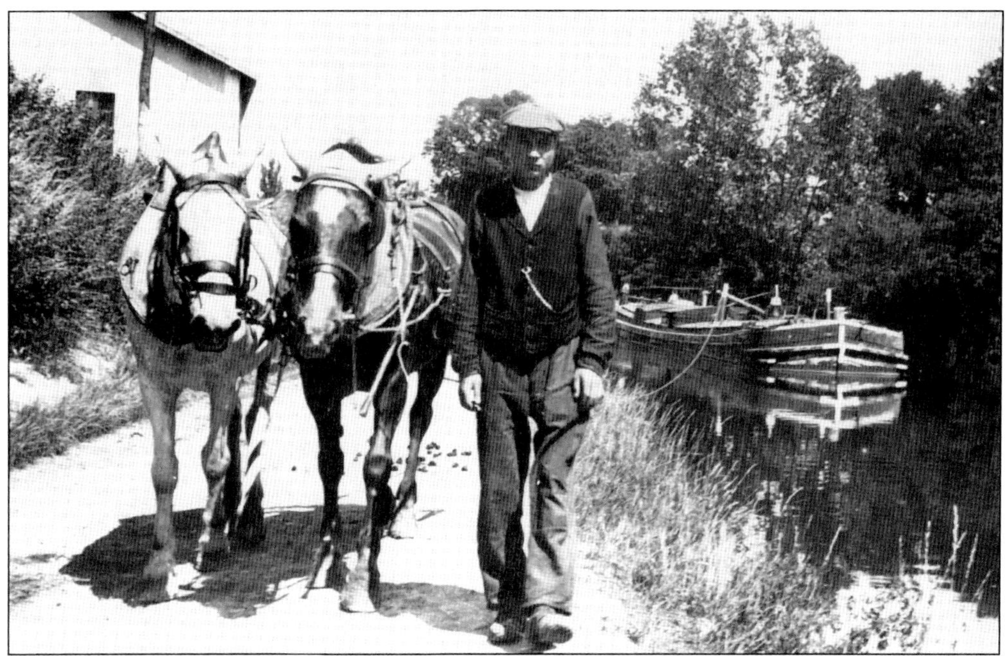

Pulling a Boat. This man is guiding a team of horses along the top of a levee as they pull a boat through a canal in the 1920s. Horses and mules were responsible for pulling barges and canal boats through America's extensive canal system for more than 150 years. Canal boats are flat-bottomed boats with square ends designed to transport freight on inland waterways. (KHS, MCA.1990ph2.5MCA10.)

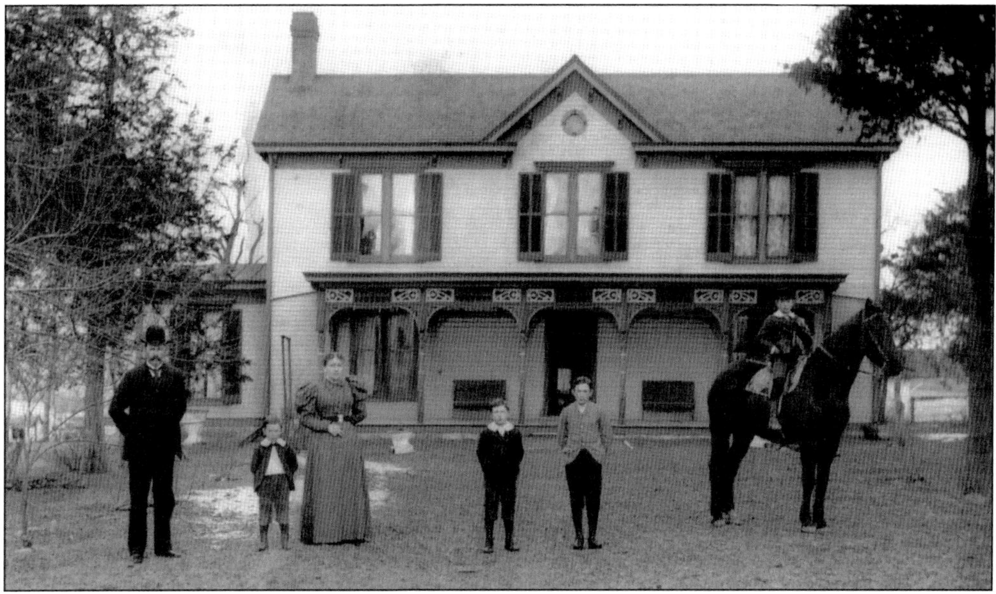

Clintonville Family. This 1890s family portrait, taken in front of the Haley home in Clintonville, in Bourbon County, includes a boy on horseback, which was often a part of outdoor group photographs in this era. The family members are, from left to right, William Haley, Isaac Haley, Amelia Cunningham Haley, Thomas Haley, Brent Haley, and William Kelly Haley, on horseback. William Kelly Haley went on to serve as a Bourbon County magistrate. (Hopewell Museum.)

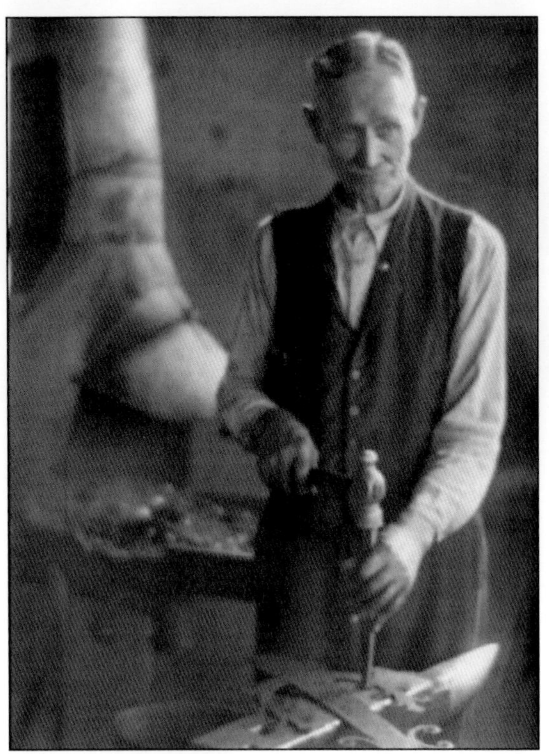

Berea Blacksmith at Work. Wesley Allen is hard at work on a large horseshoe at his anvil in this undated photograph. Blacksmiths were crucial during this era, as horses, especially those who had to travel on hard surfaces like brick or cobblestone, had to have their shoes replaced often. According to an article in the *Milwaukee Journal*, "A well-traveled horse was reshod every six weeks. The normal charge for reshoeing a draft horse was 30 cents." (Berea College Special Collections.)

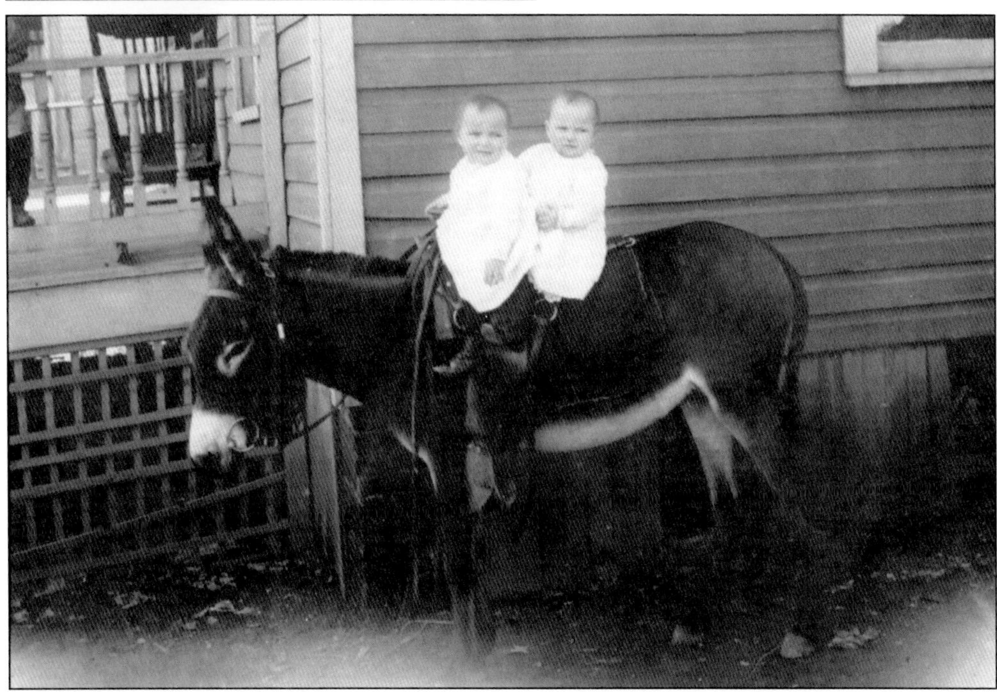

Babies on a Burro. Twins pose in white gowns and button-up leather high-top shoes in this undated photograph taken in Bourbon County. The back of the photograph reads only, "Almeda's twins," so there is no way to tell for sure if they are boys or girls. In this era, both sexes were dressed similarly when they were babies. Burros are small donkeys. (Hopewell Museum.)

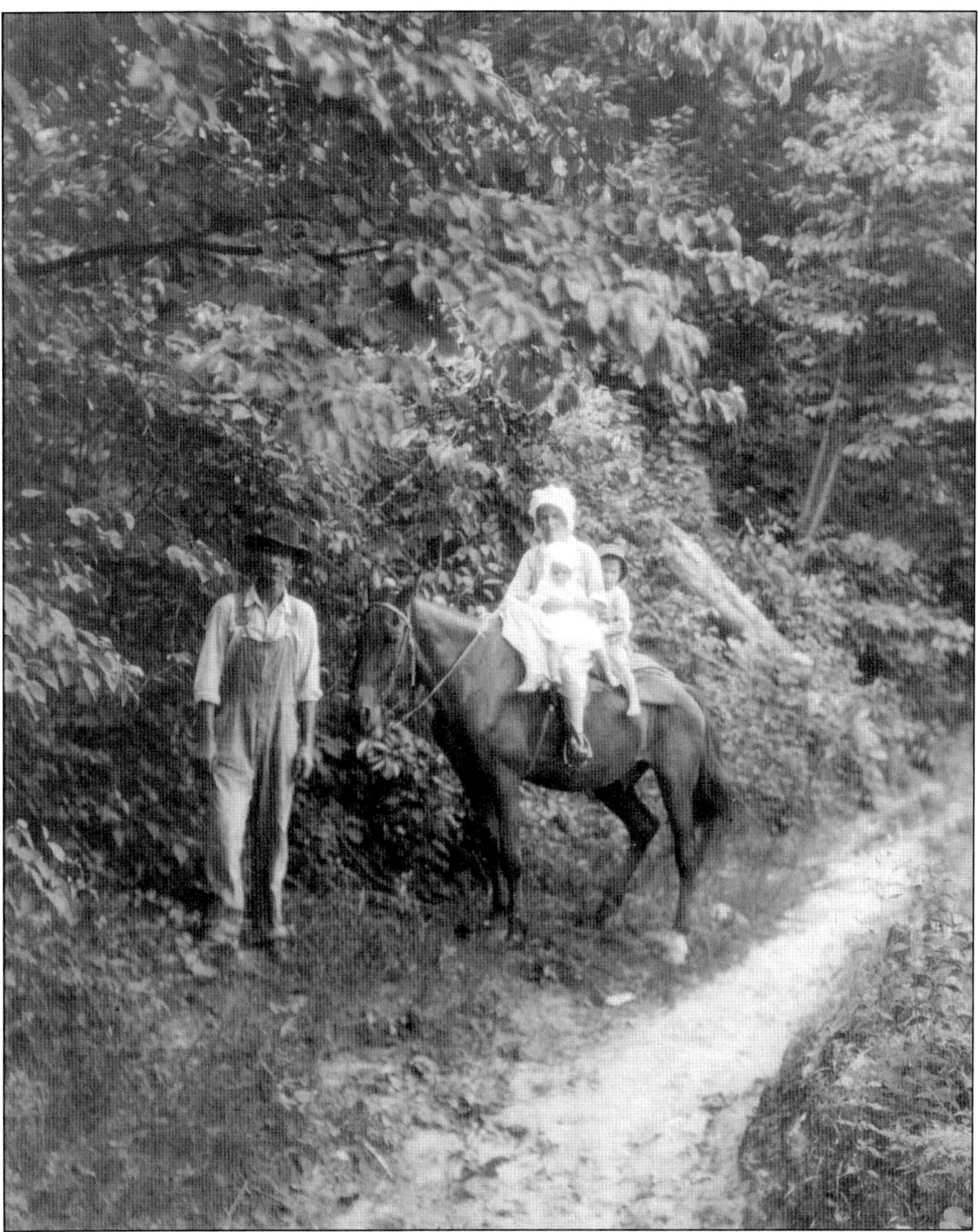

A Family and Their Horse. This undated photograph of a man and his young family was most likely taken in the mountains of Eastern Kentucky. The man is leading a horse that carries his wife and two small children along a narrow dirt path amid the riotous growth of midsummer. Residents in the remote areas of the state needed a horse or a mule to provide transportation and to assist with myriad daily chores. According to US Department of Agriculture statistics quoted in the *Equine Review*, the horse population in the United States reached its high point in 1920, with more than 25 million horses, mules, and ponies. That was three years after the manufacture of the first Ford tractor, in 1917. The growing popularity of tractors and the family automobile cut the equine population in half by 1940, and the trends in Kentucky mirrored those in the rest of the country. (Berea College Special Collections.)

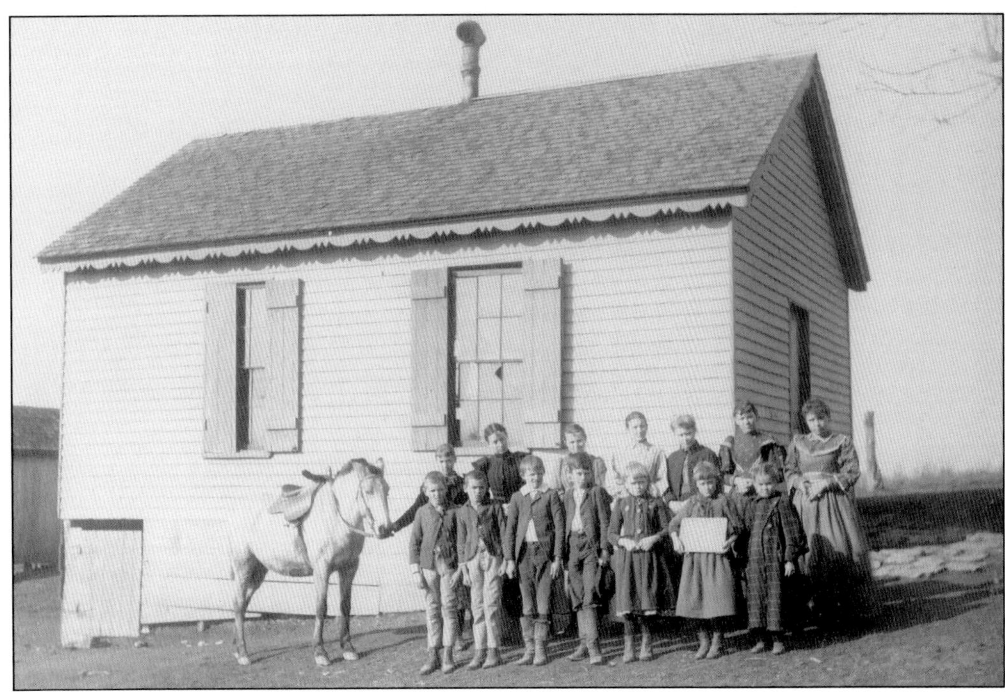

One-Room Schools. These two photographs of one-room schools in Fayette County capture the teachers, the mainly female students, and, in both cases, a horse used by one or more of the students to travel to school each day. Most children walked, and some students in the county were served by horse- or mule-drawn buses or wagons. These photographs were taken in 1901 by Massillon Alexander Cassidy, who served as superintendent of the Fayette County schools from 1885 to 1901. The school for white students (above) was the Hearne School. In the photograph below, the school for African American students is identified on the slate board held by the child in front as "Owisly Academy No. 2 H.G. Owisly Teacher." (Both, UK Special Collections.)

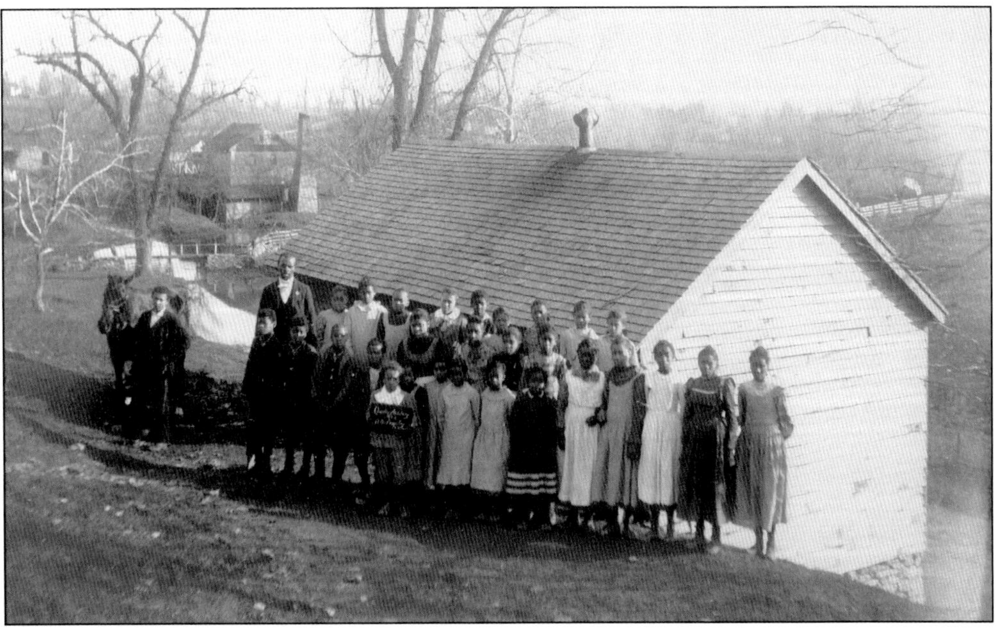

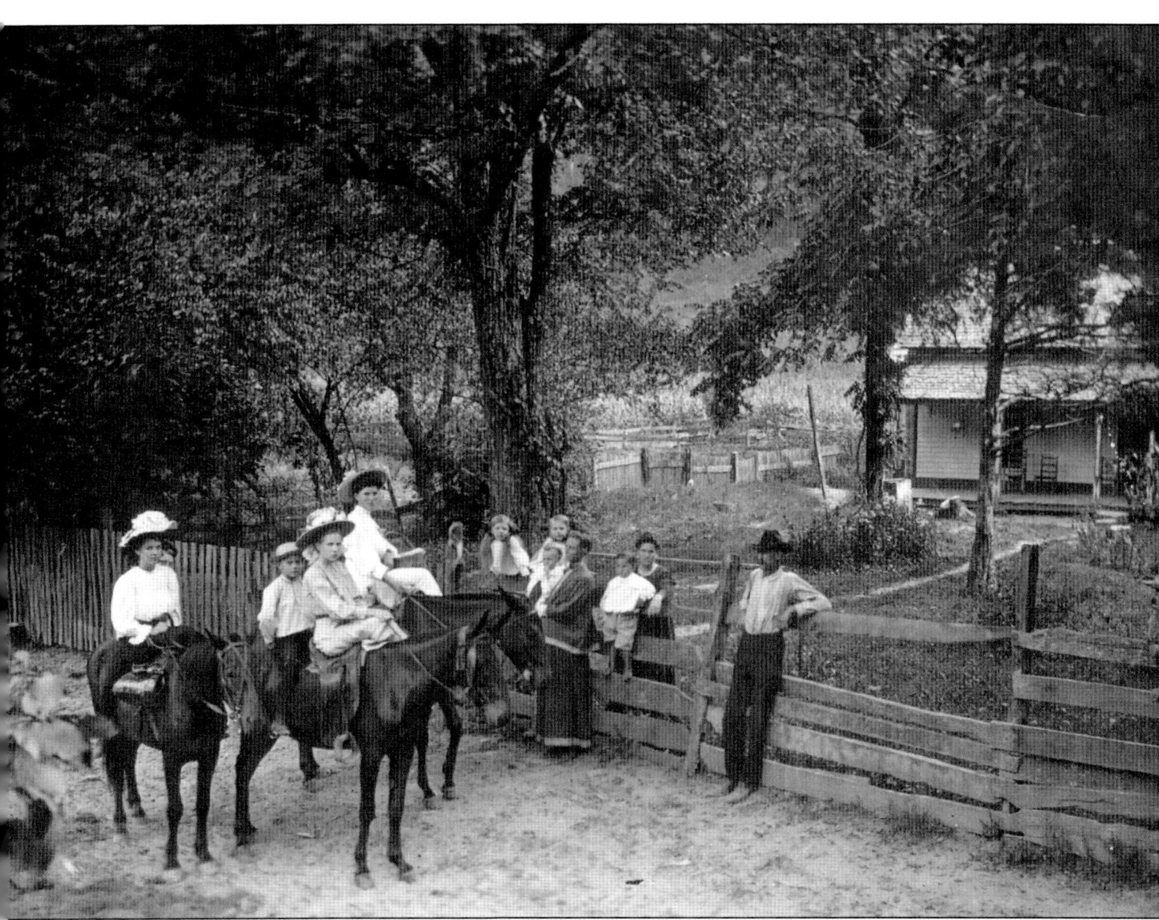

To Berea School. Here, three girls attired in neat dresses and lovely flowered hats ride sidesaddle on mules. Photographed sometime before 1901, they are ready to leave home and travel to Berea to attend school. Berea College also operated a high school and an elementary school for students from the mountain region of Eastern Kentucky who did not have educational opportunities where they lived. A small boy is perched behind the mounted girl in the center It also looks like there is a young boy or girl behind the girl at left. Perhaps they will also be attending school in Berea, or they will be bringing the mules back home after they deliver the girls to school. There is no luggage visible in the photograph, which is a bit puzzling. The girls are being seen off by parents and siblings. (Berea College Special Collections.)

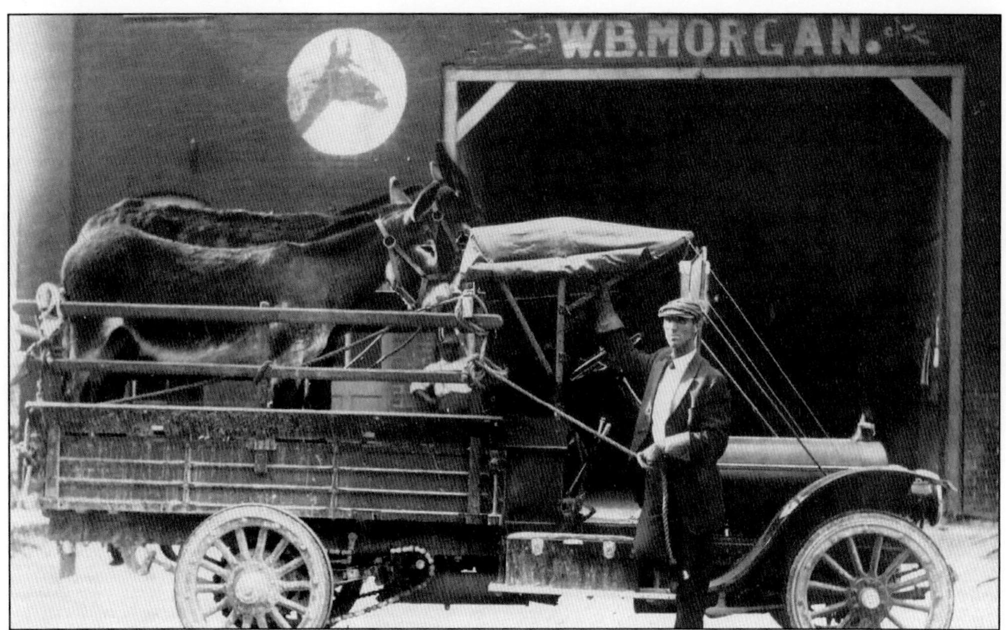

Take a Load off. It was not often that donkeys got to ride instead of using their hooves, but they did on this occasion. This undated photograph was taken in front of the W.B. Morgan Livery Stable on Main Street in Frankfort. The man with the cap is standing next to a very early pickup truck with canvas sides on the cab to keep out the rain. (Capital City Museum.)

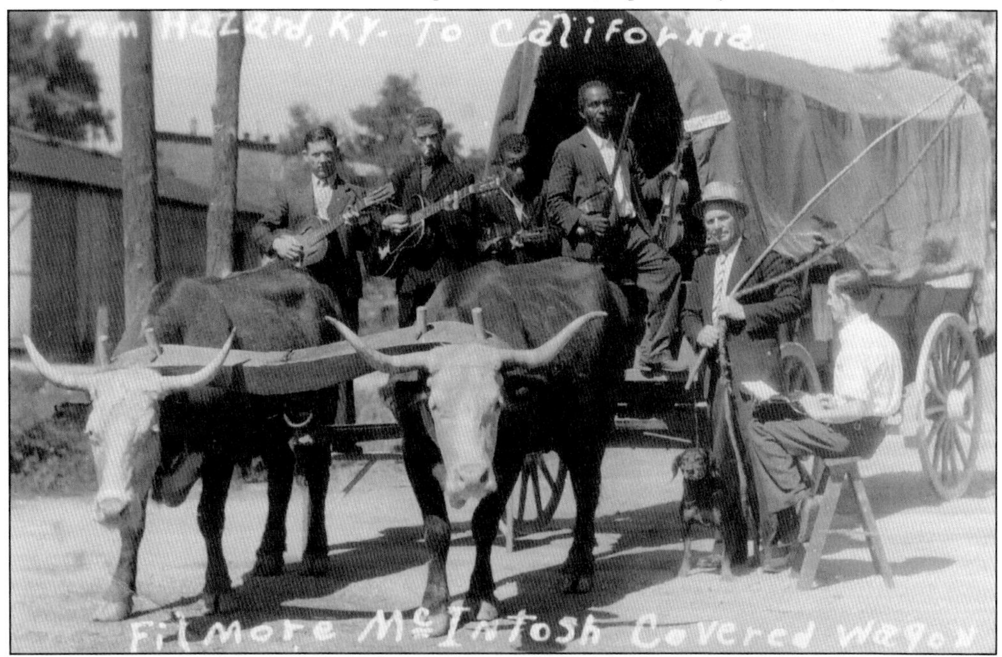

On a Long Trek. This undated photograph shows a four-man musical group and a driver holding a whip. The covered wagon is pulled by a team of oxen. Beside the wagon is a seated man with a typewriter. The handwriting at the top reads "From Hazard, Ky. to California." The assumption is that the band is planning to make the 2,395-mile trip as a publicity stunt. (Berea College Special Collections.)

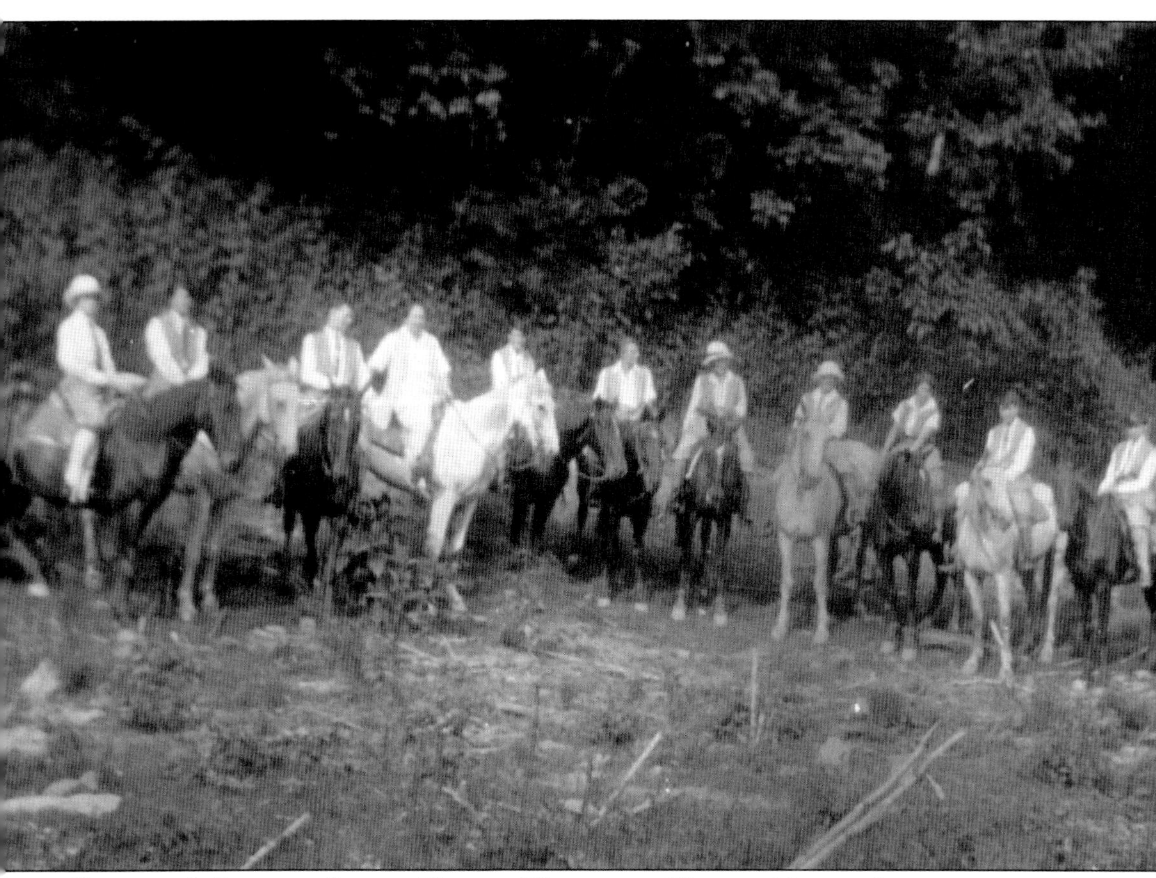

Kentucky's Frontier Service Nurses. This group of Frontier Nursing Service nurses on horseback includes founder Mary Breckinridge, according to the information on the back of the 1931 photograph. Her position in the photograph is not identified. Breckinridge started the Frontier Nursing Service in 1925 to provide health care for children in remote rural areas, a cause she felt strongly about after the death of her two children. She opened the Hospital and Health Center in 1928 and eventually opened several other nursing outposts in the mountains of Eastern Kentucky. The Frontier Nursing Service nurses were also trained midwives, and their work drastically reduced the maternal death rate for their patients compared to the nationwide average. (Berea College Special Collections.)

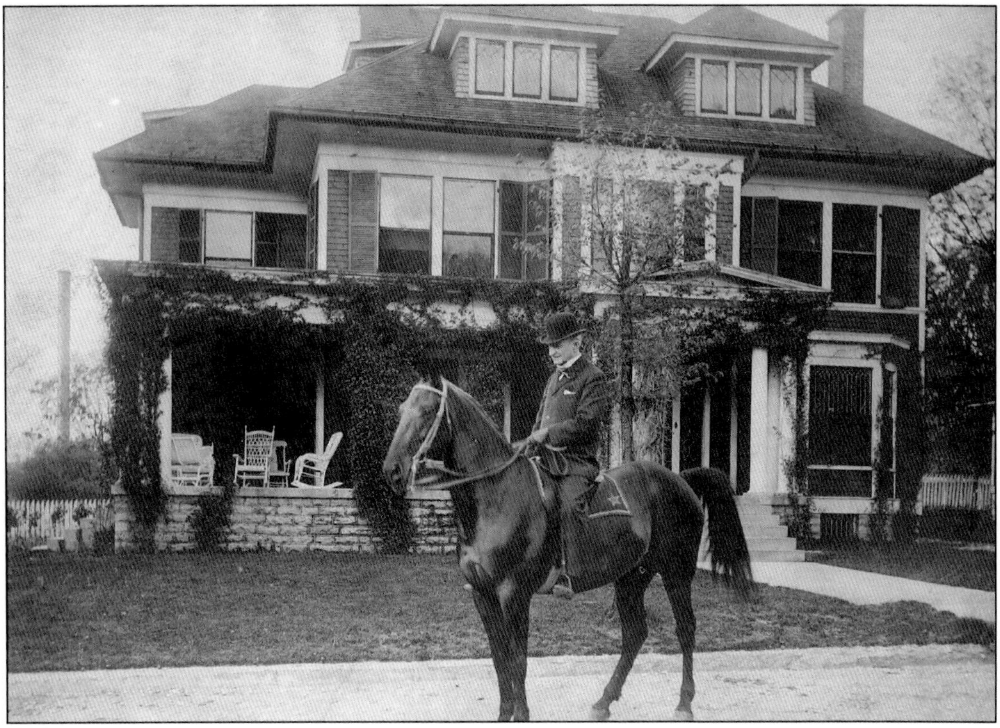

DAPPER MAN ON HORSEBACK. This 1905 photograph shows Prue Mason mounted on a handsome horse in front of his home. This was the second-to-last house on Wapping Street in Frankfort. The house looks comfortable, especially the porch and its white wicker rocking chairs. It looks like the perfect place to sit on a summer evening and watch the traffic move slowly past the house. (Capital City Museum.)

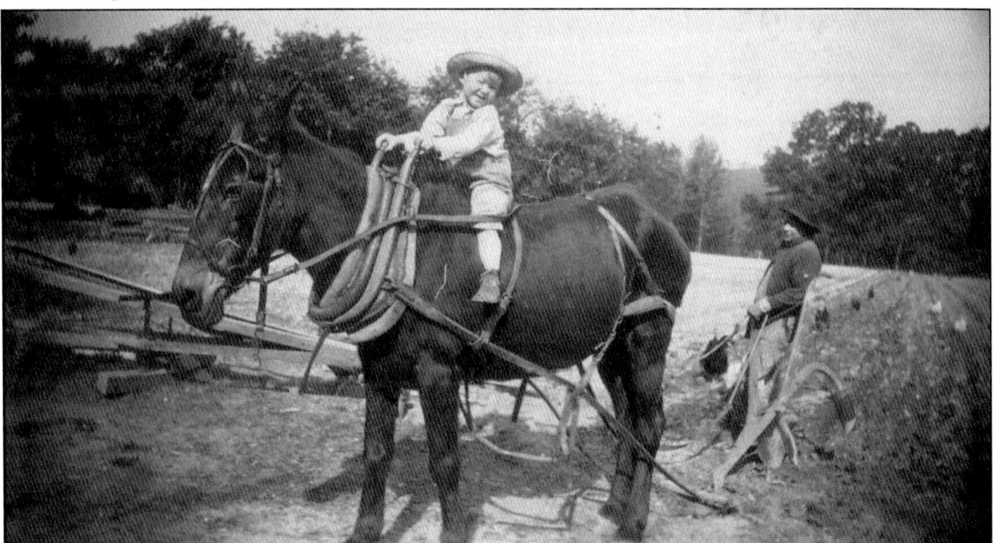

YOUNG BOY ON MULE. Young Earl Willis is "helping" Charley Morganthaler with the plowing in this 1926 photograph. He is mounted on a large mule and holding on to the mule's horse collar. Morganthaler's farm was located near White Villa in Kenton County. It looks like his chickens are looking for some meaty worms in the recently plowed area behind him. (KHS, KEN.1990ph2.a.10KEN8.)

Five

In Government Service

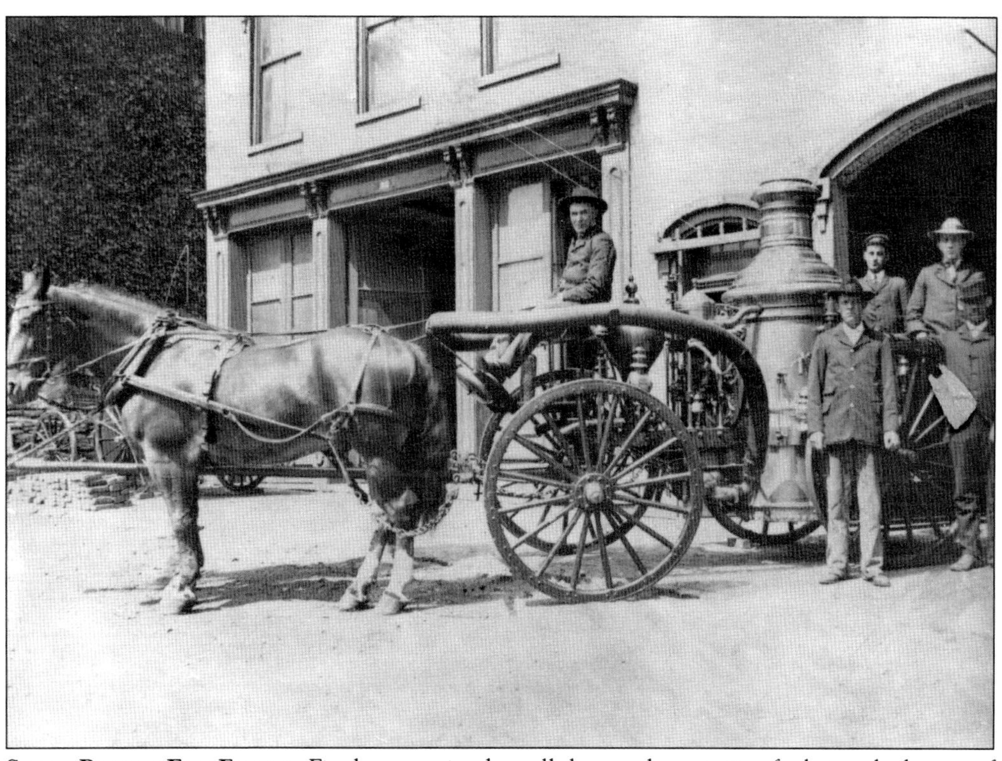

Steam Pumper Fire Engine. Fire horses gained a well-deserved reputation for being the heroes of the equine world. Highly trained and dependable, they also had to be strong and intelligent. The two horses shown here in the 1880s are hitched to an engine owned by the Paris Fire Department. Steam pumper fire engines were the backbone of most city fire departments between 1860 and 1920. (Authors' collection.)

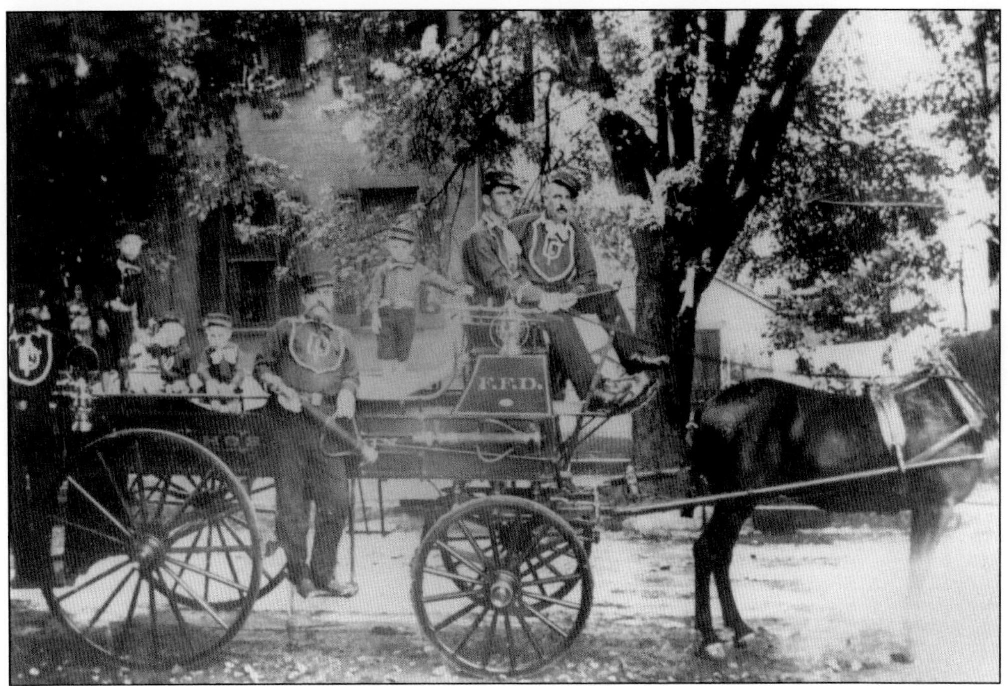

Cool Uniforms. In 1886, when this photograph was taken, members of Frankfort's fire department were known as engineers. These men took command at any fire and conducted regular fire drills. They also made sure that the engine was properly attended to and the horses cared for. One can assume that the little ones in the hose wagon are the firemen's offspring. (Capital City Museum.)

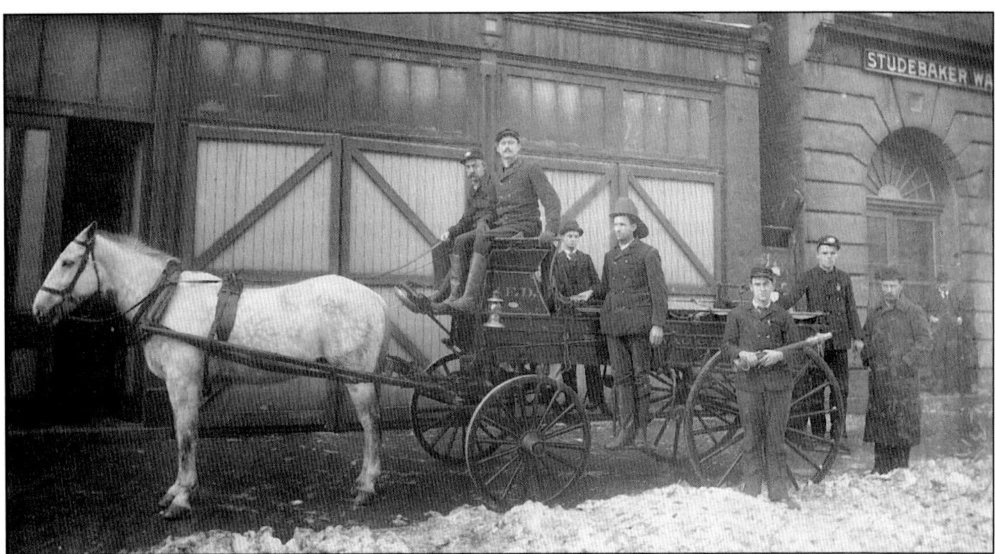

Soon to Be Paid. This 1892 photograph shows possibly the same hose wagon shown above, in front of the Frankfort firehouse on West Main Street. The man in the center is wearing the traditional "leatherhead" fire helmet. In 1895, Frankfort's common council established positions and annual salaries for firemen. The positions were: fire chief, hydrantman, drivers (pumper, hose wagon, and hook and ladder), pipeman, and two runners. (Capital City Museum.)

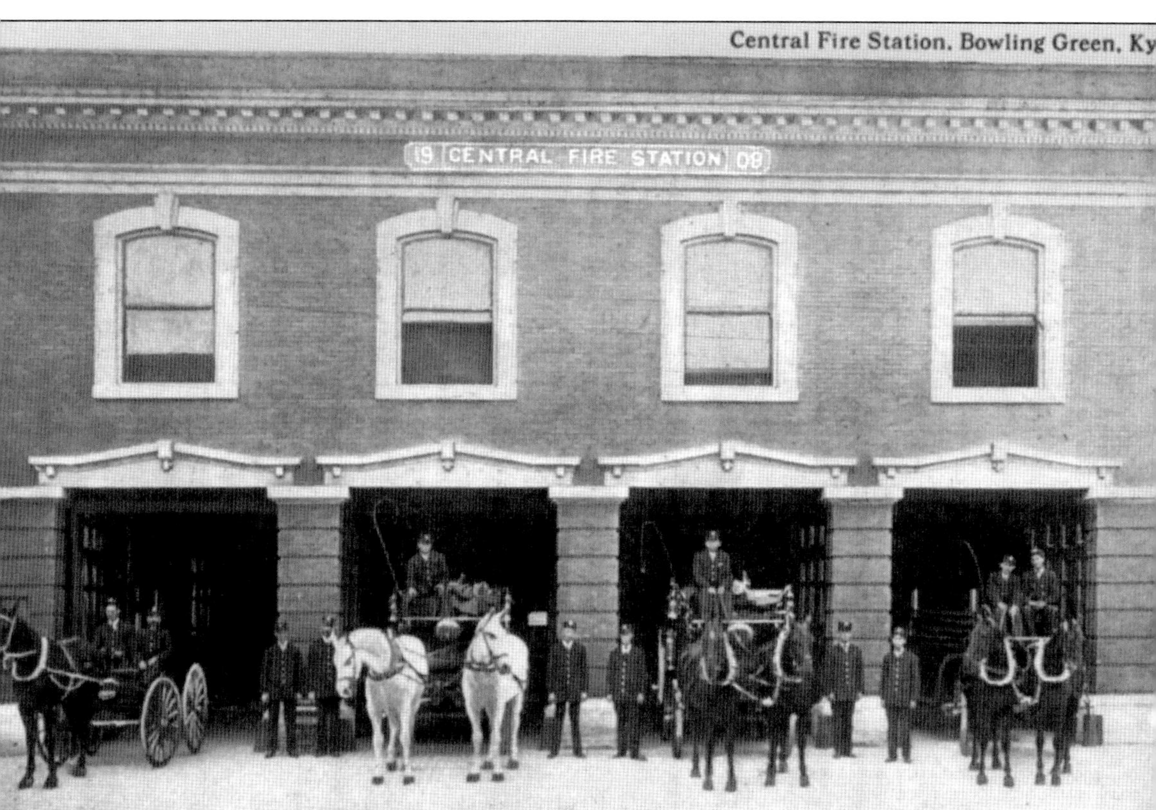

Central Fire Station. This 1908 postcard shows Bowling Green's new central fire station. The facility appears to be staffed during this shift, with twelve firefighters, four vehicles, and seven horses. In the shadows of each wagon bay, hanging from the ceiling, are what appear to be swinging harness apparatuses. The swinging harness, developed in the 1870s, allowed the horses to position themselves in front of their assigned wagon, then the special harnesses were dropped across their backs and secured with special large snap catches. This allowed the horses to be moving their wagons and men out of the station within 10 to 12 seconds of the alarm. Generally, the fire departments preferred four-to-five-year-old geldings that weighed 1,500 to 1,600 pounds and were 16 to 17 hands high. Emphasis was placed on quickness, agility, and intelligence. Because of the heavy pounding over paved streets at a gallop, the horses' hooves were given special attention and care. After a fire, the horses were walked around the street until they were dry and could be brushed and curried. (KHS, Graphic 5.Box2.182.)

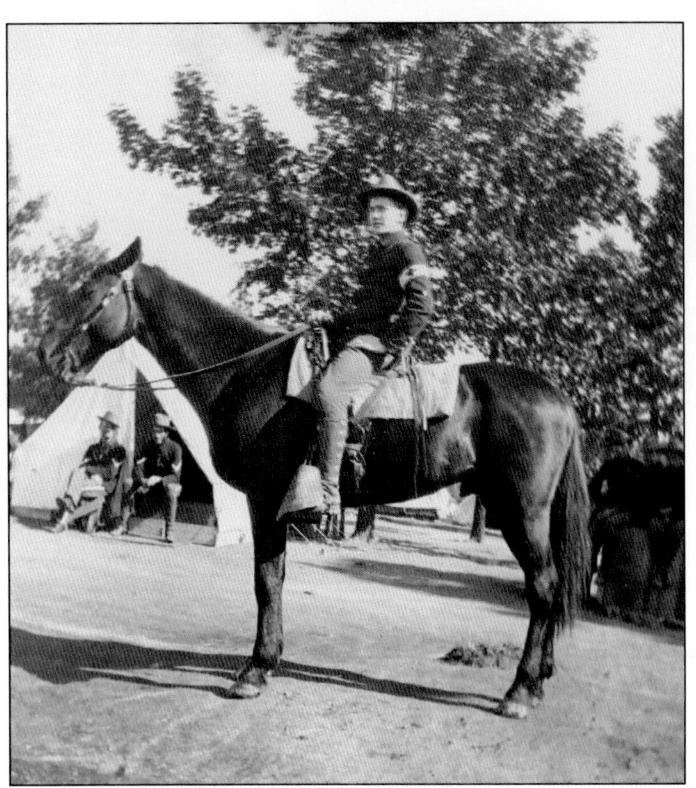

Red Cross Soldier. An unarmed medical volunteer poses on his horse in 1898. The Spanish-American War was the first time the American Red Cross provided services to members of the armed forces at war. When the United States declared war on Spain, the 76-year-old president of the Red Cross, Clara Barton, traveled to hospitals to recruit nurses to work for the Army at camps in Florida and Cuba. (KHS, MAS.1990ph2.13MAS47.)

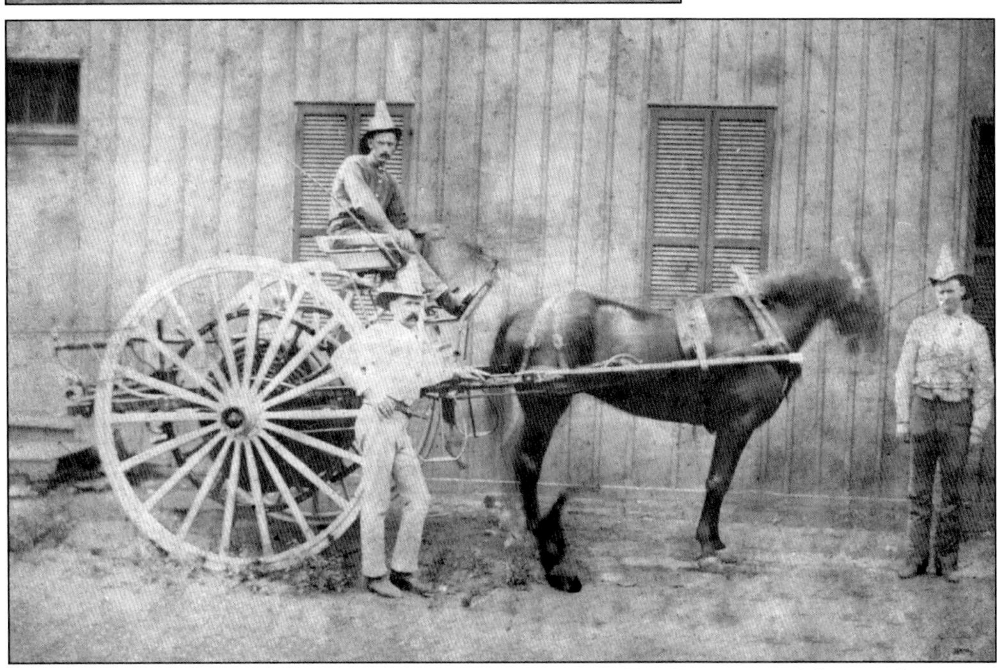

Covington Fire Department. Kenton County's Covington Fire Department's hose reel wagon is seen at the Main Street firehouse in 1877. The end of the hose was connected to the steam-powered pumper, and the horse would slowly walk forward as the hose unwound. The driver is "Blink" Bowers, and the pipemen are John Collum (left) and James Sanford. (KHS, BNE.1990ph2.1BNE1.)

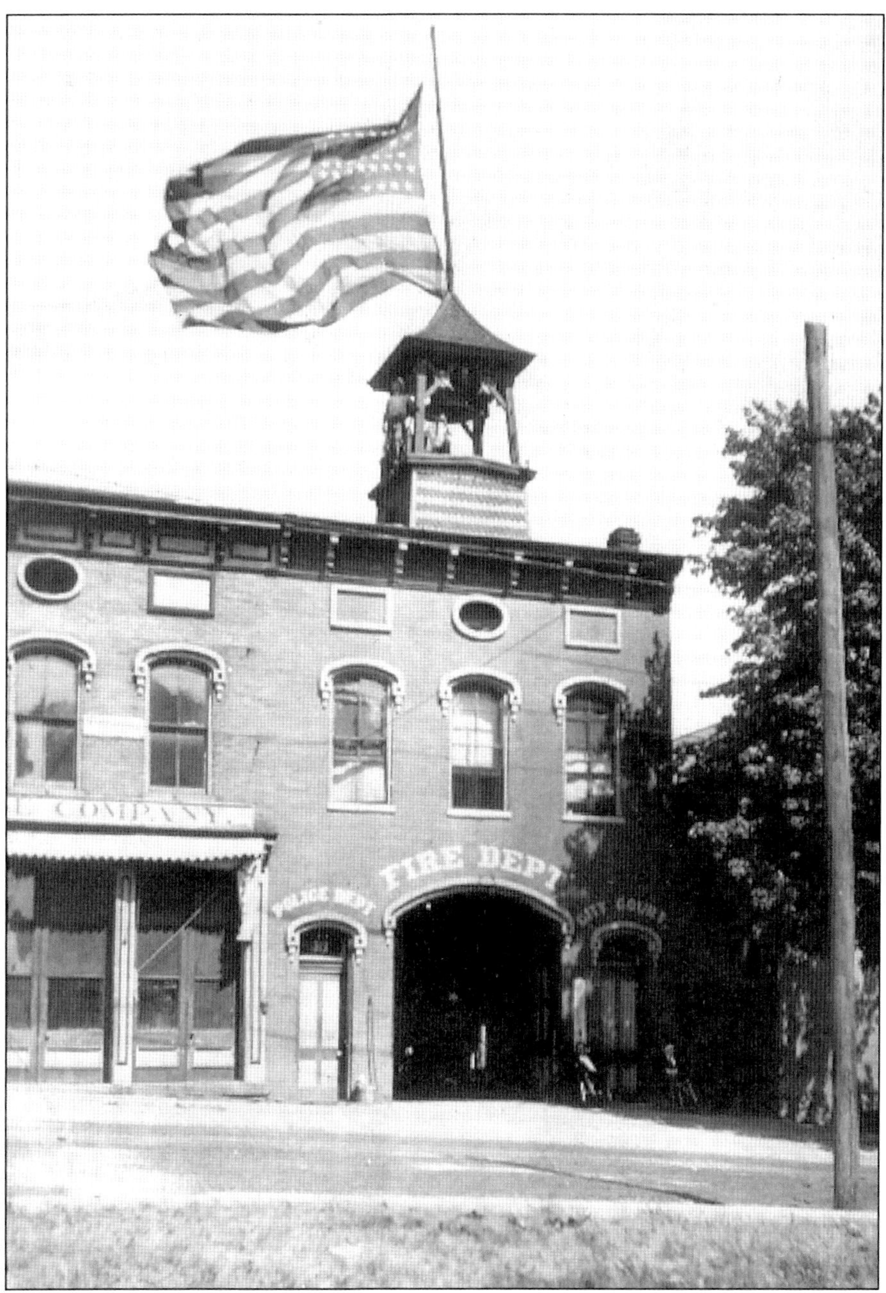

Fire Department and Flag. This building in Paris may seem unassuming, but if it could talk, it would have lots of stories to tell. The structure has housed a fire engine of some sort since it was built in 1875. Originally known as the Rescue Fire Department, an all-volunteer group organized in 1874, the Paris Fire Department was established in 1889. Paris City Hall and the police department were still housed on the second floor when this photograph was taken in the 1890s. The adjoining building on the left was built as the Holliday & Huddleston Carriage Factory. It later served as an automobile dealership until it was destroyed by fire in 1927. It was rebuilt as an extension of the fire department. The 45-star flag flying from the fire bell tower is estimated to be at least 16 feet by 30 feet in size. (Hopewell Museum.)

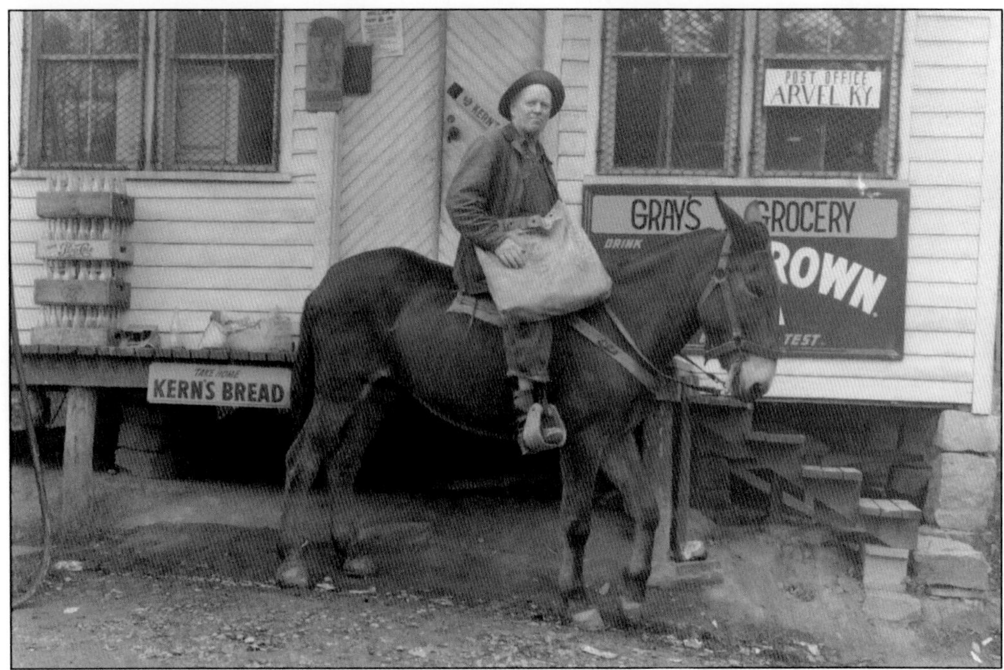

MULEBACK MAILMAN. Herbert McQueen delivered mail from Evelyn to New Zion, in Estill County, six days a week for nearly 20 years. He claimed to wear out two mules a year. He is seen here at Arvel, a post office near Brushy Mountain. Mules were perfect for this kind of work. Hardy and sure-footed, they were also easier to care for than horses. (Berea College Special Collections.)

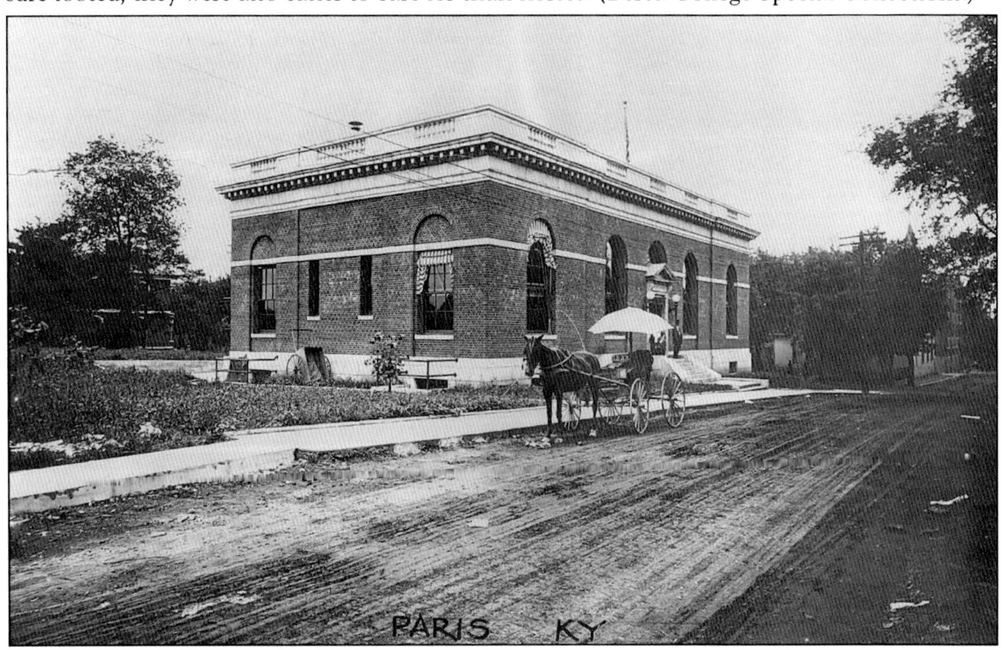

POST OFFICE NOW SERVES AS MUSEUM. This handsome Beaux Arts building on the corner of Pleasant and Eighth Streets in Paris was originally built as a post office. It was then used as the Paris City Hall before becoming the Hopewell Museum. In this early photograph, a horse and buggy are parked on the unpaved street next to the building. (Hopewell Museum.)

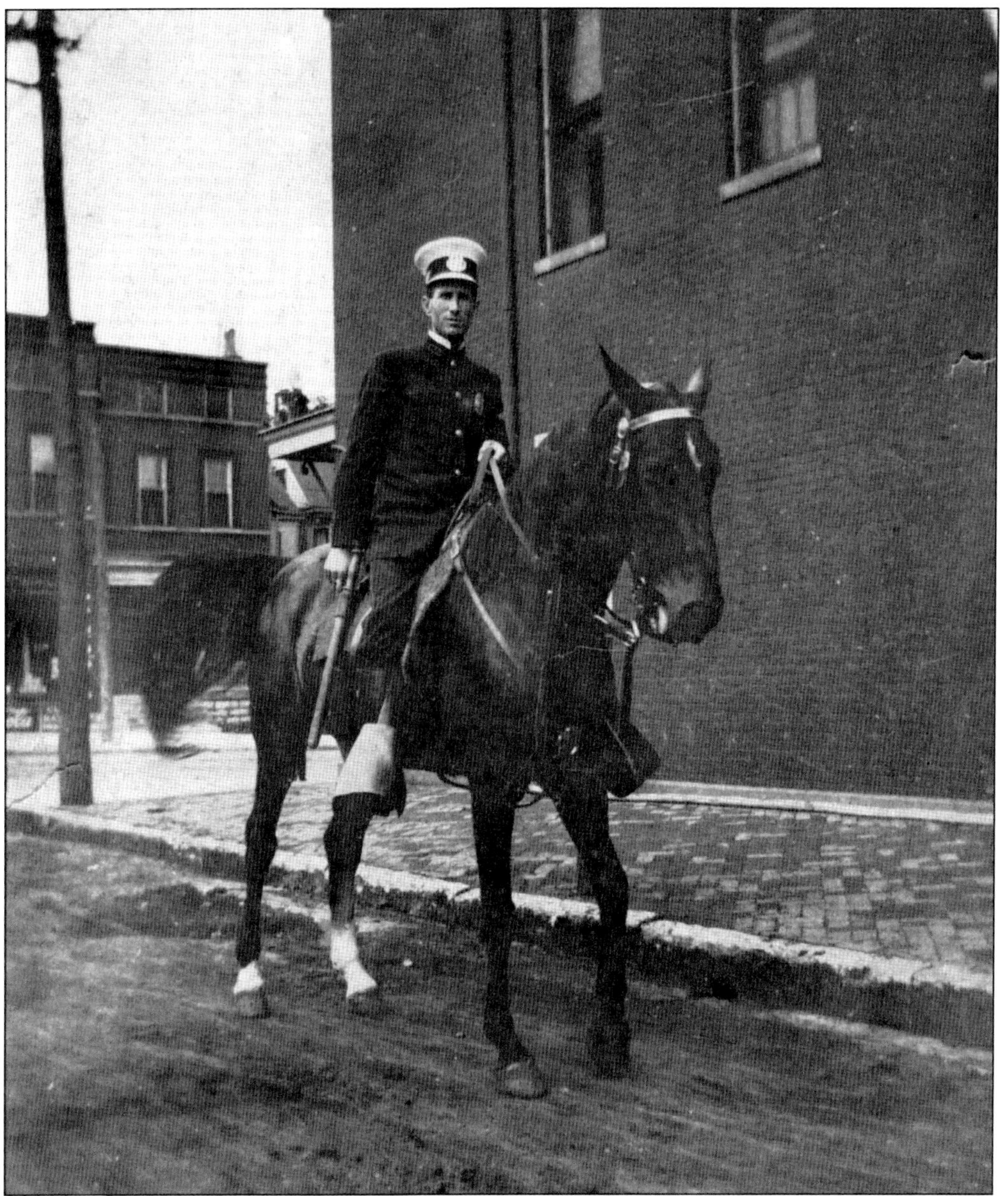

Lawman on Horseback. Mounted policemen, like Louisville officer Clem Yeager, pictured here in 1908, were a common sight in Kentucky's cities during this era. Almost without fail, their mounts were as well-turned-out as the lawmen who depended on them. The 1907 Louisville police budget was $311,851. The largest expense was for 340 policemen; the second-largest was for horses. Feed expenditures totaled $4,801, purchased horses cost $1,925, and horseshoes were $1,206. One of the police chief's biggest concerns was that the budget did not include funds to acquire the new horseless carriages. It was difficult, if not impossible, for his horses or bicycles to apprehend most of the "fast" horseless carriages. In March 1937, the mounted patrol was disbanded, and 12 horses, with an average age of 11 years, were auctioned off for an average price of $138.75. One of the horses, Kelley, was, judging by his teeth, between 27 and 32 years old. Kelley was pulled from the sale at the last minute and declared a duly pensioned member of the force. (KHS, JFL.1990ph2.9JEFL9.)

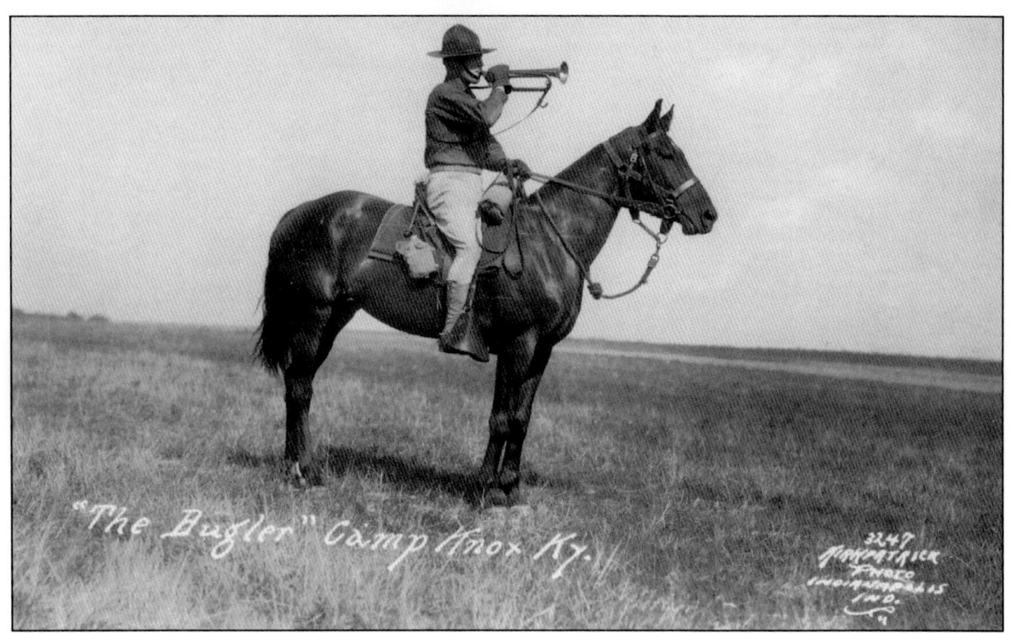

The Bugler. The horse in this 1918 photograph, taken at Camp Knox, had learned to stand at attention when the bugle calls were made. Historically, the bugle was used in the cavalry to relay instructions to soldiers during battle. Bugle calls also indicated changes in the daily routines of camp. Since cavalrymen had horses to look after, they heard twice as many signals as did regular infantry. (KHS, Graphic5_Box4_414.)

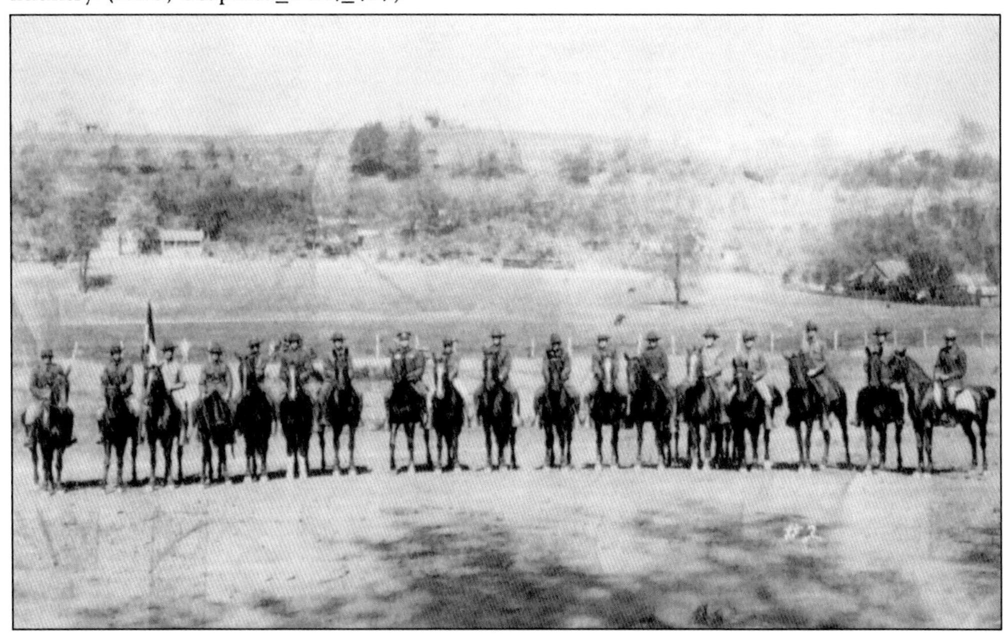

Kentucky Guard Cavalry. Pictured here is First Squad, Troop A, of Kentucky's proud 123rd Cavalry Regiment. The men are drilling outside of Frankfort in the late 1920s or early 1930s. Several units of the regiment were sent by Kentucky governors to quell problems during elections in Harlan County and at several coal-mining labor disputes in Eastern Kentucky. (Capital City Museum.)

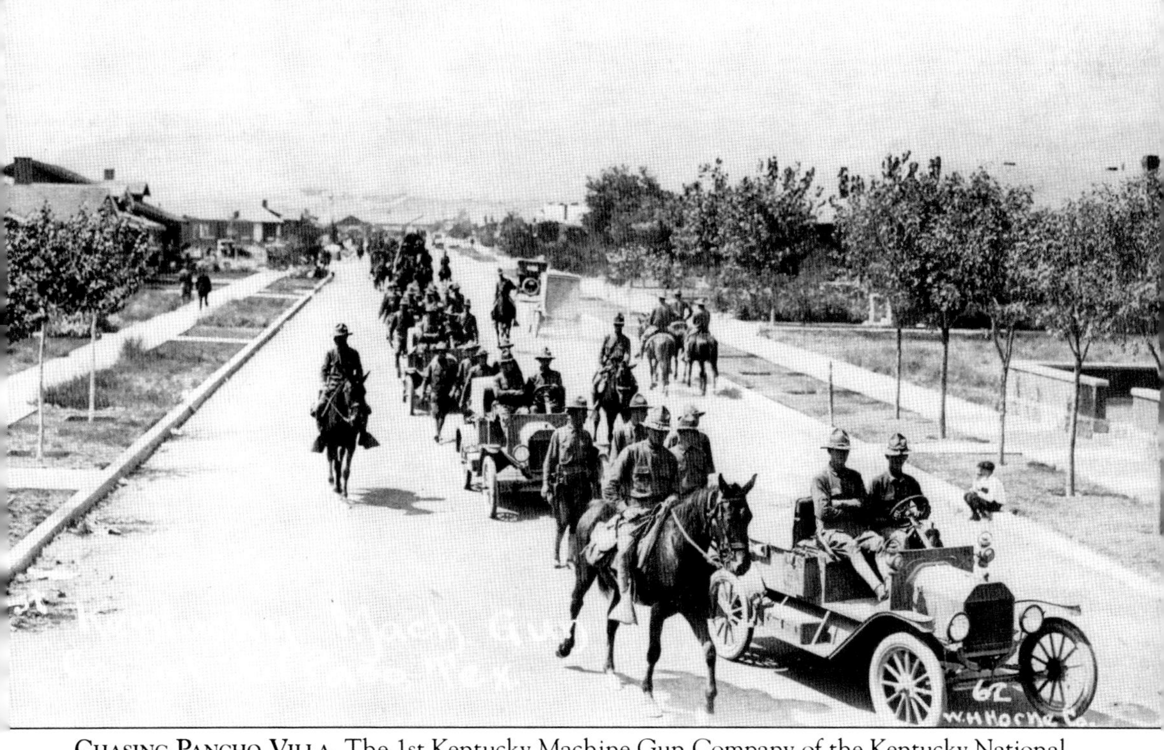

CHASING PANCHO VILLA. The 1st Kentucky Machine Gun Company of the Kentucky National Guard is seen in this 1916 photograph in El Paso, Texas. It had been ordered there as part of a larger force to patrol a 60-mile stretch of the Rio Grande to prevent incursions into the United States by the Mexican revolutionary Pancho Villa. The soldiers were armed with Lewis light machine guns mounted on the hoods of their Ford Model T trucks. Here, officers and noncommissioned officers ride alongside the trucks on horses. The unit saw little or no action and was ordered back to Kentucky in February 1917. However, the maneuvers in Texas and Mexico provided valuable experience for the approaching war in Europe. (KHS, 98MO3.B20.440.)

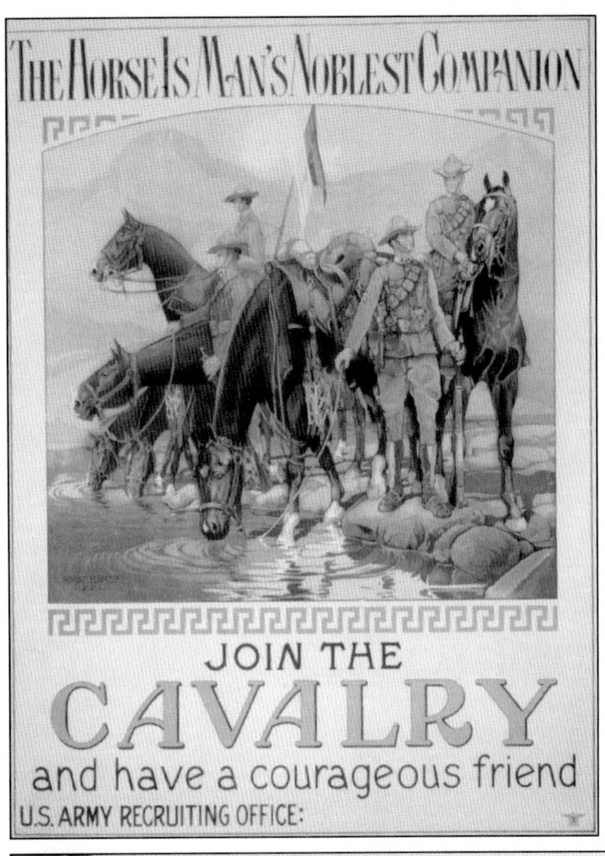

"Join the Cavalry." This patriotic appeal was for a military force that the United States would hardly use during World War I. The units that saw action did so mainly dismounted. But the military used horses and mules in great numbers for transport and remounts for allied cavalry units. An estimated one million horses and 350,000 mules were sent from the United States to Europe during the four years of the war. (LOC.)

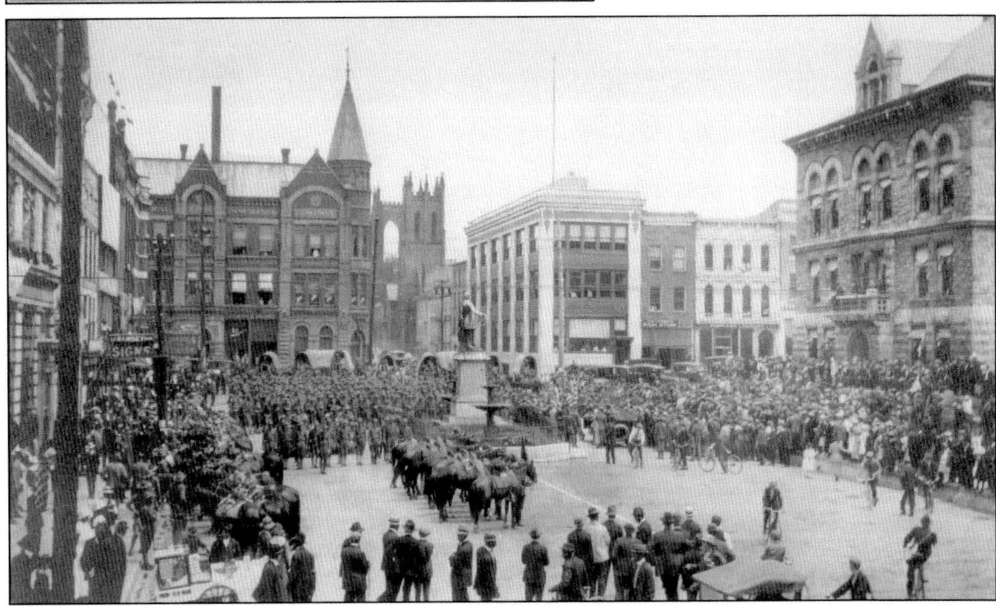

Troops in Lexington. This photograph, taken sometime during the World War I years, captures what is probably a Kentucky Guard unit gathered at Cheapside Square, next to the Fayette County Courthouse. Note the officers' horses drawn up in front of the troops and the horse-drawn wagons at the rear. Early automobiles are seen to the right of the wagons. (UK Special Collections.)

Six

Hauling the Loads

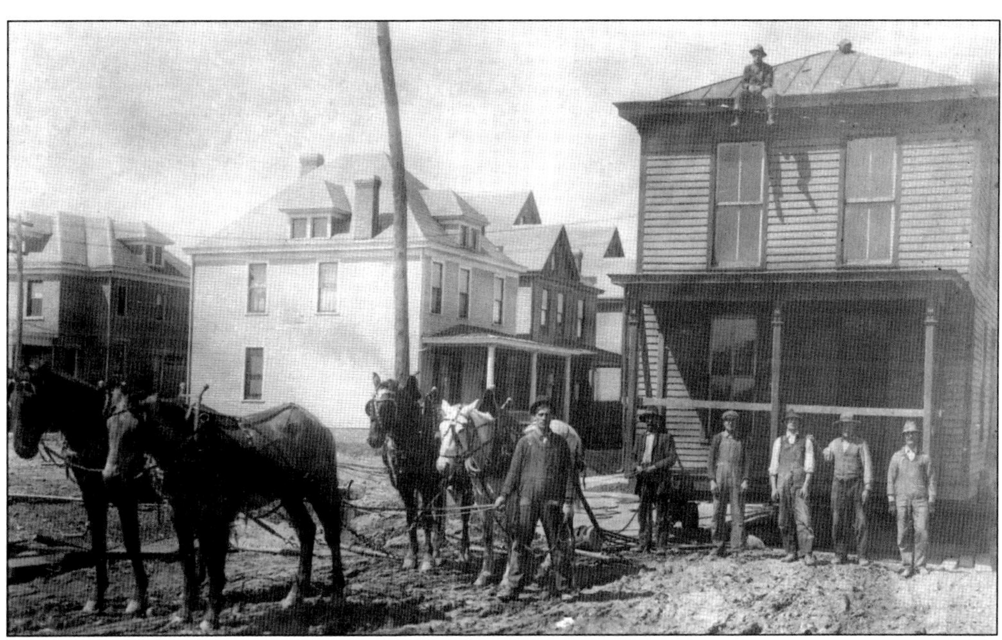

Moving Day. Tandem teams of horses are shown pulling a two-story frame house down a dirt street in Ashland around 1920. Moving houses was easier during Kentucky's horse-drawn era, as there were not as many electric lines to worry about. Even though it was easier to accomplish in the 1920s, it must have been an unusual sight to see a house slowly moving past one's window. (KHS, BOD.1990ph2.1BOD29.)

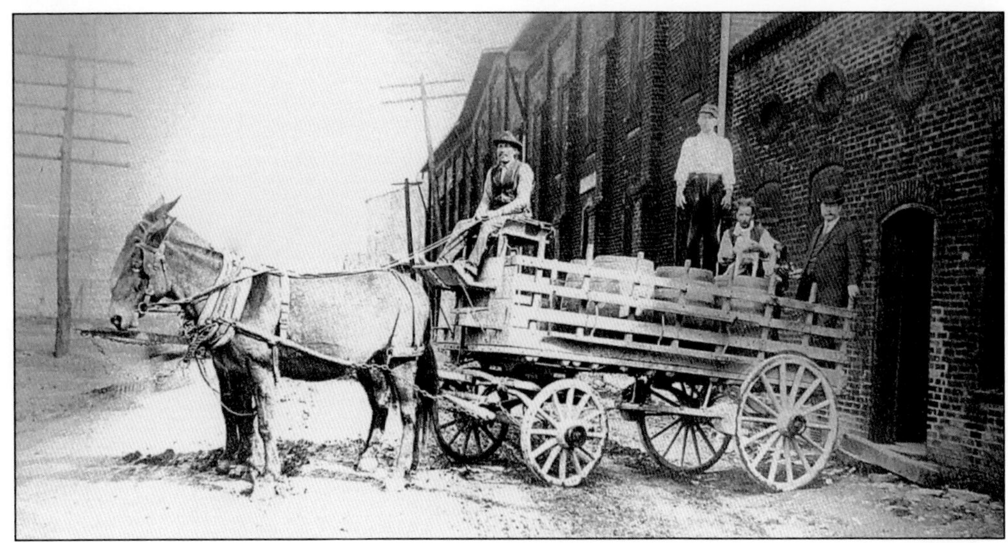

Wagonload of Bourbon Barrels. These men are either picking up or dropping off a load of bourbon barrels in Bourbon County in the 1880s. During that time, bourbon and tobacco warehouses were scattered throughout Paris, and there were seven operating bourbon distilleries in the county. The last one closed for good at the beginning of Prohibition. Despite claims to the contrary, Bourbon County is not a dry county. (Hopewell Museum.)

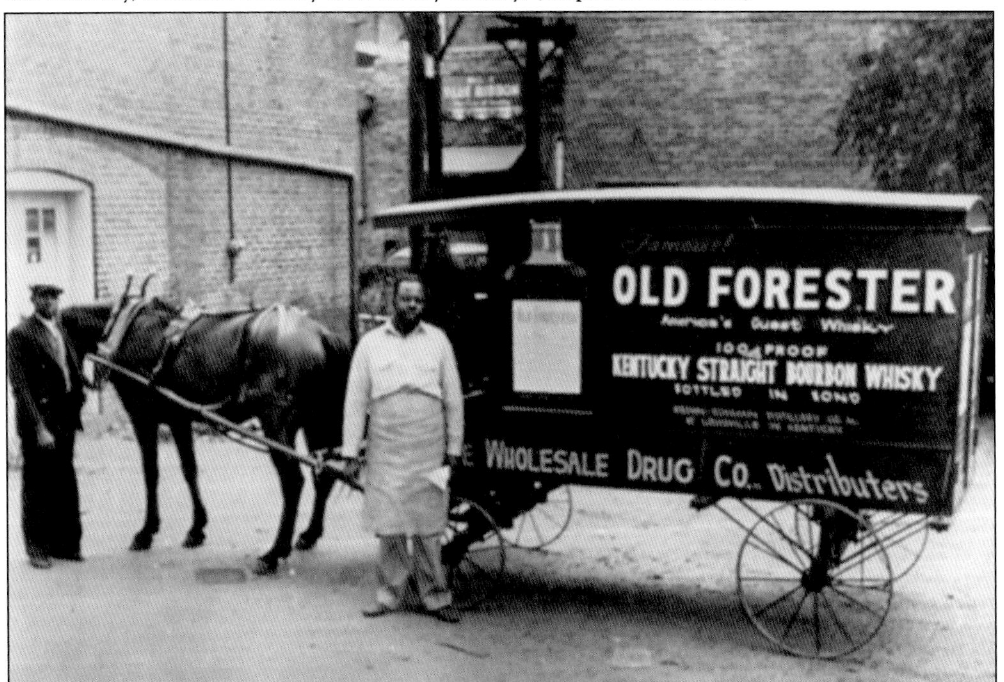

Medicinal Whiskey. This horse-drawn wagon delivered Old Forester "whisky" in Louisville. Old Forester was the flagship brand of the partnership formed by George Garvin Brown and his brother J.T.S. Brown. The company went through several name changes, eventually becoming Brown-Forman. It was the only Kentucky distilling business still controlled by its founding family at the time. Old Forrester (original spelling) Straight Bourbon Whisky was the first product sold in sealed bottles. (Brown-Forman Corporation.)

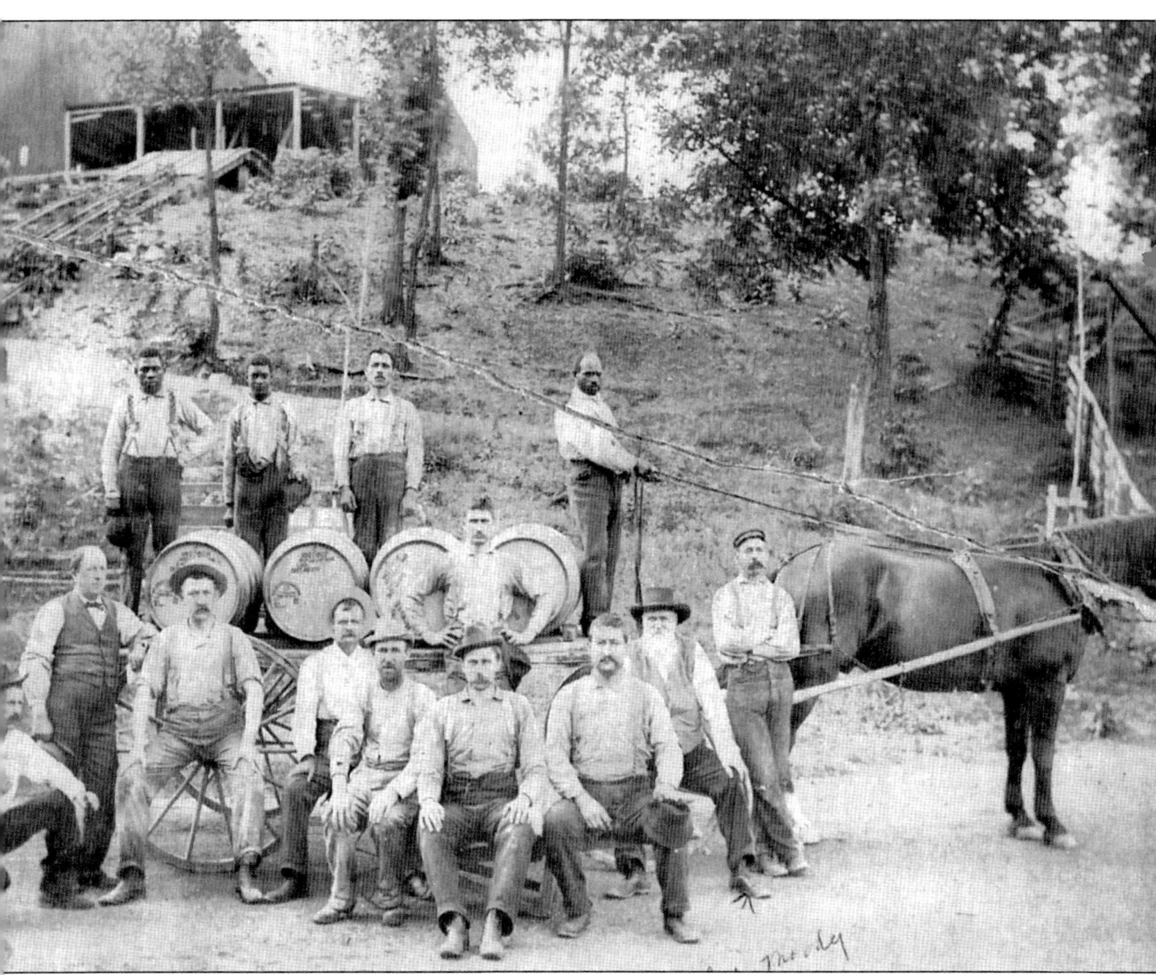

Barrel-Hauling Wagon. Around 1885, this crew turned out to have its photograph taken with a horse-drawn wagon carrying barrels of bourbon at Boldrick & Callaghan Distillery. Richard Wathen operated the distillery, on the Rolling Fork River in Marion County, from 1852 to 1875. After several ownership and name changes, the facility became the Boldrick & Callaghan Distillery and operated under that name until it was closed by Prohibition. The 19th Amendment meant the end of most of the hundreds of distilleries that were operating in the state at the time. A handful produced "medicinal whiskey" during Prohibition, and a few others reopened, but a great many never operated again. For more on Kentucky bourbon distilling, see the Arcadia Publishing book Images of America: *The Kentucky Bourbon Trail.* (Oscar Getz Whiskey Museum.)

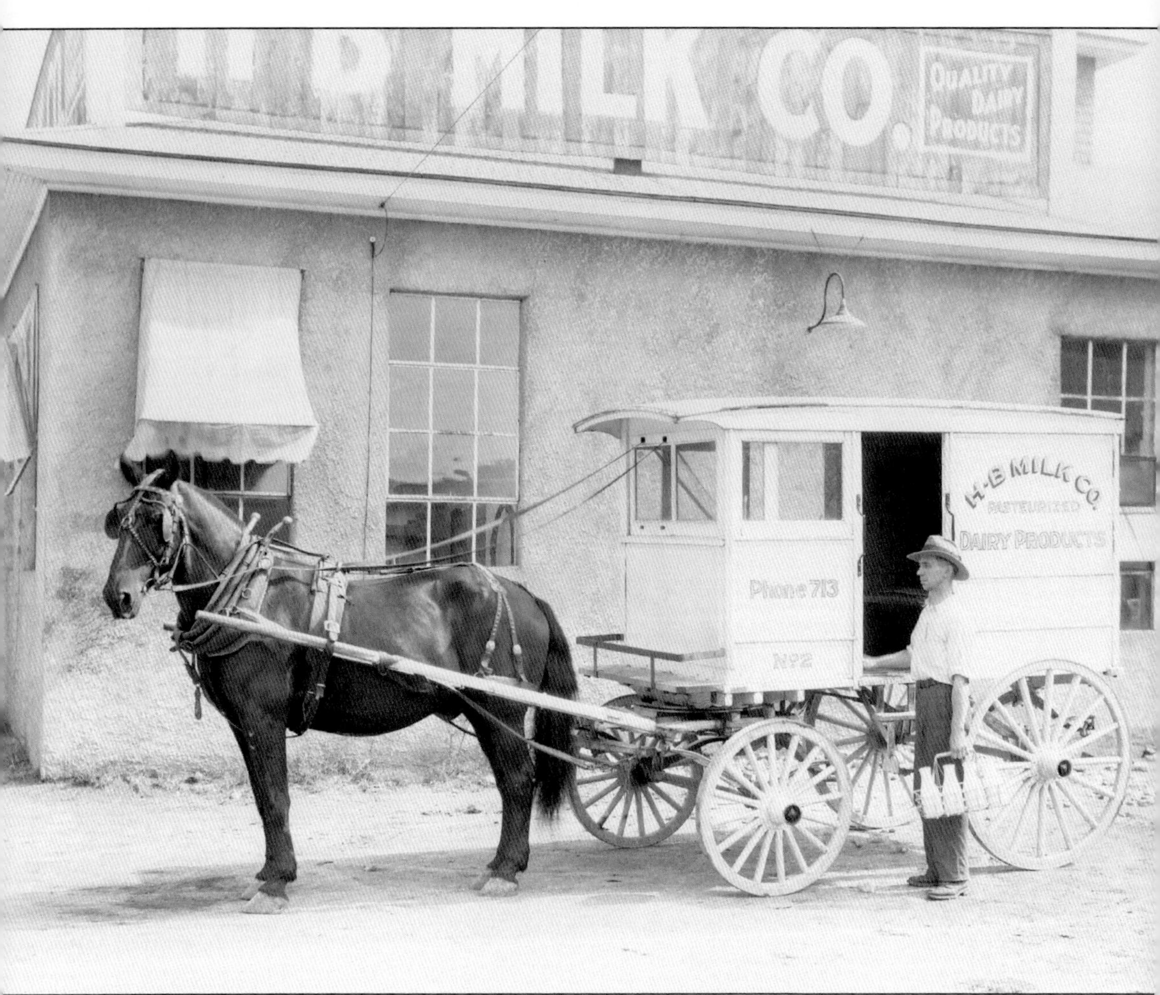

Milk Delivery Wagon. The H-B Milk Company in Frankfort was proud of its pasteurized milk products, which it advertised on the side of this natty delivery wagon. In this 1927 photograph, the deliveryman holds a wire rack carrying four quarts of milk. The horse provides the power to pull the wagon using a horse collar. Horse collars were designed to distribute a load around a horse's neck and shoulders, greatly increasing its pulling power by utilizing its strong hindquarters. In the late 1920s, both horse-drawn vehicles and early cars and trucks were used. Another photograph in this collection at the Kentucky Historical Society shows the H-B Dairy with a couple of Ford Model A trucks, filled with milk and cream cans, pulled up outside in 1927. The day of the horse was fading. (KHS, Graphic2_FreezerBag20_5768.)

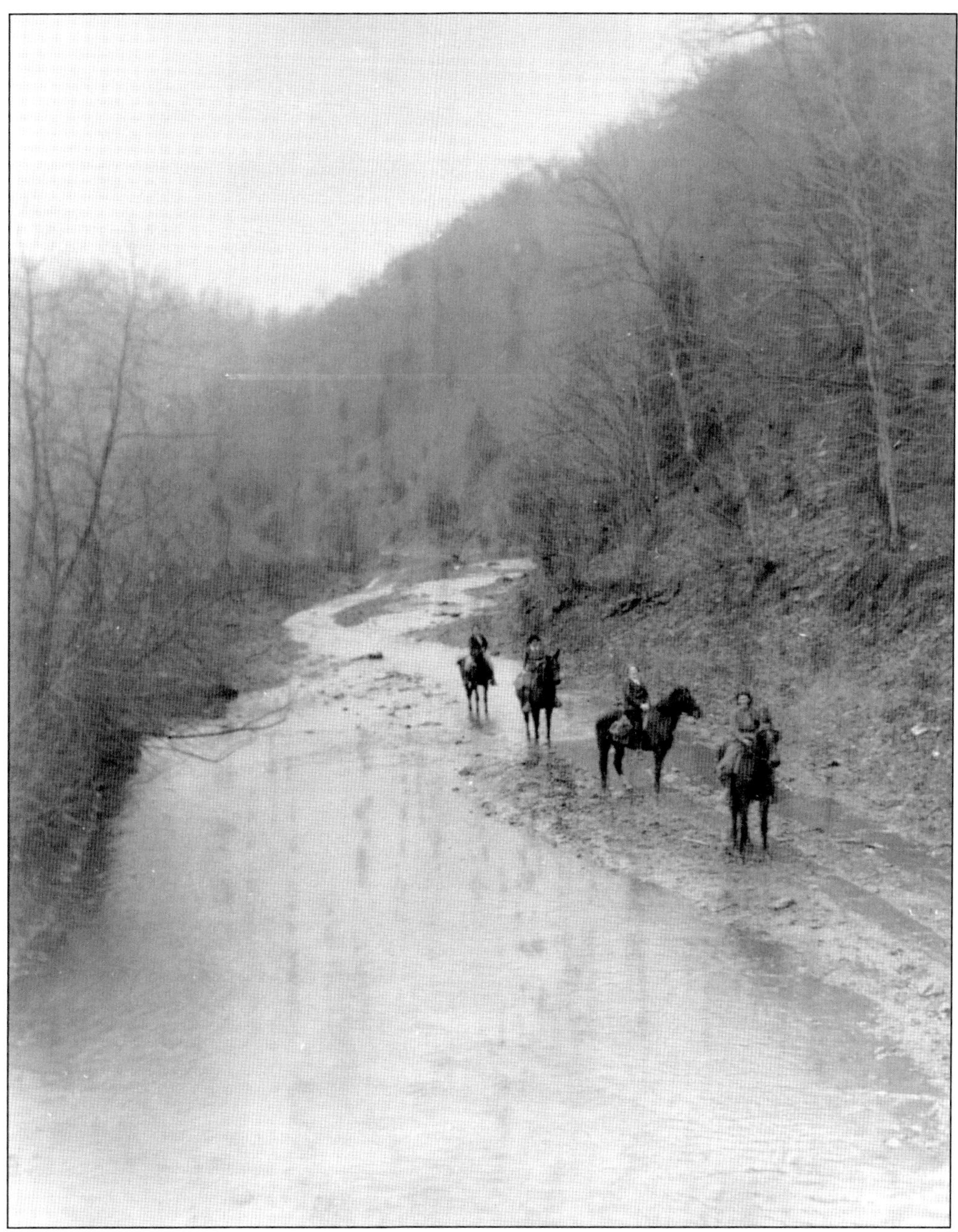

Pack Horse Librarians. The Pack Horse Library was founded in Owsley County by the Works Progress Administration (WPA) in the 1930s to provide reading materials to rural areas. As an example of how much ground the mounted librarians covered, four of them rode a total of 564 miles in October 1936, distributing new books and magazines to patrons and picking up previous deliveries. This 1936 photograph shows four librarians on horseback as they travel down the clear area along the banks of Grassy Creek. The Pack Horse Library was one of several projects that worked to bring needed services to the isolated families in the mountains of Eastern Kentucky. (UK Special Collections.)

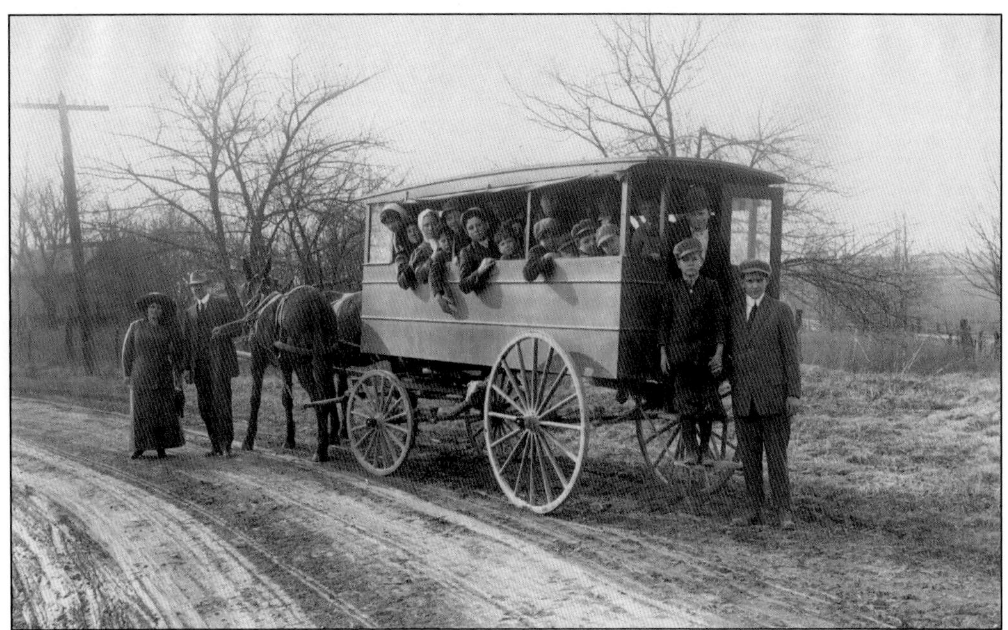

SUPERINTENDENT WITH SCHOOL WAGON. Nannie Faulconer (far left) was the superintendent of the Fayette County Schools from 1904 to 1921. She stands with the driver, Sam Brooks, in front of the Greendale School wagon. There are more than 16 students in the bus, along with two teachers (in white head scarves). Greendale was one of the first consolidated high schools in Kentucky. (UK Special Collections.)

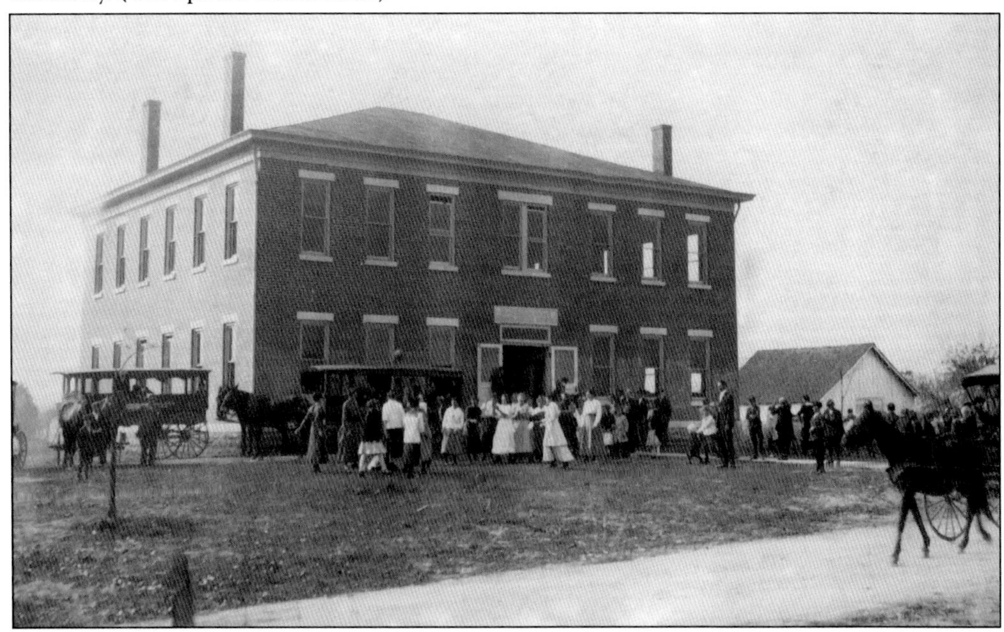

BOARDING SCHOOL BUSES. In a scene repeated countless times every school day across Kentucky, teachers marshal schoolchildren into lines to board the correct horse-drawn school bus for the trip home. This photograph was taken in October 1916 in front of the Woodburn Consolidated School in Warren County. Horse-drawn or mule-drawn school buses were used for decades before being replaced by the yellow, motorized versions. (LOC.)

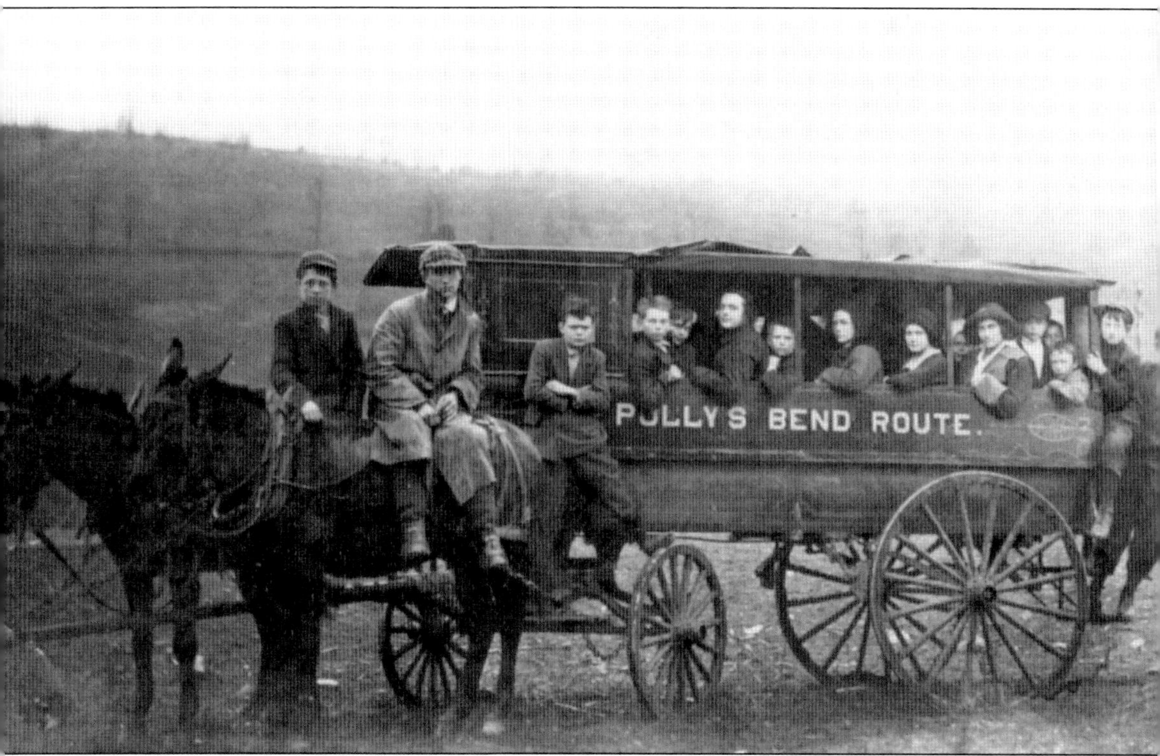

MULE-DRAWN SCHOOL BUS. This undated photograph, taken in Mercer County, shows a bus loaded with children and teachers. There are at least eleven children, plus the four women assumed to be teachers. The young man with the heavy coat and checked hat seated on one of the mules (second from left) appears to be the driver. The bus has a canvas top and probably two doors, one at the far side of the bus in the front and one in the back of the bus. The doors were located as they were so that people getting on and off would not scare the mules. People inside sat on two long benches along each side, not in rows as in today's buses. Another difference was the lack of heating—everyone had to bundle up to stay warm. (WKU Special Collections.)

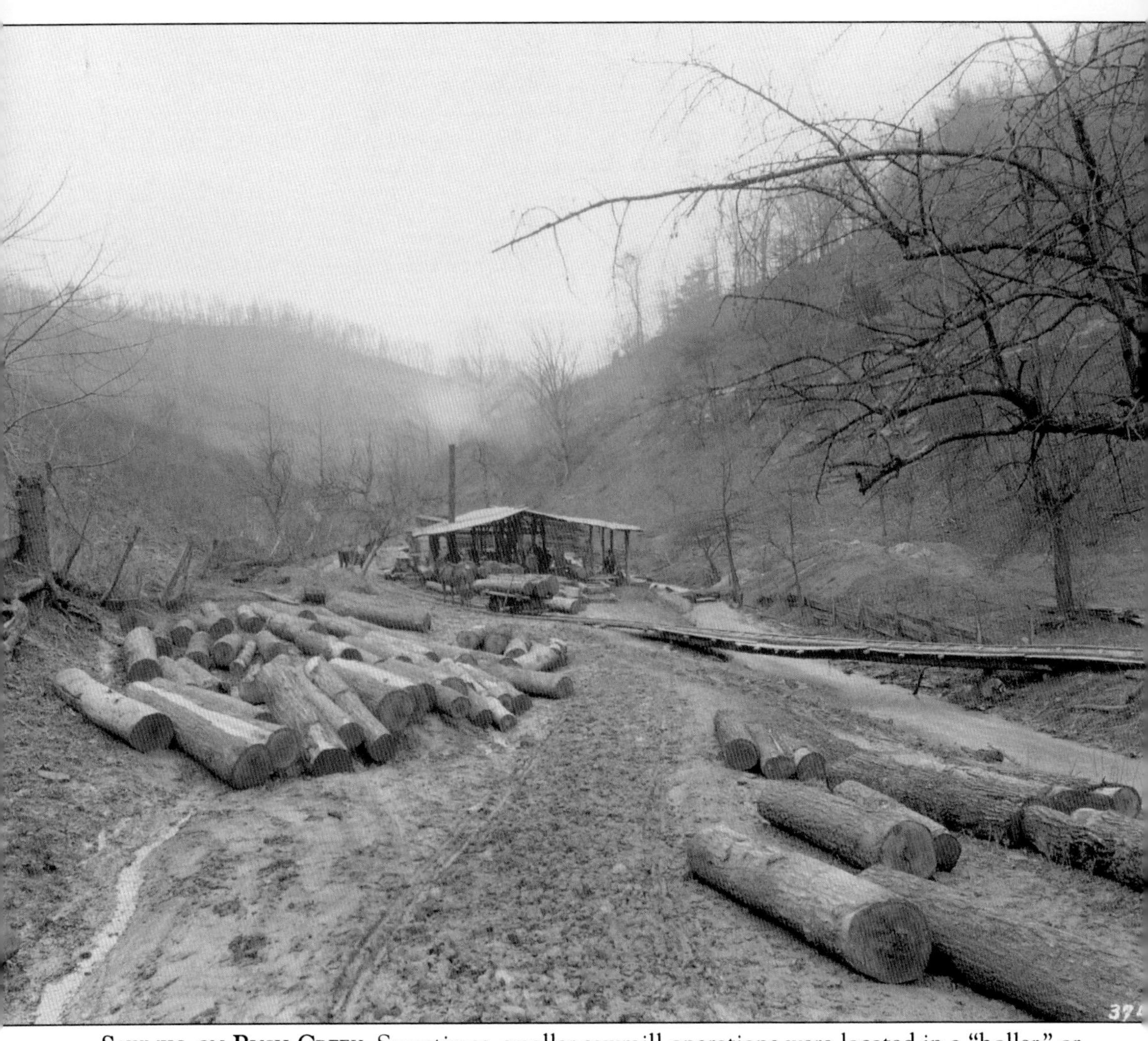

Sawmill on Bush Creek. Sometimes, smaller sawmill operations were located in a "holler," or valley, in the mountains in Eastern Kentucky so that the timber harvested in the area had to be hauled only a short distance. This 1920 photograph shows a sawmill on Bush Creek in Breathitt County. In the foreground are cut logs. In front of the structure is a team of mules pulling a wheeled cart containing three large logs. The cart traveled along a track that runs back across Bush Creek on the small bridge at right. Unfortunately, the valuable virgin timber was irreplaceable, and, once it was cut and sold, harvestable timber all but disappeared from the landscape, leaving nothing for the sawmills to process. By 1927, lumber production in the state had fallen to just 30 percent of what was sold in the decades between 1870 and 1920. (KHS, 1987.ph08.d37.)

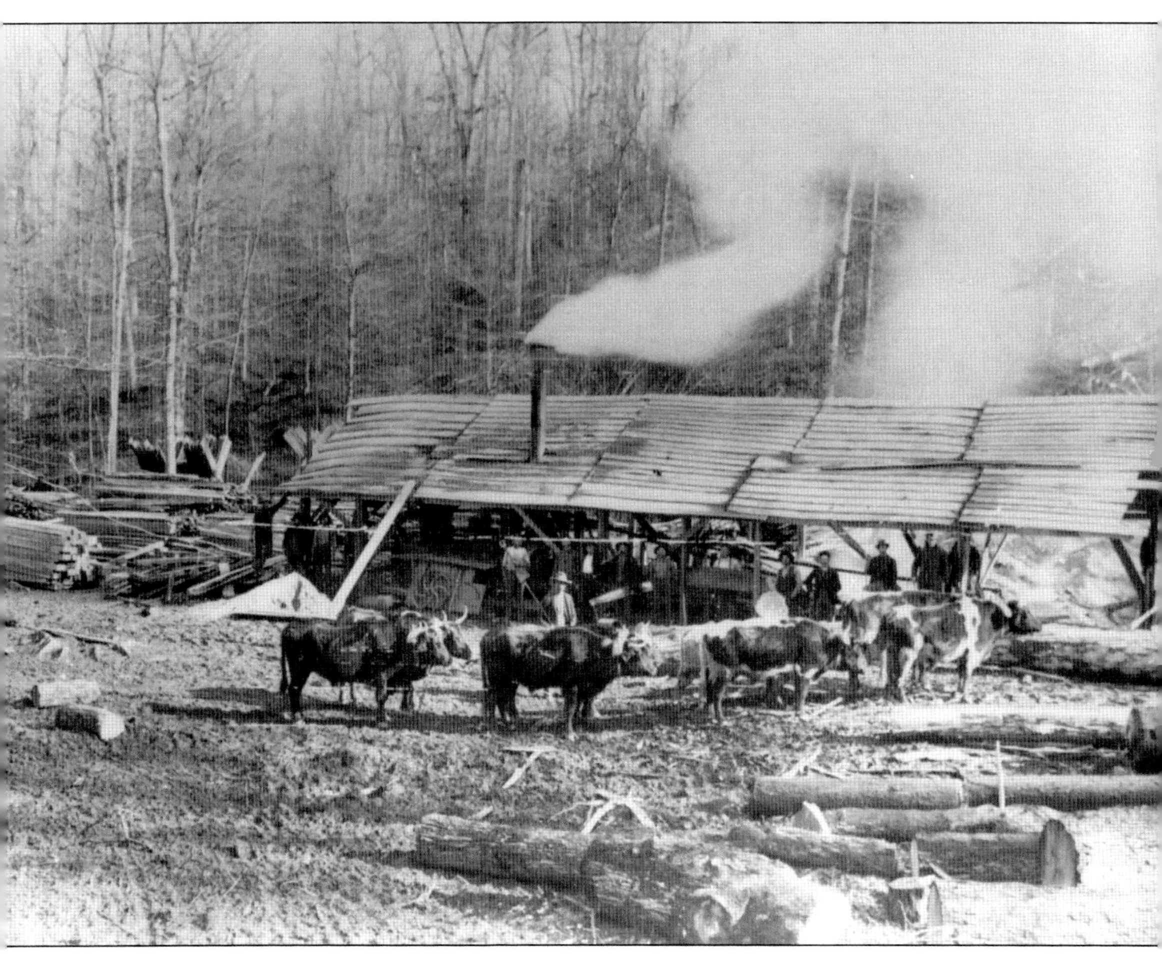

Oxen Team at Sawmill. In this 1900 photograph, a handsome eight-oxen team waits at a sawmill at Hylton Branch, in Carter County. Standing behind the oxen in the center of the photograph is the teamster in charge of the oxen. He is holding a goad, used to help guide the animals. Almost directly beneath the sawmill's chimney, wearing a white shirt, is a man identified as W.W. Walls, holding a saw blade. Another man in the center group, identified as Nathan Hylton, is holding a long crosscut saw blade. The oxen were used to "snake" or skid logs along the ground from where they were felled to the sawmill or, in some cases, to a river to be floated to a more distant sawmill. (KHS, BOD.1990ph2.8BOD10.)

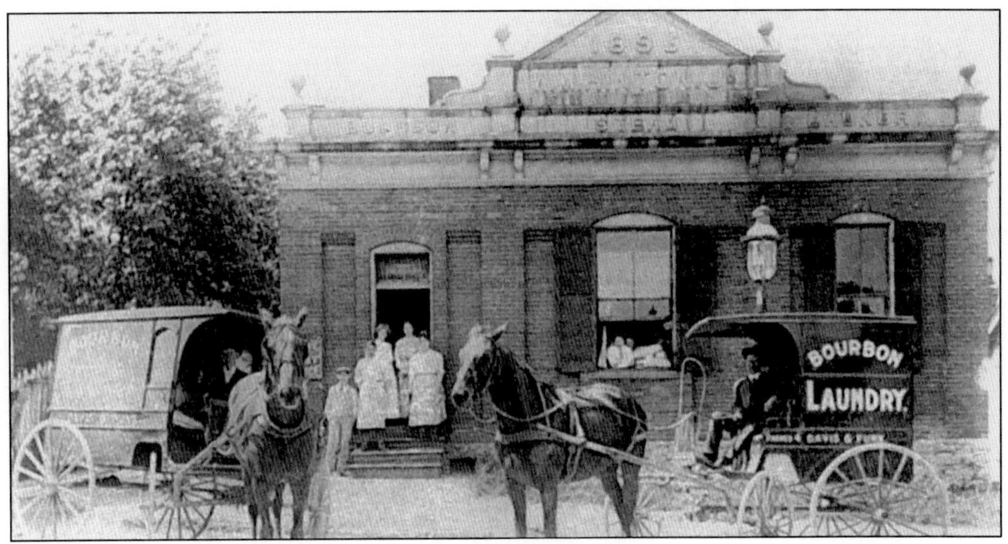

STEAM LAUNDRY. The Bourbon Steam Laundry's building in Paris, seen in this 1908 photograph, was a handsome structure. Gathered in front of the building are two delivery wagons drawn by well-fed horses, as well as the drivers and laundry employees. One of the wagon drivers is identified as Homer Shy. The other laundry listed in the 1908 Paris Business Directory belonged to Hop Lee. (Hopewell Museum.)

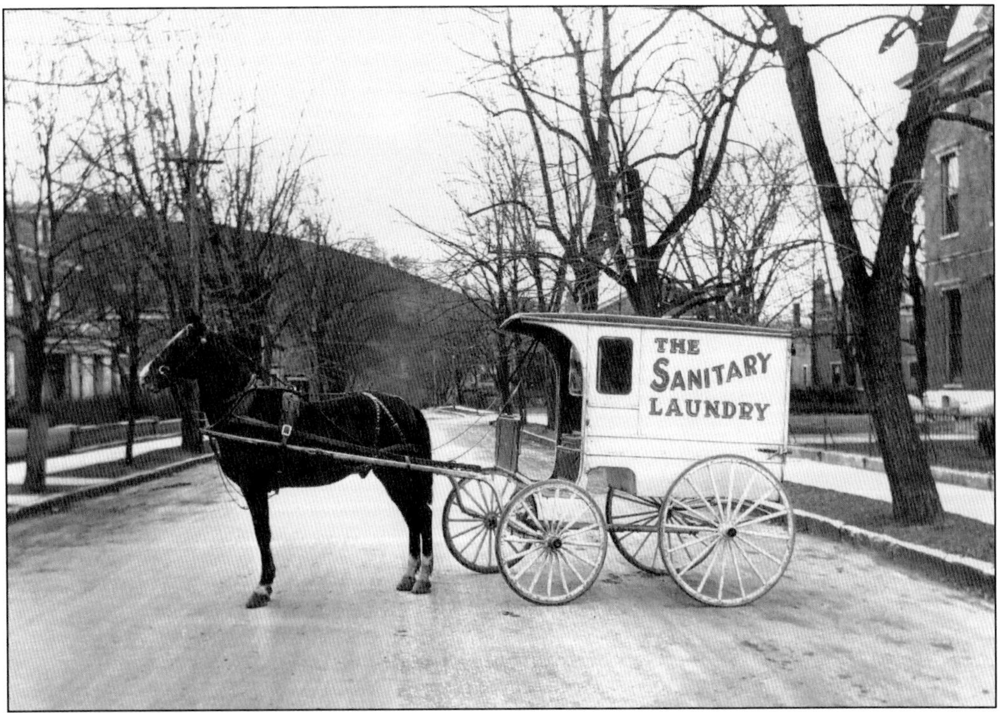

UNATTENDED WAGON. This wagon's driver may be at a nearby house making a delivery. It appears that the horse has been trained to wait patiently until the driver returns. This undated photograph was taken on Wilkinson Street in Frankfort. In the days before permanent press, some households sent off their tablecloths and bed linens to be cleaned and pressed, in addition to their clothes. (Capital City Museum.)

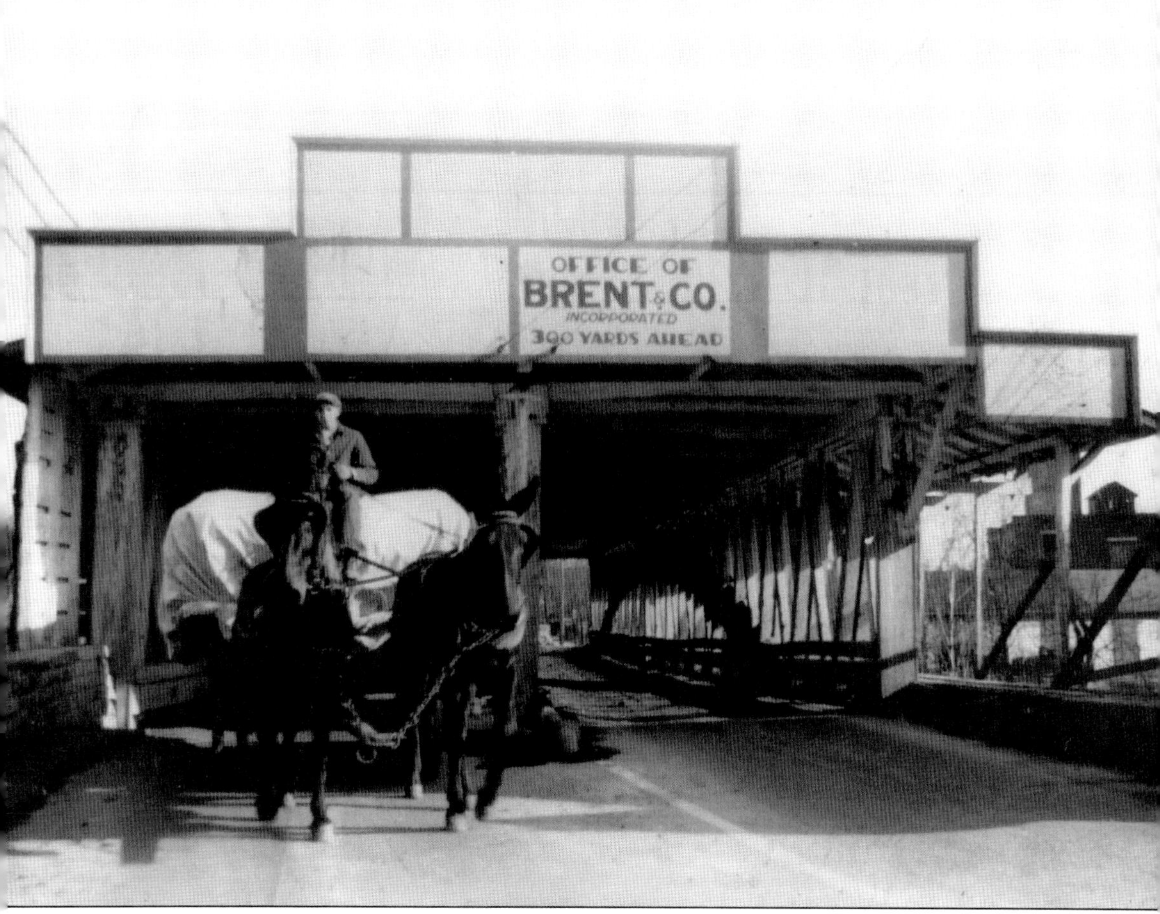

Cottontown Covered Bridge. This two-horse team pulling a heavy load was photographed emerging from one side of the "double-barreled" covered bridge that spanned Stoner Creek in Bourbon County from 1833 to 1933. The load under wraps could be blocks of ice, which had to be covered when it was hauled from the icehouse. The covered bridge was built by Lewis Wernwag, a German immigrant who built several bridges in the state and who was one of the first to use a cantilevered bridge design. The bridge had two "drive-ways" for vehicles, each 12 feet wide, separated by a partition. It also had a six-foot-wide walkway for pedestrians. It was called the Cottontown Bridge because it linked the Paris business district with an area where a cotton mill once stood. (Authors' collection.)

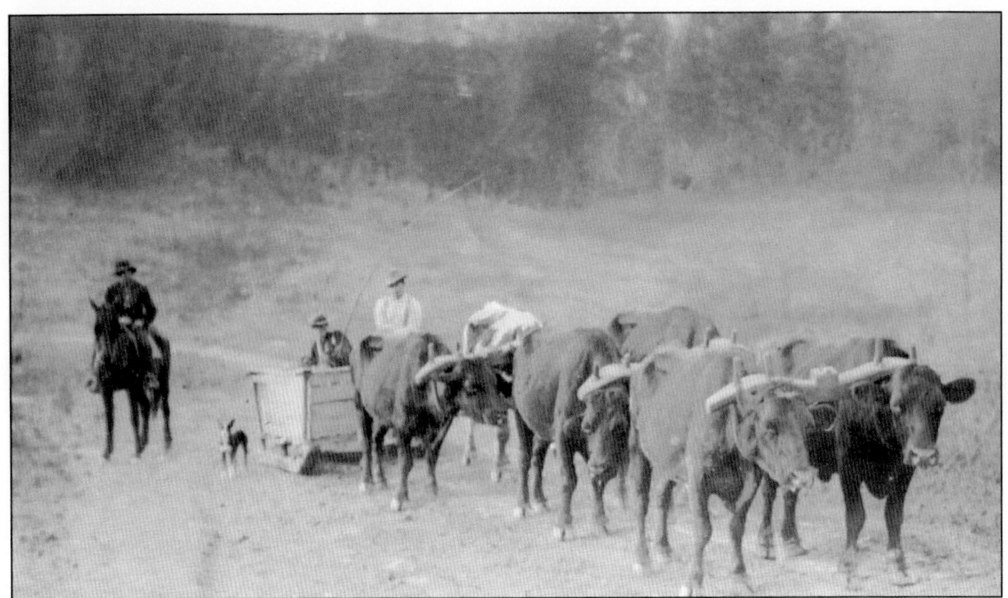

Sleds Are Not Just for Snow. Wooden sleds were sometimes used in the mountainous regions of Kentucky to haul loads. Unlike wheeled vehicles, sleds moved more smoothly over the rocky terrain and were less likely to break. This undated photograph features a six-oxen team pulling a sled, with one man driving, another man riding one of the oxen, and a third man on horseback. The group is accompanied by a small dog. (Berea College Special Collections.)

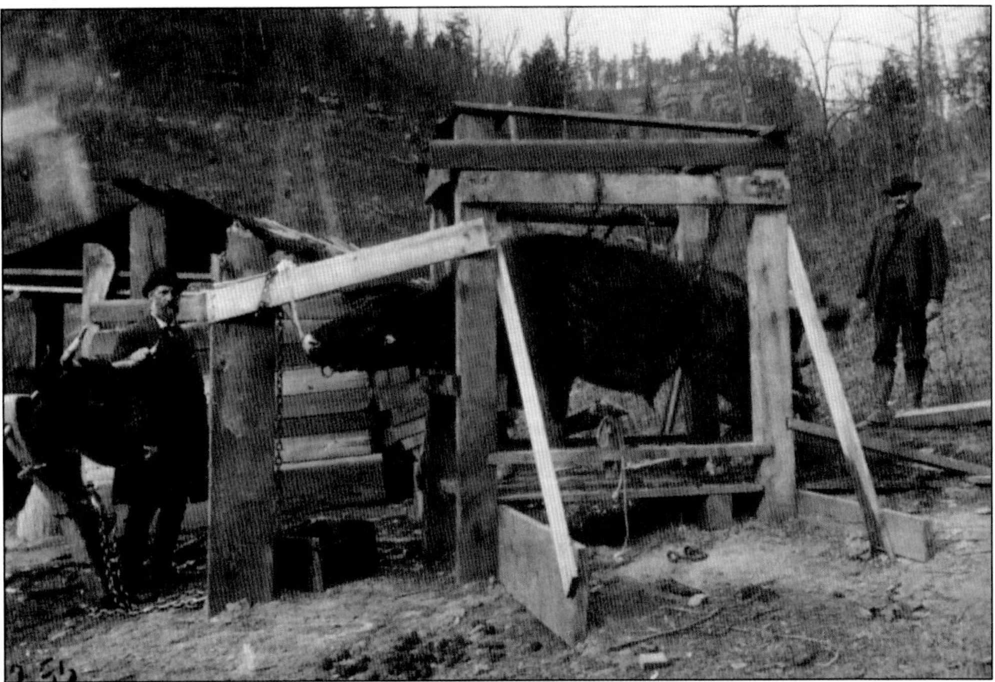

No Easy Task. It is one thing to shoe a horse or a mule—they are accustomed to the process, which begins when they are young. Shoeing an ox, however, is much more difficult. This 1892 photograph, taken in Powell County, shows the sturdy framework built to hold the weight of an ox as it is lifted off the ground with a sling so that it can be shod. (Berea College Special Collections.)

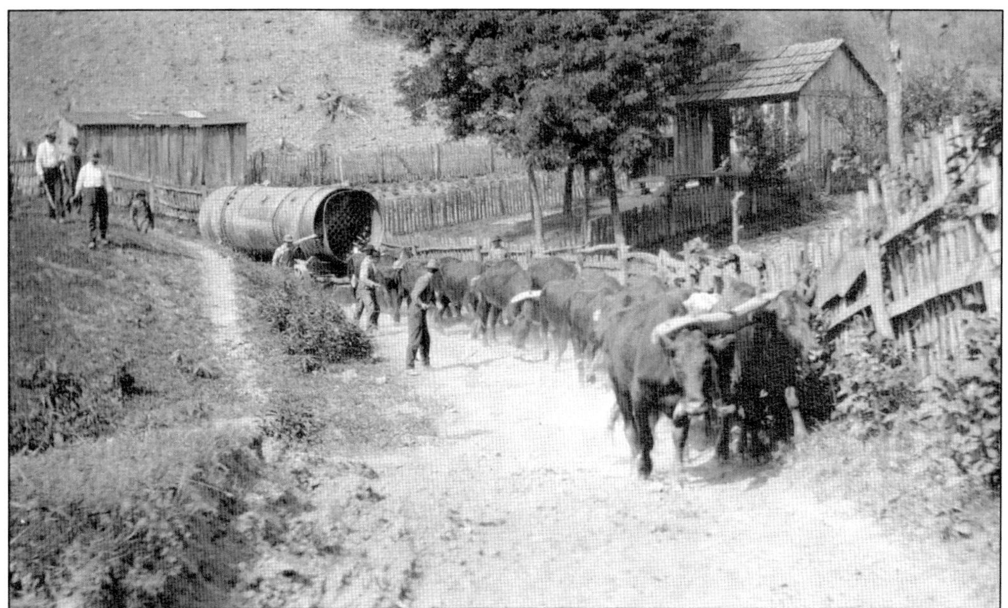

Oxen Pulling Oversized Load. Today, oversized loads are hauled by huge trucks on interstate highways. When this mammoth 16-oxen team pulled a heavy boiler up the rocky, rutted roads of Eastern Kentucky, the sight no doubt amazed residents. In this photograph, taken between 1910 and 1912, six men can be seen guiding the oxen and the load. (Berea College Special Collections.)

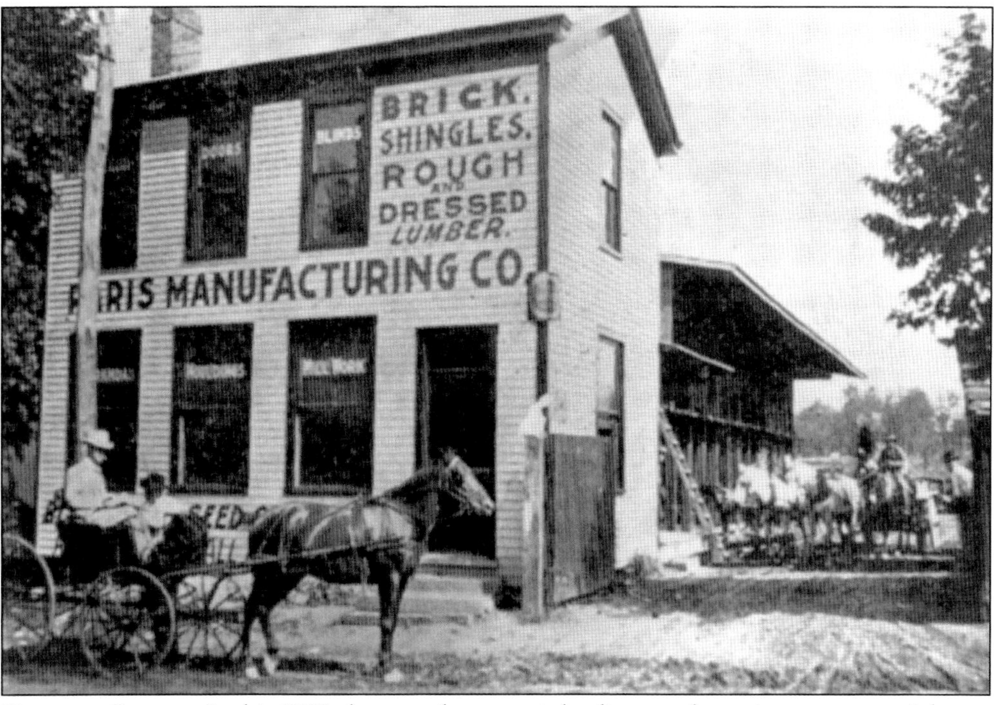

Curbside Service. In this 1902 photograph, a man is loading purchases into a customer's buggy at Paris Manufacturing. In the rear of the building, men load wagons, pulled by teams of horses, with some of the materials advertised on the building's facade. The materials included rough and dressed lumber, bricks, shingles, doors, blinds, and moldings. (Hopewell Museum.)

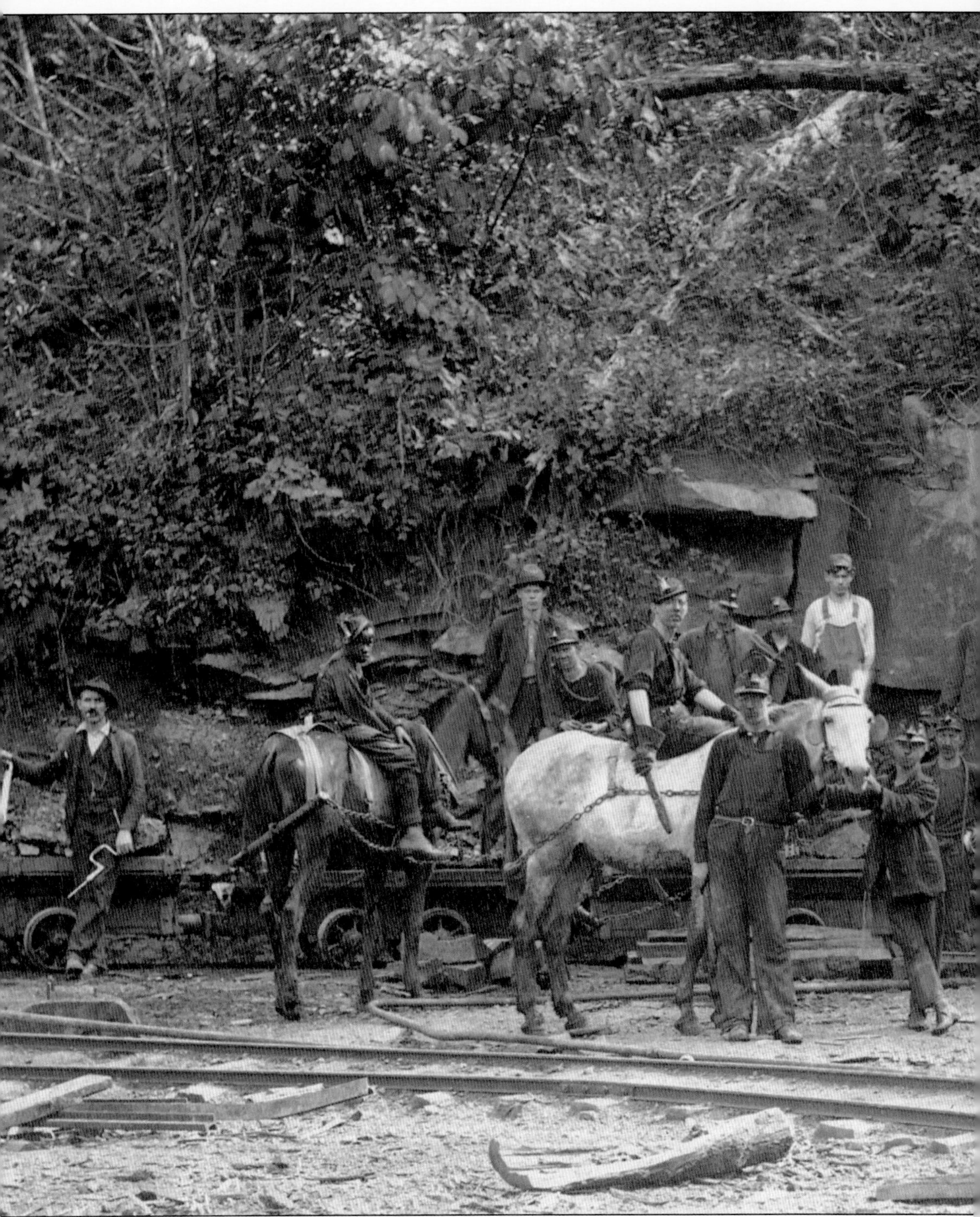

MEN AND MULES AT MINE. This 1918 photograph of a coal-mining crew in front of an unidentified Kentucky mine shows some of the men and mules employed in the industry. The group of more than 25 miners is somewhat racially diverse, with a young black boy on the mule at far left and a group of African American miners standing just outside the mine entrance at right. Visible

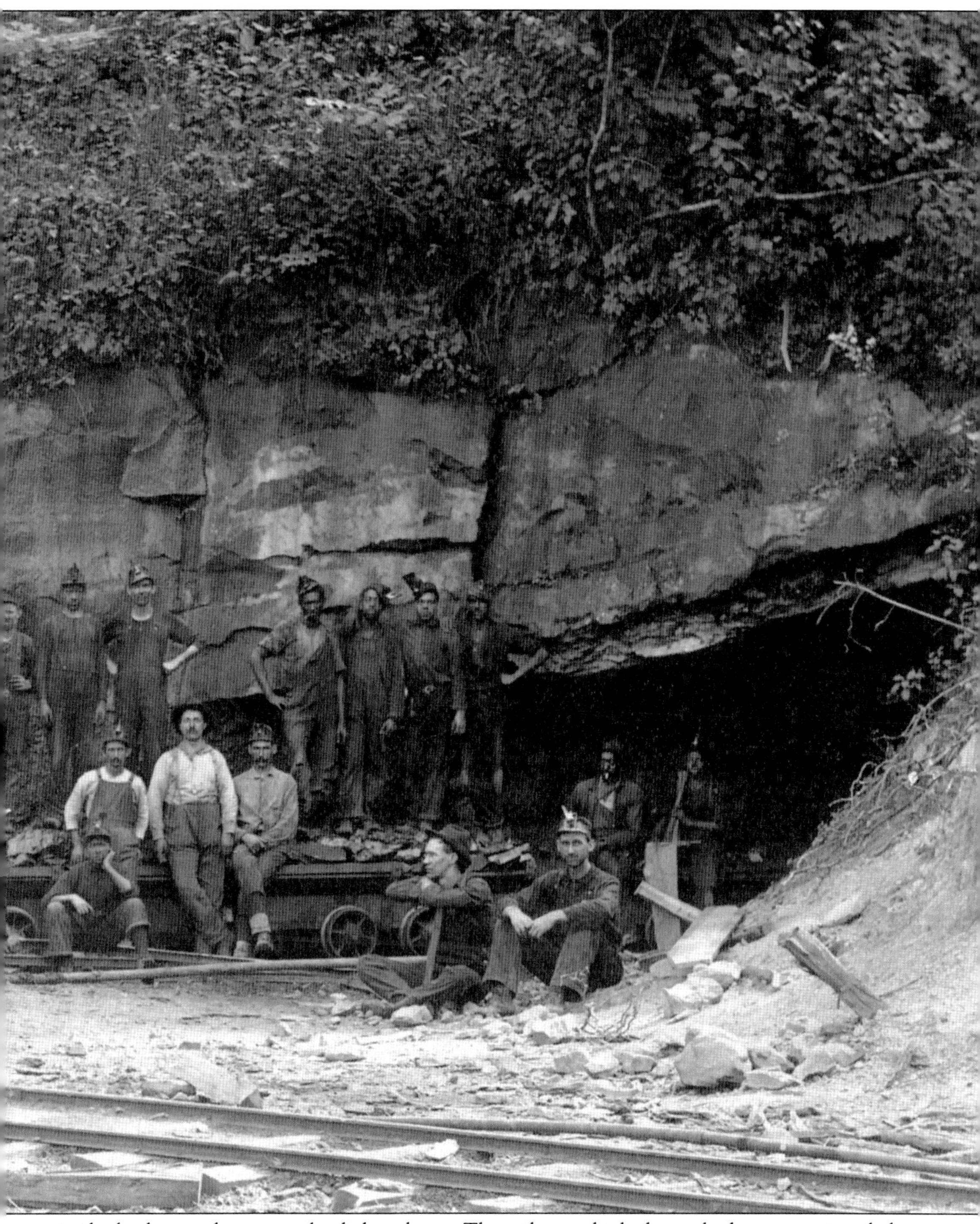

in the background are some loaded coal cars. The rails on which the mule-drawn cars traveled can be seen in the foreground. Expanding railroad lines in Kentucky made mining in previously untouched areas easier, changing the landscape forever. By 1920, Kentucky was producing more than 38 million tons of coal a year. (KHS, 1999PH10.29.)

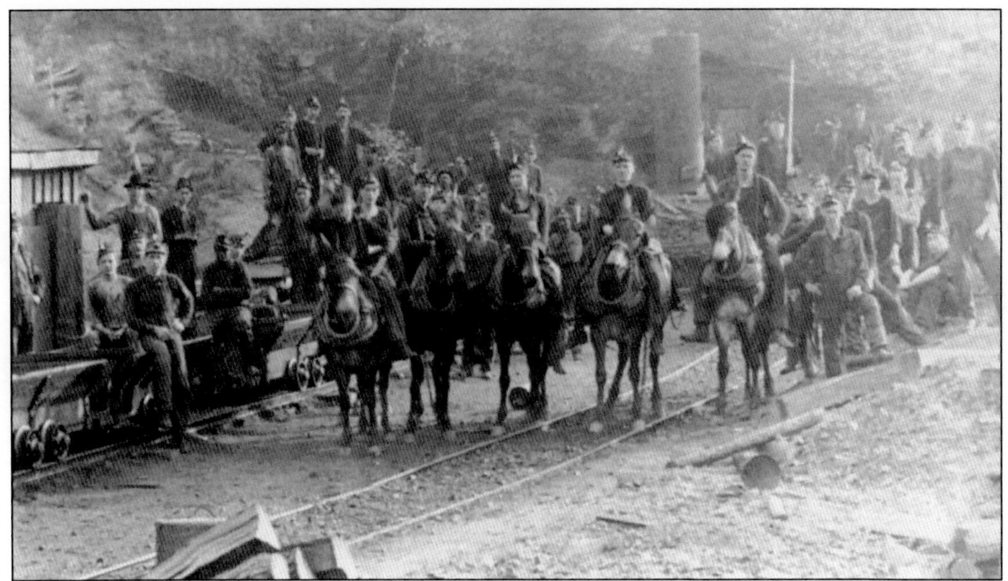

Barren Fork Mining Camp. These miners, along with their five mules, gathered to have their photograph taken in 1910 at the Barren Fork Mining Camp. The site is in what would soon be McCreary County, formed in 1912. Today, the Barren Fork Horse Camp is situated on the Barren Fork Mining Company's former site in the Daniel Boone National Forest, near Whitley City. (Rebra Perkins, US Forest Service, and the McCreary County Museum.)

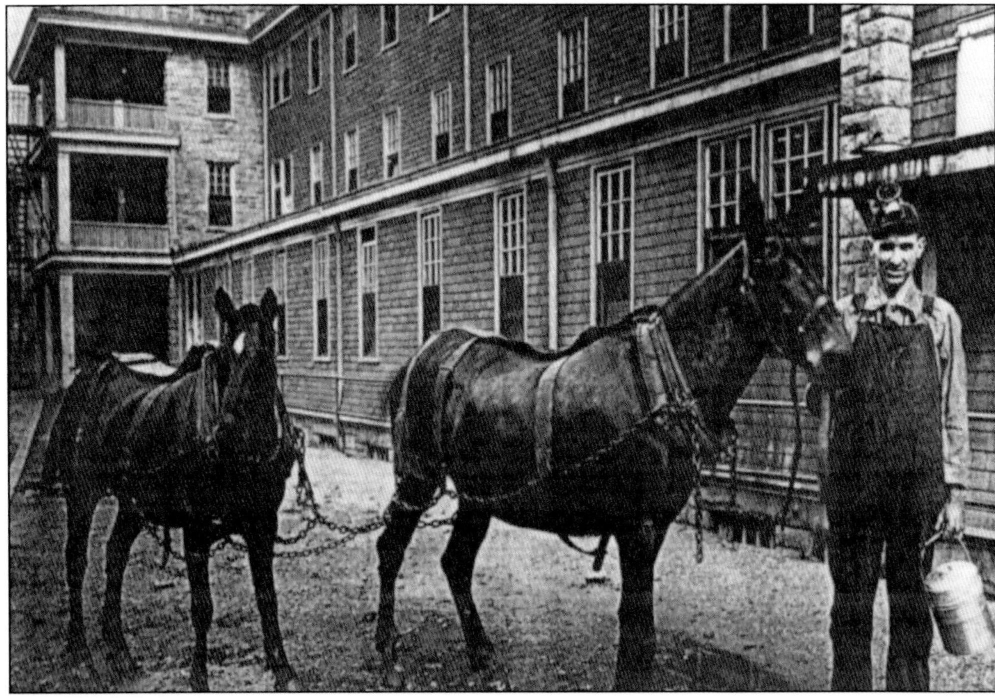

Coal Miners Hotel. Holding his metal lunch pail in one hand, this coal miner leads a team of mules behind the Coal Miners Hotel in Lynch. The hotel, built by the US Steel Corporation, had four floors, with 110 sleeping rooms, a barbershop, a beauty shop, a bowling alley, and a ballroom. This photograph was taken in 1918 or 1919. (Mike O'Bradovich.)

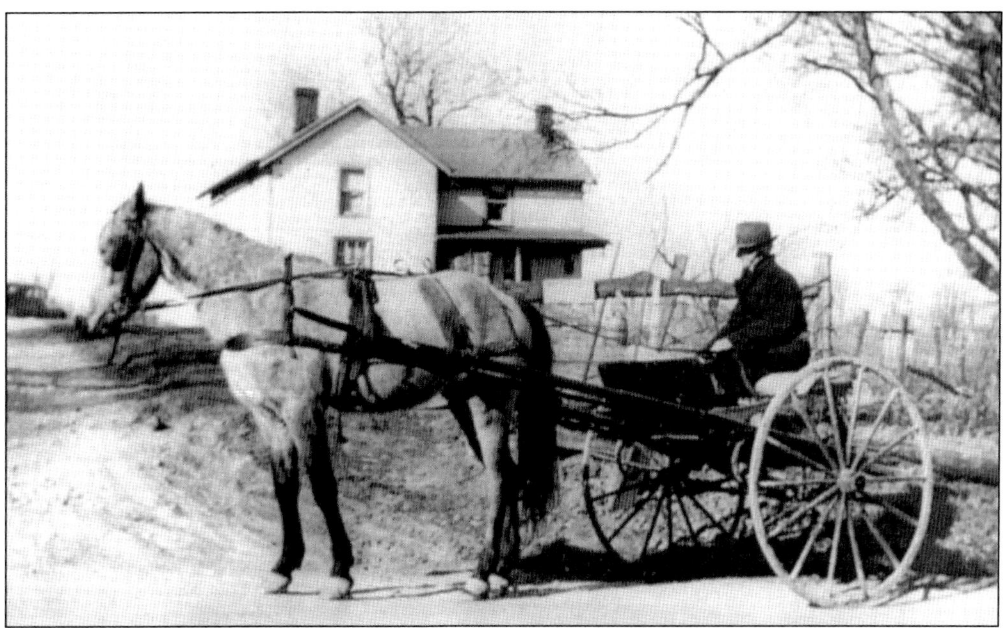

Last Hoof-Powered Mail Delivery. For 28 years, Larry Buchanan delivered mail in the rural areas of Bourbon County, never missing a day. He used a mule-drawn or horse-drawn buggy or rode mule-back or horseback. Mail was delivered six days a week, including holidays. Buchanan made his last delivery in 1958 at age 74. The pony pulling the buggy in this photograph was named Molly Mc. (Authors' collection.)

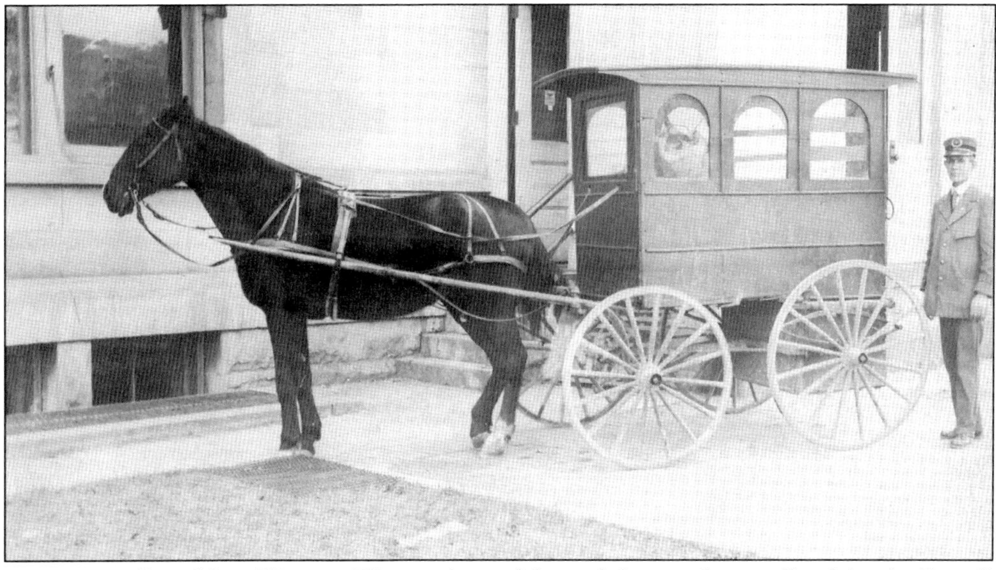

Frankfort City Mail Wagon. The mail was delivered door-to-door in Frankfort by Russell H. Wertzel, pictured here in 1910 in front of the post office on Wapping Street. The mail was transported via the railroad in special cars and picked up directly from the railway car by US Mail personnel using horse-drawn wagons like the one seen here. (Capital City Museum.)

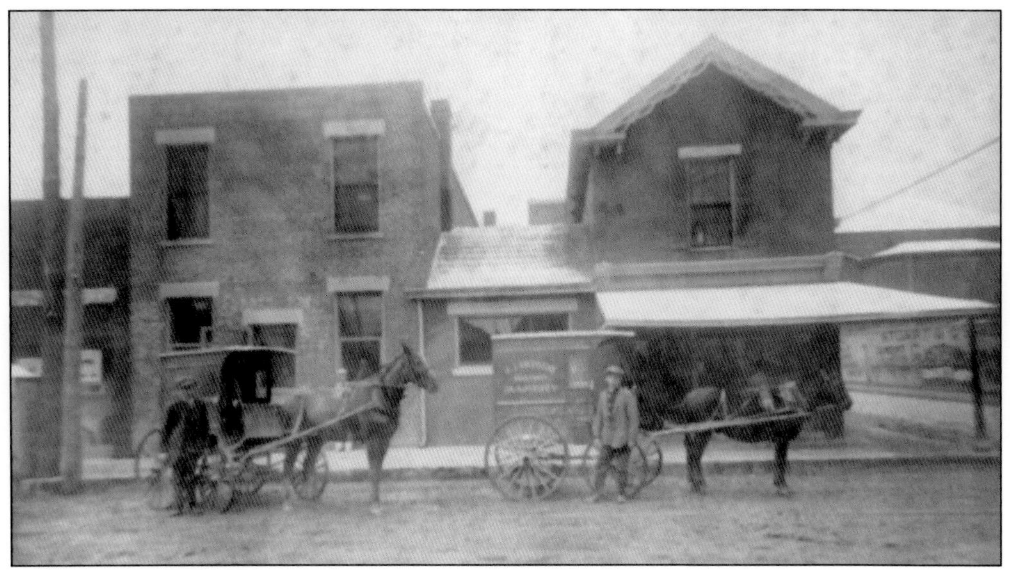

Grosche Sanitary Bakery. This bakery, located on High Street in Paris, delivered its products to customers using these two sharp-looking delivery wagons pulled by sleek horses. They are seen here in front of the bakery. Many types of items were delivered regularly to residential areas, including bread and other bakery products; blocks of ice for pre-electric iceboxes; milk, cream, and butter; and groceries. (Hopewell Museum.)

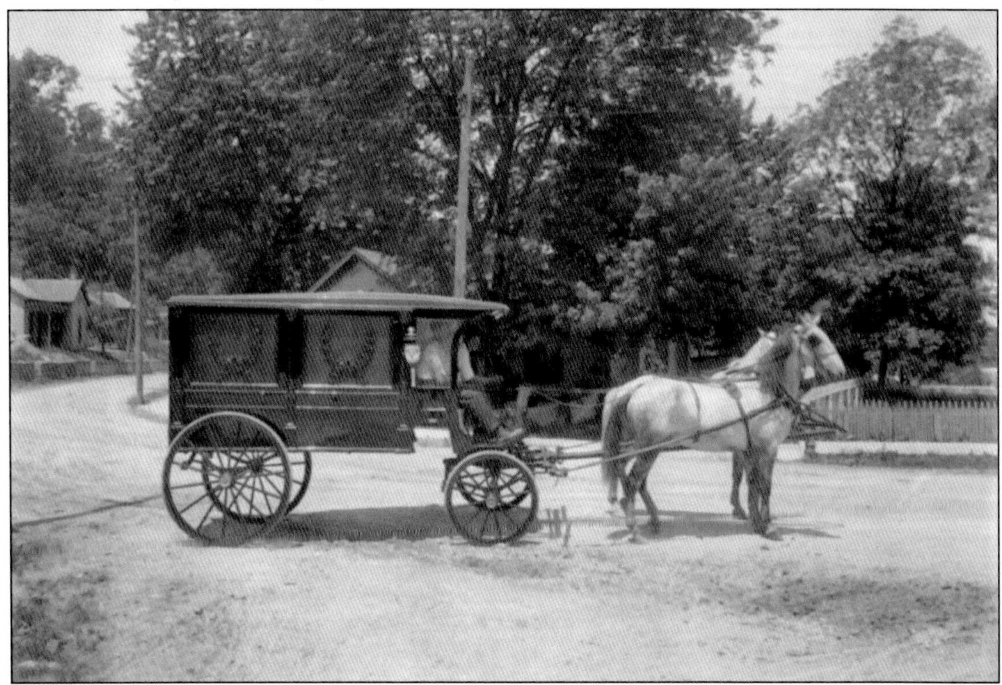

Going out in Style. In 1890, when this photograph was taken, and throughout the horse-drawn era in Kentucky and around the country, hearses like this one were used to transport the deceased to the cemetery. This handsome equipage, drawn by a pair of white horses, was owned by the Rogers Funeral Home in Frankfort. The firm opened for business in 1802 and is still in operation today. (Capital City Museum.)

Seven

The Horse Business

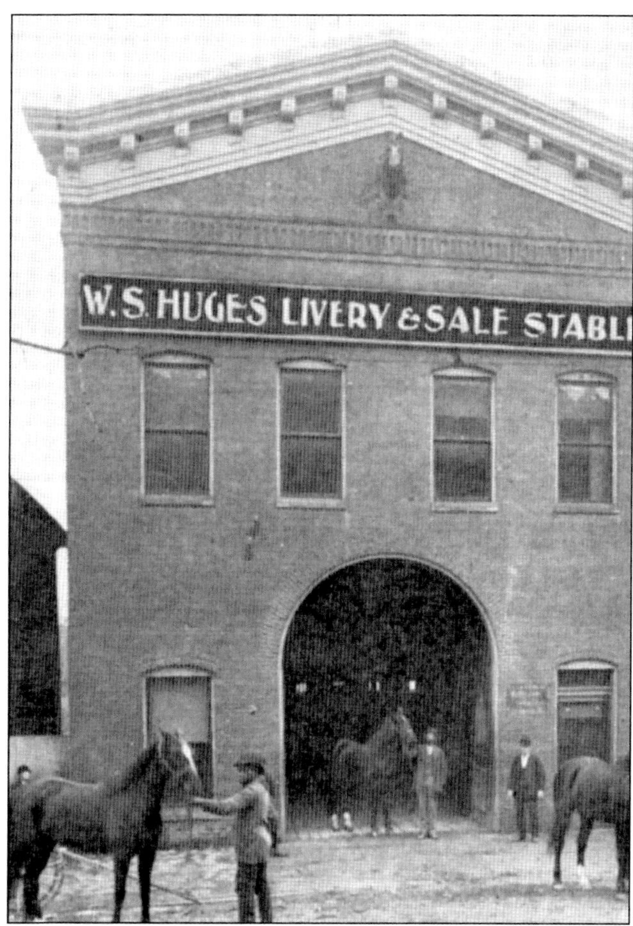

Rental Facilities. Especially in the city, not everyone owned a horse or had a place to stable one. Every city and most towns had livery stables, like the W.S. Hughes Livery & Sale Stable in Frankfort, pictured here in 1898. Residents or out-of-town visitors could rent a horse, buggy, or wagon, or they could board their own animal at a daily or monthly rate. (Capital City Museum.)

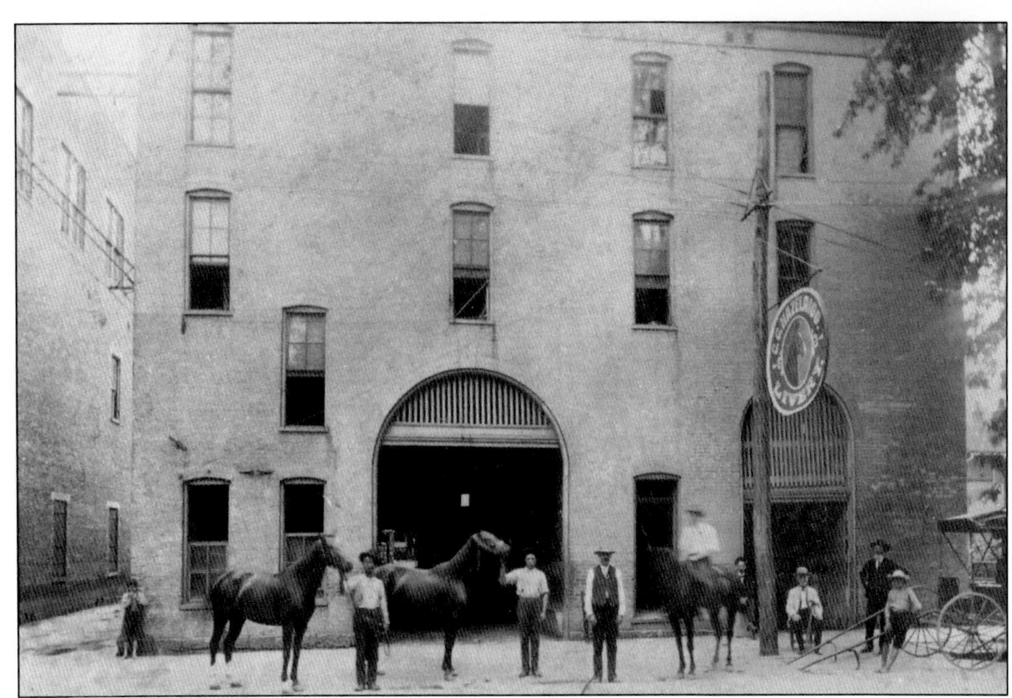

Hazelrigg's Livery. C.C. Hazelrigg, who is perhaps the man seated with a light-colored jacket in the 1890 photograph above, had possibly the largest livery operation in the state capital of Frankfort. The following is a typical price list of services offered at a livery stable of the time: horse rental per day, 50¢; horse and buggy rental, $1; carriage and team, $2; carriage and driver, $4; horse to pasture, 50¢; feed, 25¢; bucket of oats, 50¢; stall rental, $1.50; stall plus hay, $2.50; one month board on horse, $10; currying horse, 10¢; and saddling horse, 25¢. The advertisement below reveals that Hazelrigg was a smart businessman, offering facilities for the ladies and maintaining a phone attached to both of the town's telephone companies. (Both, Capital City Museum.)

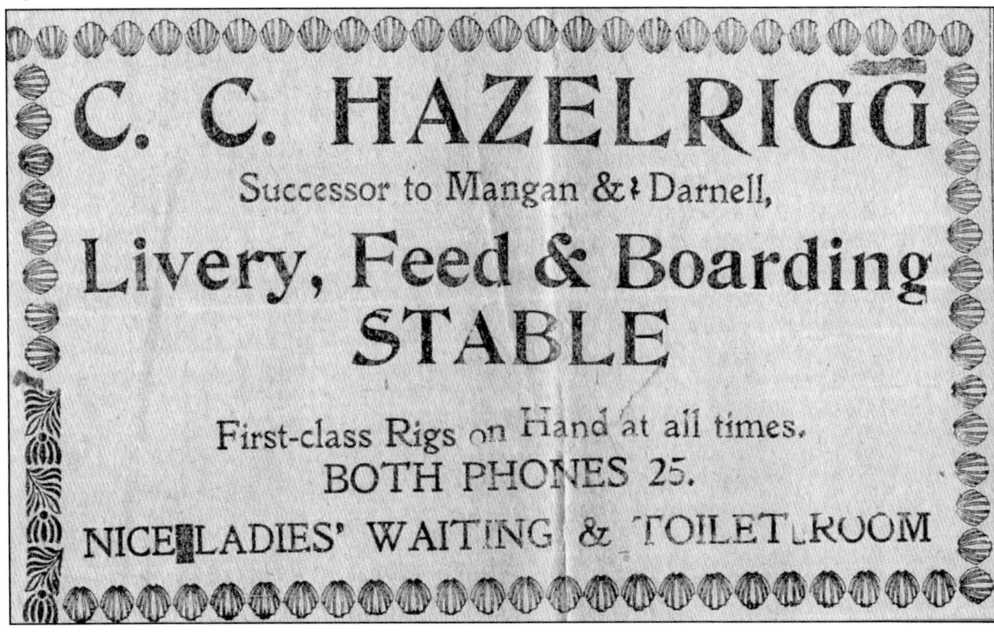

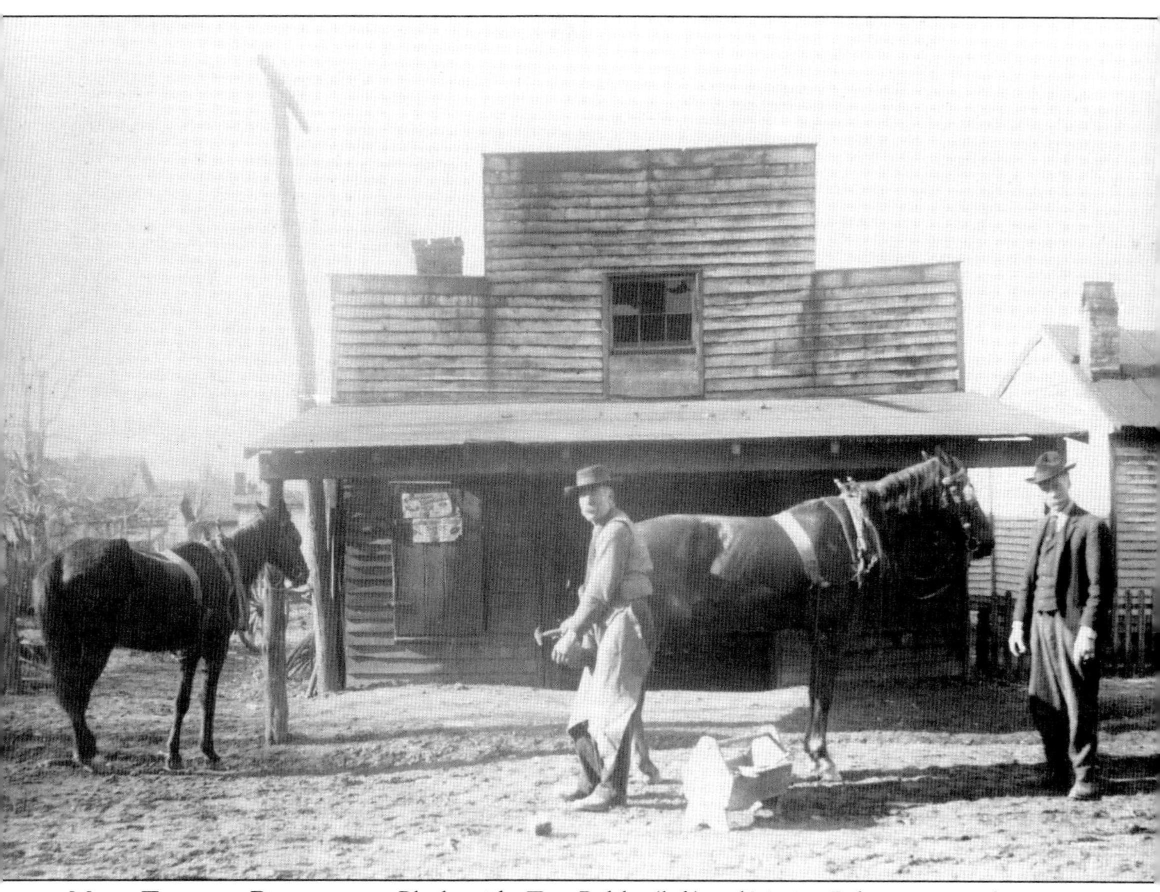

Multi-Talented Blacksmiths. Blacksmiths Tom Bohler (left) and Marion Behen are seen shoeing a horse in front of their stable in the river town of Cloverport, in Breckinridge County, in 1910. One can see from their collars that the horses in the photograph were used to pull wagons or possibly farm equipment. Blacksmiths used a variety of hammers, tongs, chisels, and punches to create, repair, rivet, or weld. With a vise and files, he refined the rough edges of his ironwork. The ability to shape iron by heat and tools has been a highly valued skill throughout history. By the early 1900s, an American blacksmith's work had grown to include repairing all types of manufactured, horse-drawn farm machinery, wagons, carriages, and sleighs. He also sharpened plows, saws, and other tools. For raw materials, the blacksmith ordered lengths of heavy iron and steel (iron with carbon), which were delivered to town by the railroad. (KHS, JFA.1990ph2.4JEFA15.)

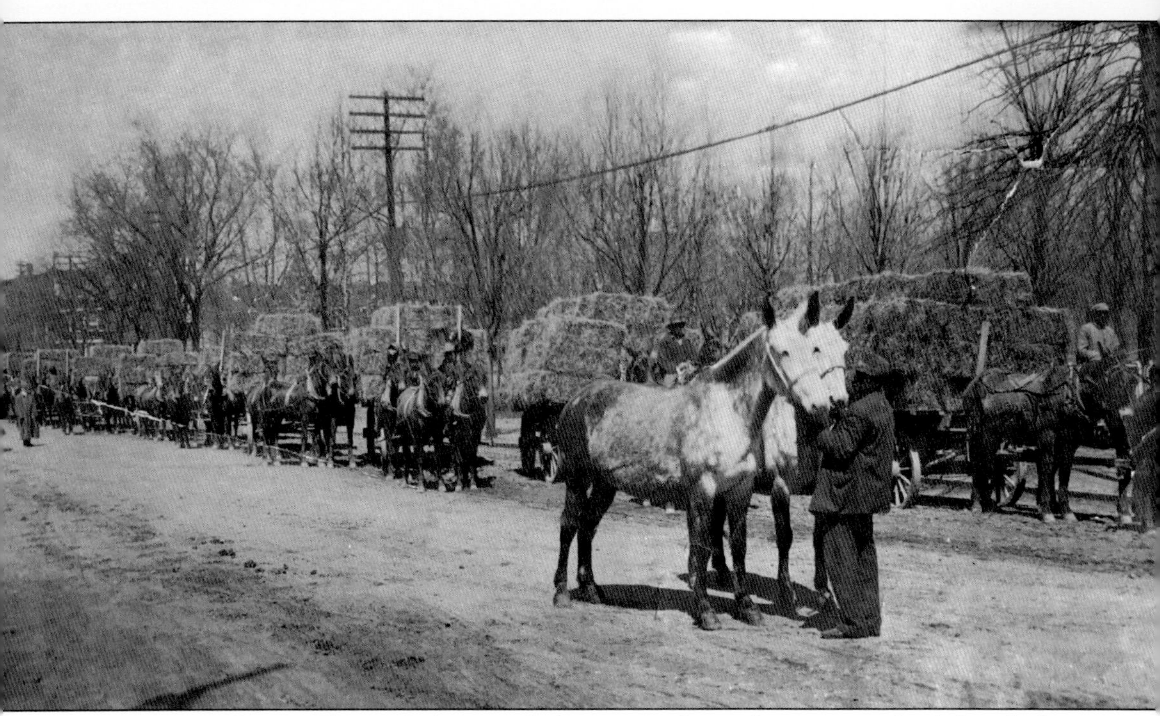

Hay Is for Horses. This 1918 photograph shows more than a dozen wagons loaded to the brim with hay in Henderson County, headed for the war effort. Good, clean, dry hay was and is the most common food for horses. In Kentucky, the most popular hay choices are alfalfa, timothy, orchard grass, and alfalfa-grass mixes. Tons of hay and grains, like oats, were consumed daily by horses in the state. The average working horse consumed 10 to 25 pounds of hay each day and an almost equal amount of oats, depending on its size and job. Cities like Louisville, Covington, and Lexington had commissions that monitored the quality of hay, oats, and straw sold in the large feed markets. (KHS, HED.1990ph2.29HED1.)

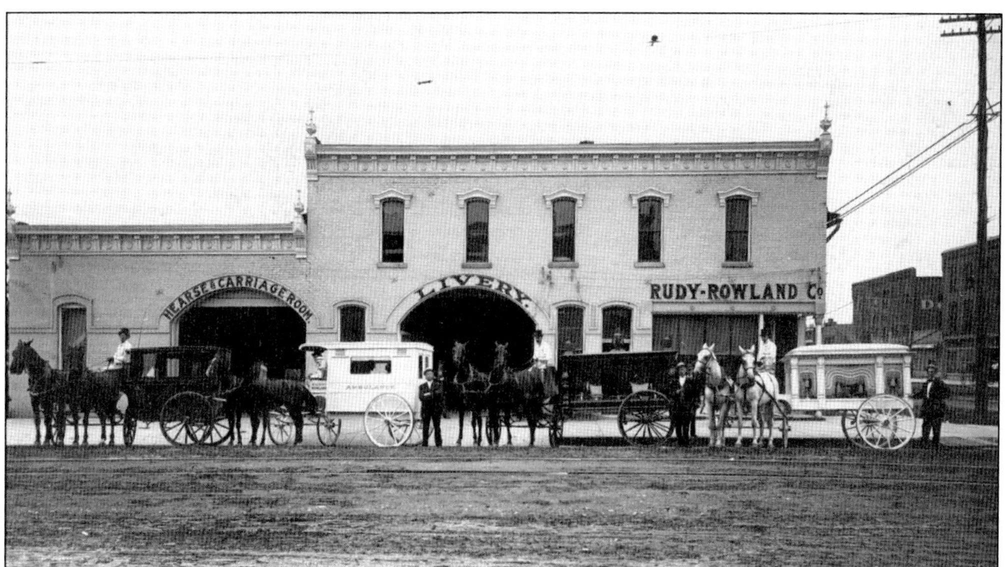

Livery and Funeral Services. The Henderson firm of Rudy-Rowland Company was a full-service livery stable in 1900. Besides offering the usual array of services, it rented hearses and coaches for funerals. It also offered the use of an ambulance before such services were provided by local governments or hospitals. The business name Rudy-Rowland lives on in Henderson as a full-service funeral home. (KHS, HED.1990ph2.16HED15.)

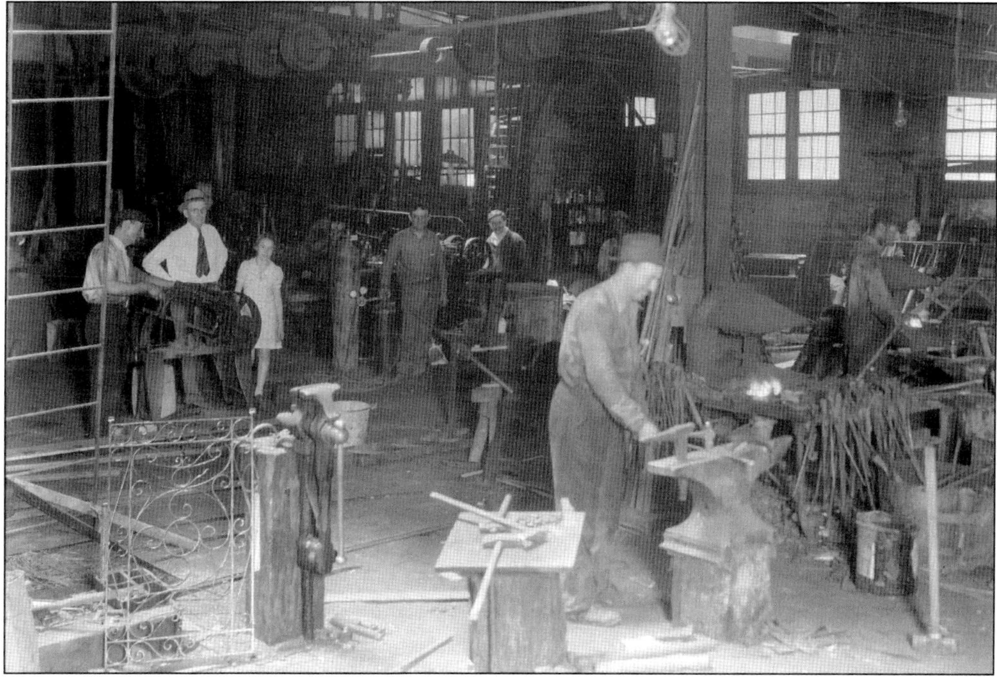

"New Age" Blacksmith. The blacksmith seen here in 1933 at Saunier Brothers in Lexington had adjusted his craft to fit in with the 20th century. He expanded his business to include automobile body repair, tool and die work, and decorative metalwork. While others in the shop depended on complex machines, all he needed was a hot fire, an anvil, a hammer, and his strong right arm. (UK Special Collections.)

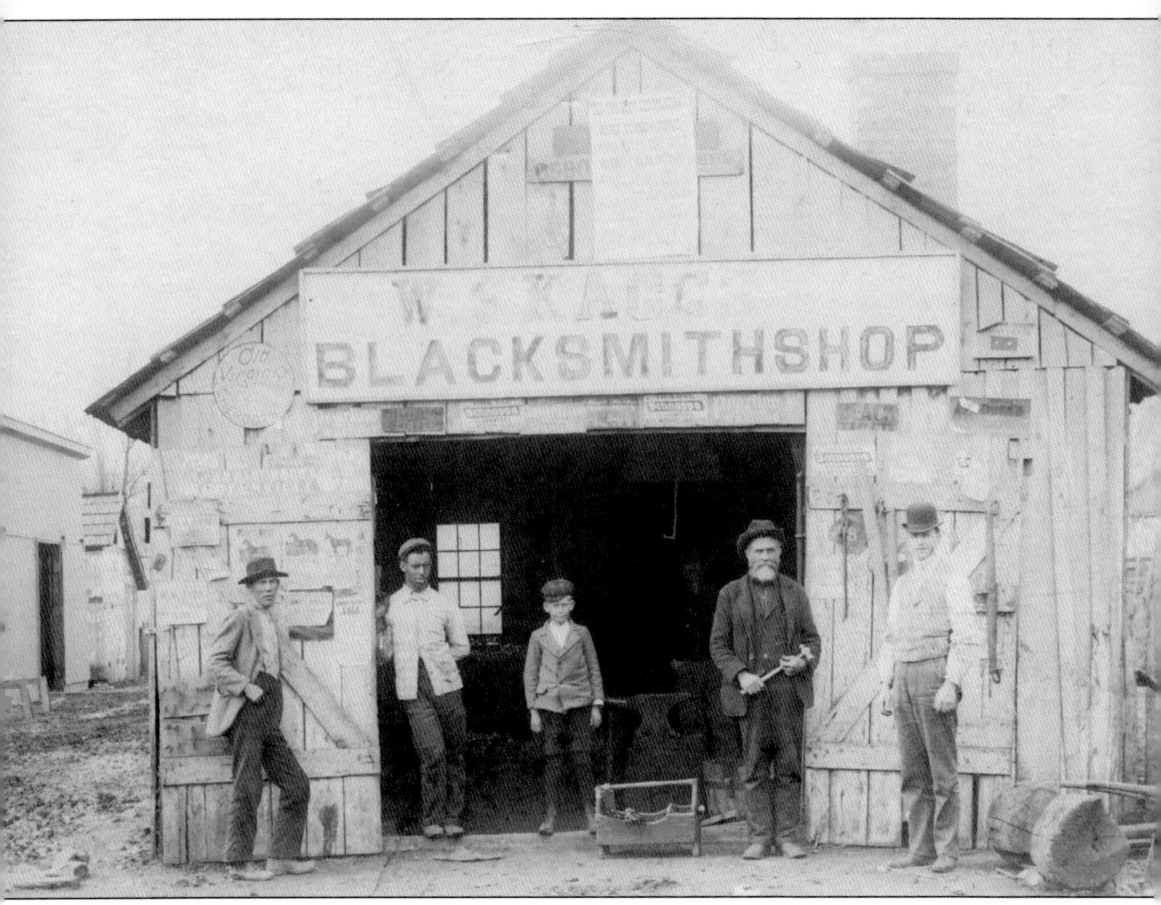

GATHERING AT THE BLACKSMITH. Wyllys Skaggs, the blacksmith holding a hammer in this 1892 photograph, made his living in Sonora, near Elizabethtown in Hardin County. Blacksmith shops were natural gathering places for men and boys to hear local gossip and watch someone else work. The town blacksmith shop was a busy location throughout the year, but it felt especially welcoming on cold winter days, when heat from the glowing coals in the forge warmed the building. The rhythmic sound of hammering metal and the distinctive smell of burning charcoal identified a workshop. At the beginning of the 20th century, farming was done with the power of horses, and the skills of a blacksmith were important to the local economy. The shop was a popular destination to wait for repairs of equipment, have horses shod, and hear the latest news. (KHS, WadeHall.Box19#181.)

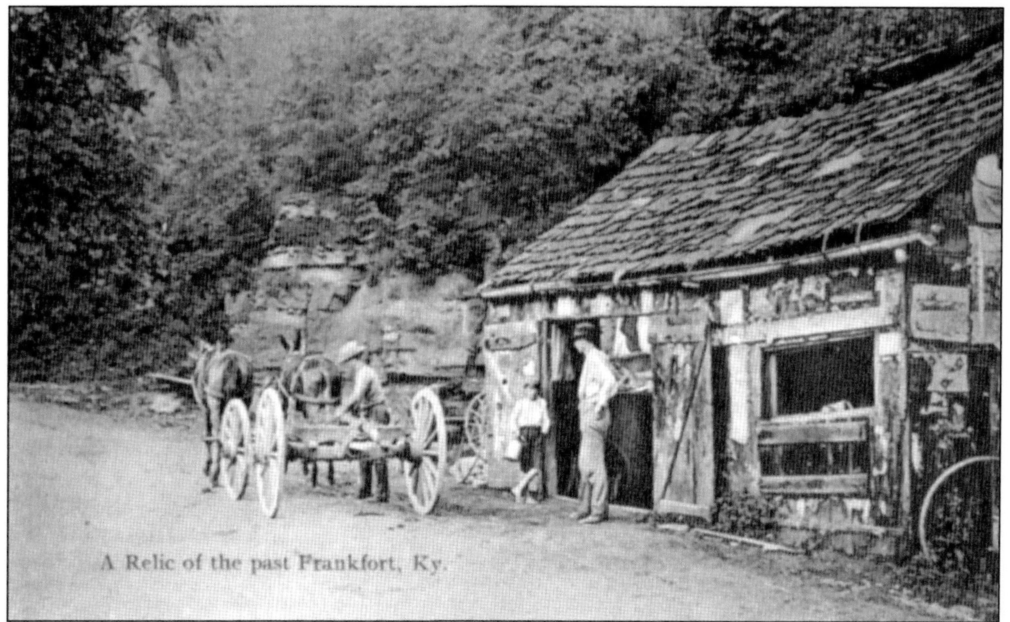

RUSTIC LIVERY STABLE. This postcard image shows a country livery stable outside of Frankfort on Old Louisville Road. This shop probably catered to rural folks in need of a wagon or other heavy equipment, with the appropriate team of horses or mules to pull it. The wagon shown is heavy-duty in nature, with large wheels and horse collars on the team, ready for a heavy load. (Capital City Museum.)

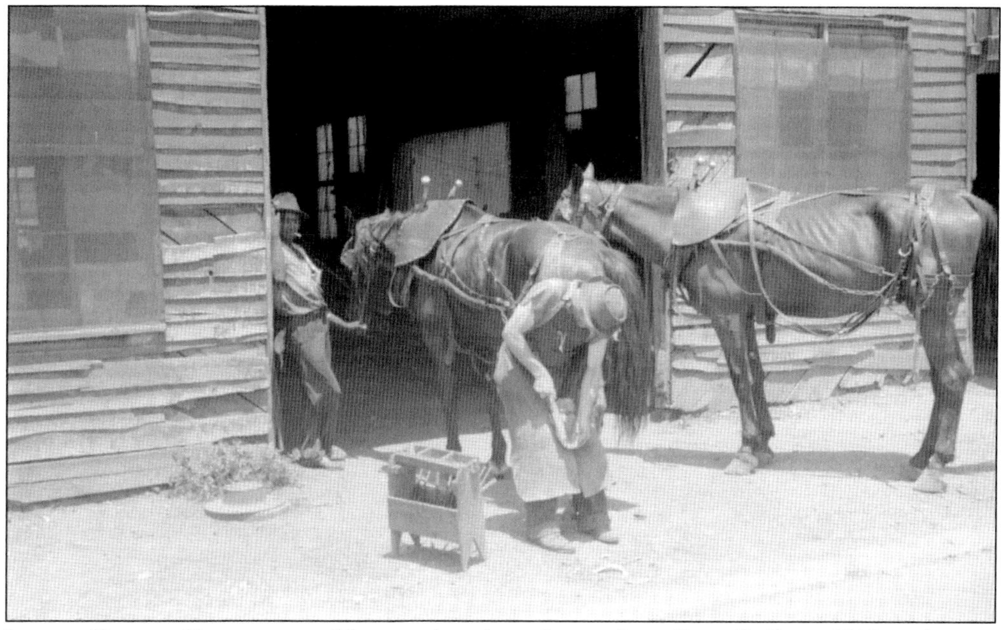

LOGAN COUNTY BLACKSMITH. This smithy, plying his trade in Russellville in 1910, is shoeing a team of farm horses. When the use of horses for farming and transportation came to an end, it forever changed the blacksmith's role in the community. Traditional, small-town blacksmith's shops gradually went out of business or evolved into the first automobile repair shops, as the horsepower of mechanical engines replaced the power of horses. (LOC.)

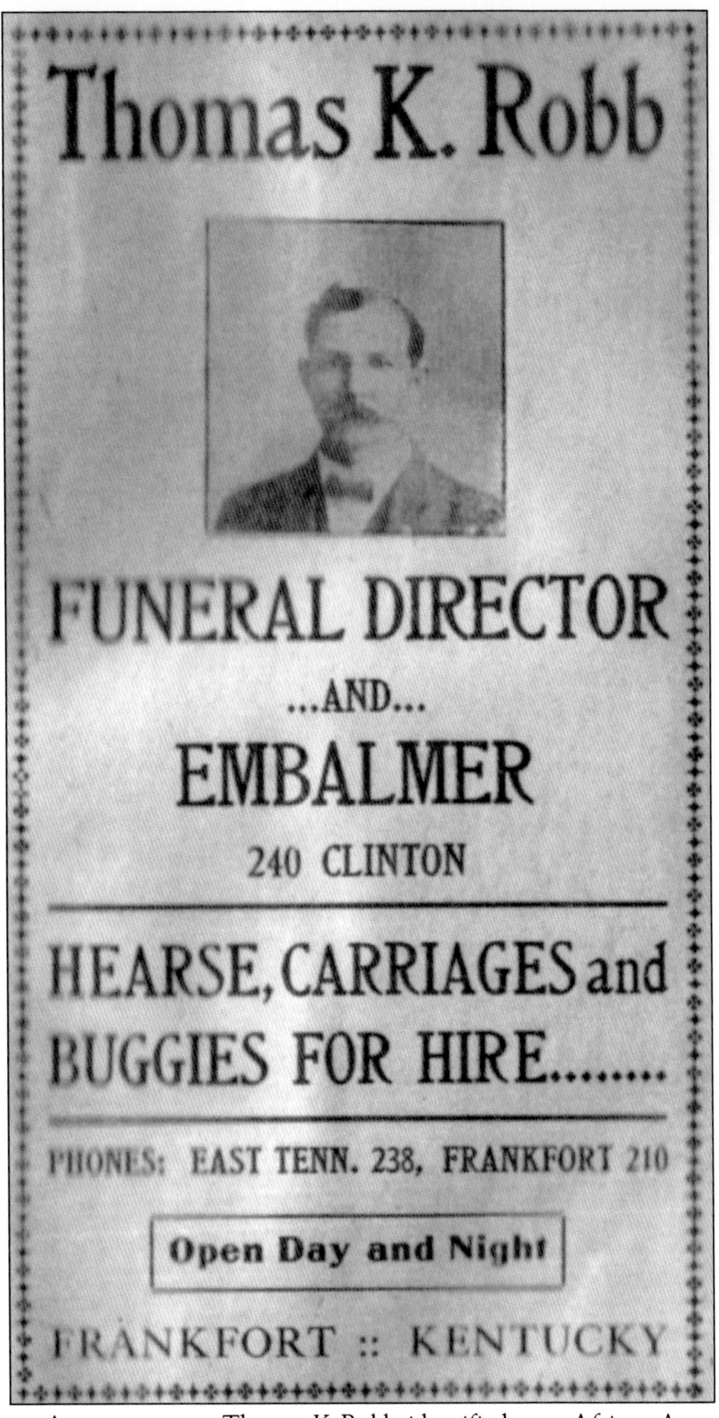

City Directory Advertisement. Thomas K. Robb, identified as an African American of mixed race, placed this advertisement in the 1908 Frankfort City Directory. Like many livery stable owners, he got into the funeral business by renting out the use of hearses and carriages. Other professions that entered into the funeral business about this time were furniture makers and dealers who had been selling coffins to the bereaved. (Capital City Museum.)

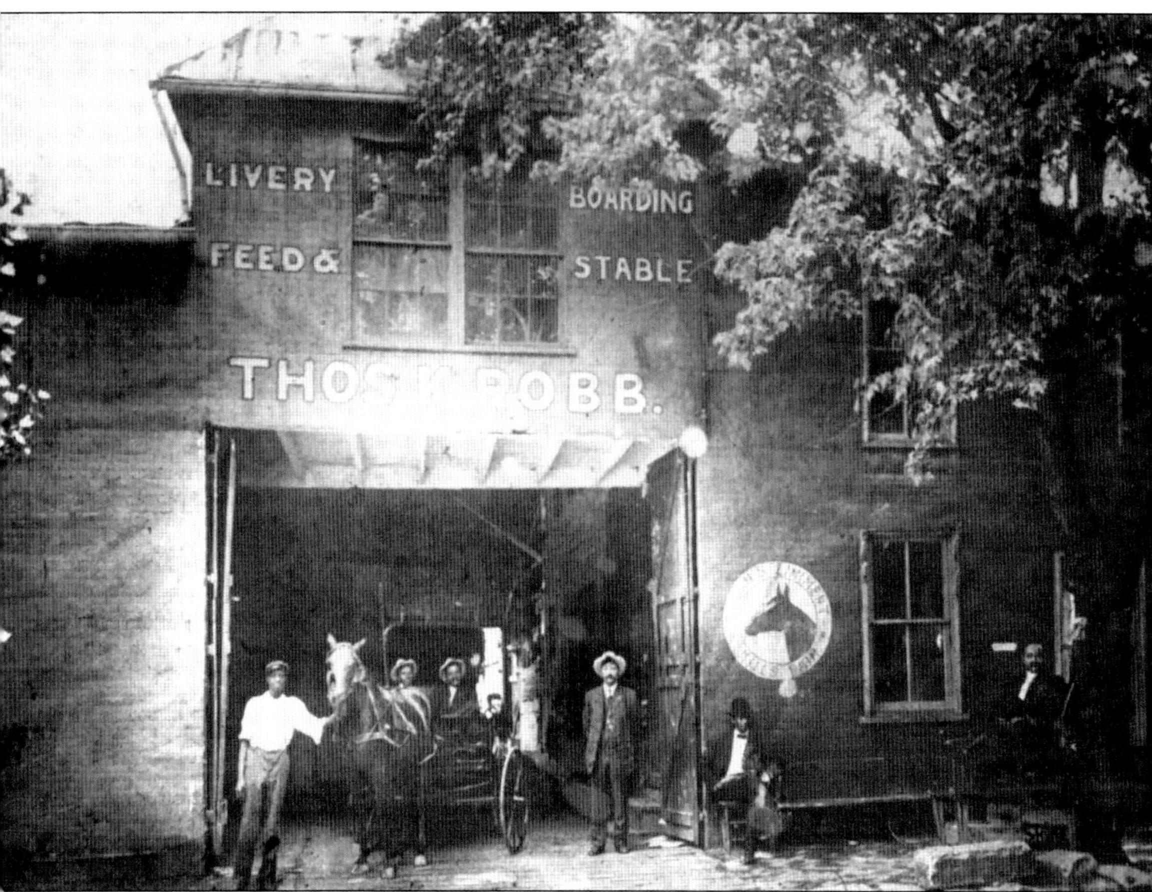

Man of Many Skills. This photograph shows Thomas K. Robb (standing, center) in front of his Frankfort stable in the 1890s. The round sign displaying the head of a horse was seen on many stables and blacksmith shops of the day. It reads "Sloan's Liniment—Kills Pain." Born in Frankfort, Robb initially worked in lumber. In 1896, he was elected lumber inspector for the Frankfort Penitentiary by the state, beating out 11 competitors, all of whom were white. In 1918, Robb's undertaking business and his livery stable were destroyed by fire, resulting in $5,000 in damages. Robb rebuilt and continued to have a prosperous business. (Capital City Museum.)

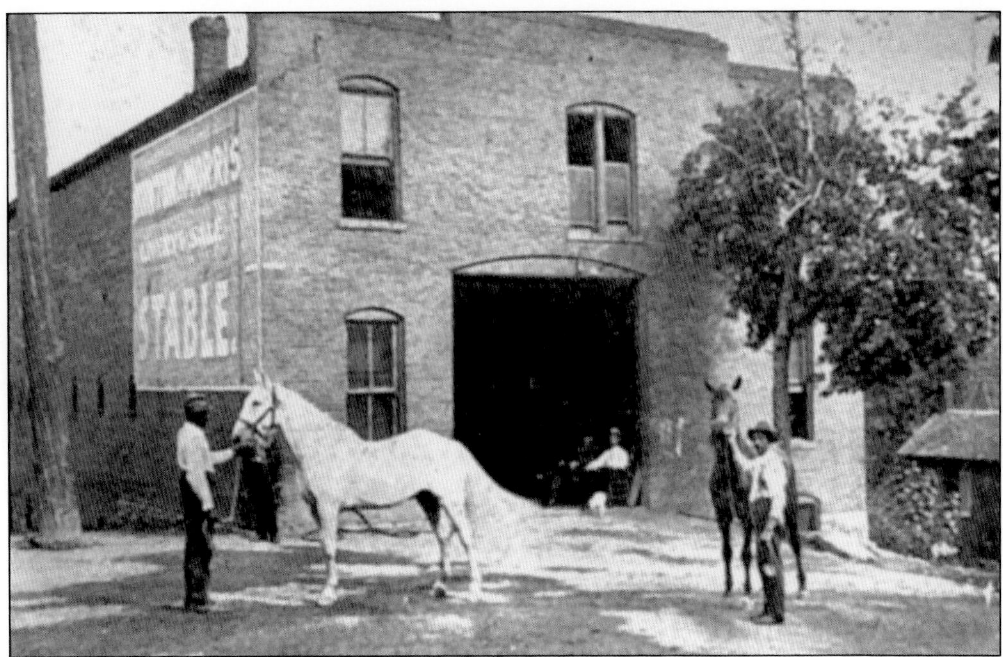

Hinton's Livery Stable. This Paris livery enjoyed the advantage of being across the street from the town's largest hotel and near the railroad station. In 1905, it advertised offering "a good horse or team of horses and comfortable, light, easy running vehicles at any and all times." Once the automobile took hold, many workers sought new careers, many of them as coachmen, wagon makers, harness or saddle makers, blacksmiths, or teamsters. (Hopewell Museum.)

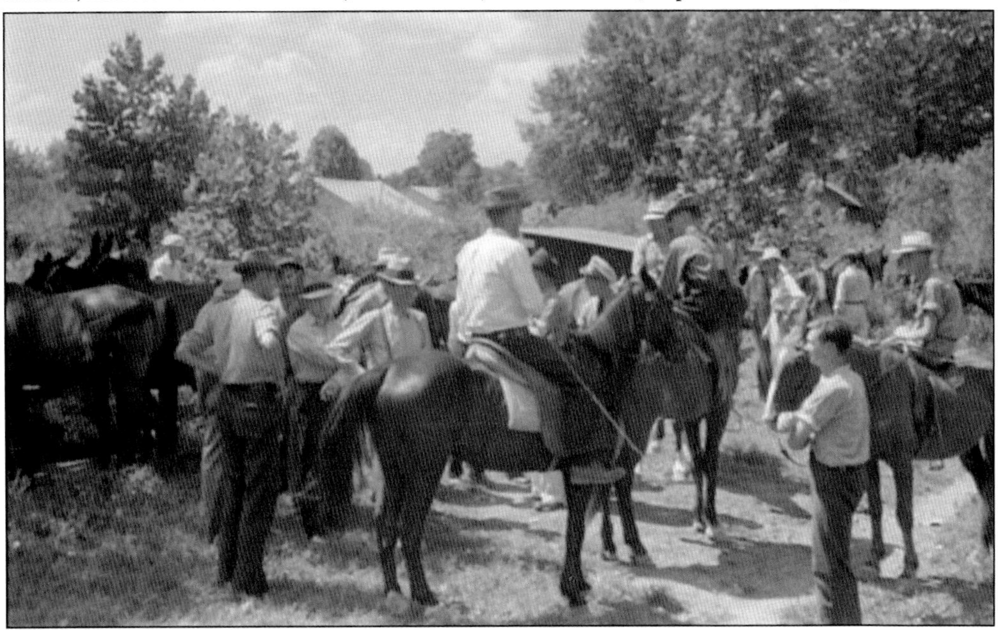

Mule Market on Jockey Street. Trading and selling mules was still going on in Campton, in Wolfe County, as late as 1940. These mules were put to good use in some farmer's field after they had been trained to work together. During World War II, when gasoline was rationed, many Kentucky farmers were happy to return to the old ways with horses and mules. (LOC.)

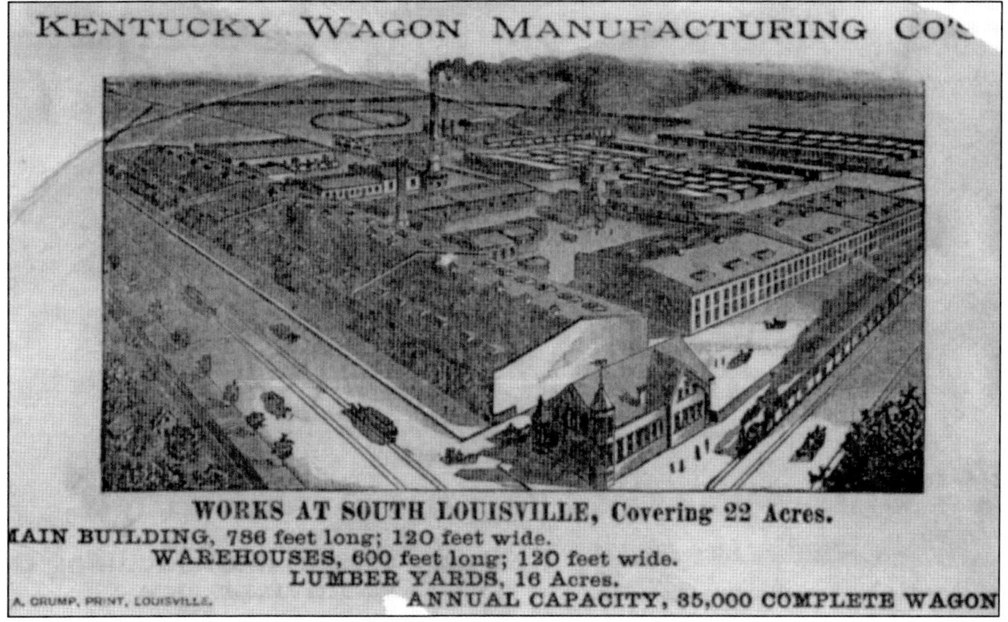

KENTUCKY WAGON IN LOUISVILLE. The Kentucky Wagon Manufacturing Company was founded in Louisville in 1879. Kentucky Wagon produced the Old Hickory and the Tennessee, two of the nation's most popular horse-drawn wagon models. The quality and durability of Kentucky Wagon's products were unmatched, and the firm became the largest wagon manufacturer in North America. As the advertisement above indicates, the manufacturing plant at its height, in 1891, covered more than 22 acres and employed 500 to 600 workers. The main building alone encompassed nearly three acres and could produce up to 35,000 wagons a year. Below, a postcard, in full-color lithography, promotes the company's best-selling Old Hickory farm wagon. By 1919, the production of horse-drawn vehicles was curtailed, and the company concentrated on manufacturing the Dixie Flyer automobile. It only lasted until 1923. In 1936, the company was renamed Kentucky Manufacturing Company, and it does business today as Kentucky Trailer, building made-to-order semi-trailers, truck bodies, and large, expandable marketing and command-center trailers. (Above, Kentucky Trailers; below, WKU Special Collections.)

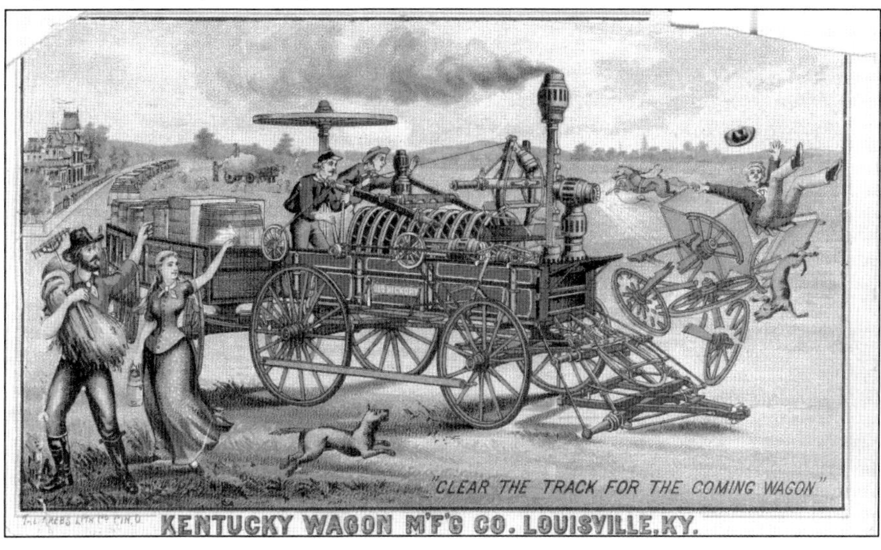

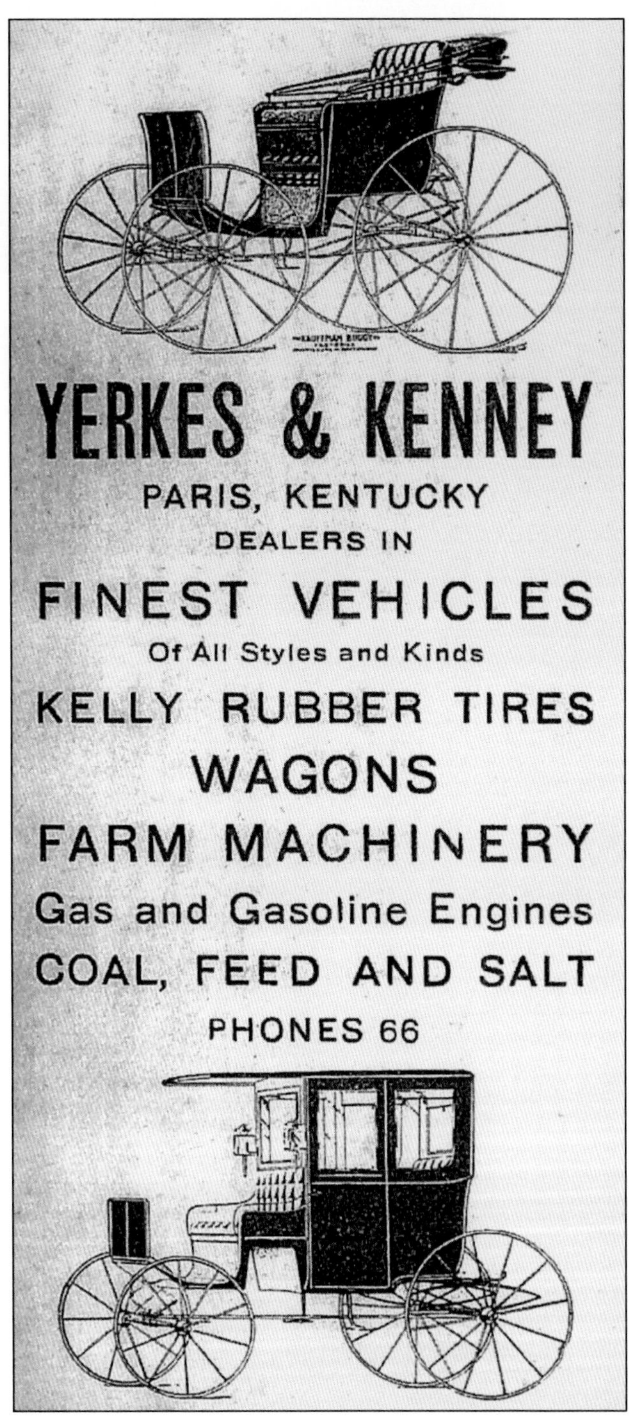

Yerkes & Kenney. The Bourbon County firm featured in this 1895 advertisement specialized in the sale of horse-drawn vehicles in Paris. It ordered the parts for most of its vehicles from manufacturers and assembled them after receiving the parts by rail. The firm sold "A full line of . . . Buggies and Run Abouts, Handsome Dept Wagons, Surreys, Phaetons and Stanhopes." (Authors' collection.)

Eight

Special Occasions and Unusual Sights

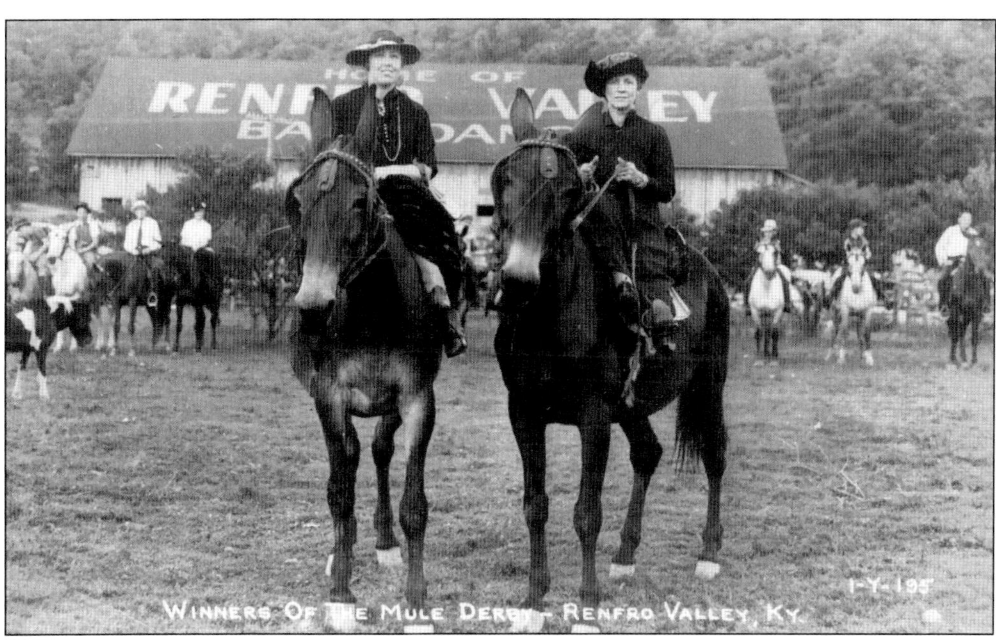

Derbies Are Not Just for Horses. This was not the traditional "Run for the Roses" that takes place in Kentucky on the first Saturday in May each year. Here, two of the horse's less-speedy "cousins" had their moment in the spotlight when they won the 1940 Mule Derby at Renfro Valley in Rockcastle County. The winning riders are dressed in black, with matching hats, and both are riding sidesaddle. (KHS, Graphics5_Box15_286_1_dm.)

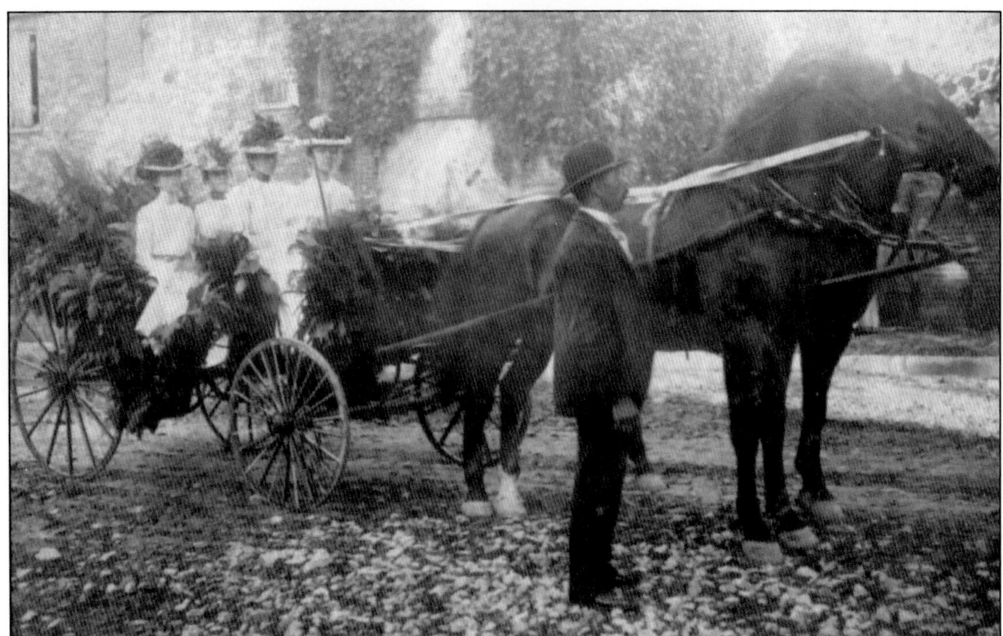

Ready for a Parade? These ladies do not look too happy about the upcoming parade or garden fete they are bound for, but, hopefully, they cheered up after this photograph was taken. Their groom is keeping an eye on the horses while the ladies prepare to depart in their carriage decorated with ferns and greenery. This photograph was taken in 1890 in Frankfort. (Capital City Museum.)

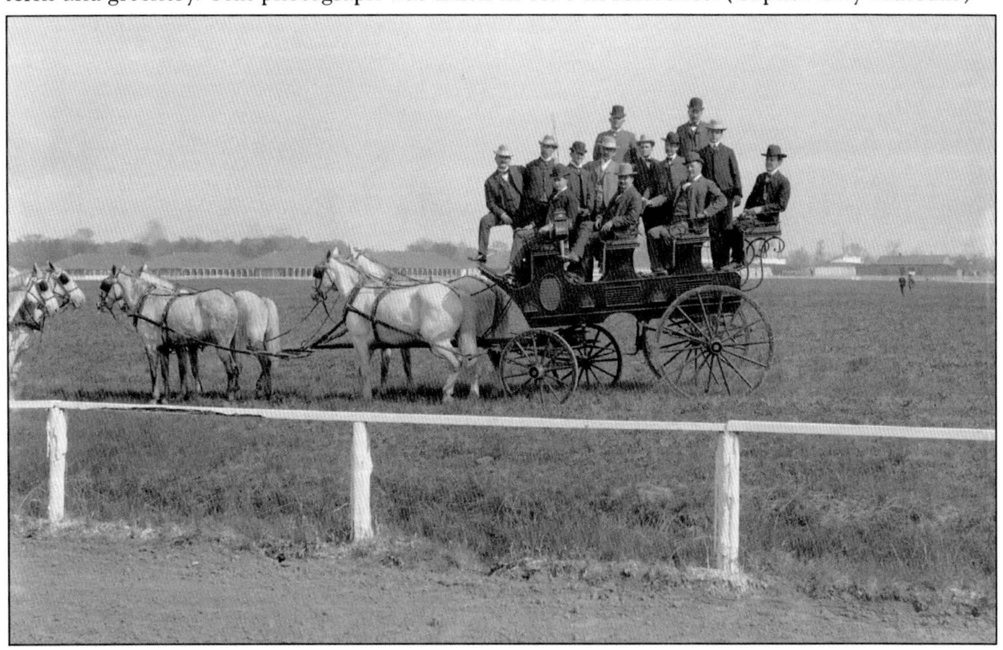

1901 Kentucky Derby. Kentucky governor J.C.W. Beckham is shown with a group of men at the Kentucky Derby. Beckham was William Goebel's lieutenant governor when Goebel was assassinated in 1899. Beckham then became governor. He narrowly won a special election in 1900 and was reelected in 1903 for a full term. He is tentatively identified as the man in the driver's seat. (International Museum of the Horse at the Kentucky Horse Park.)

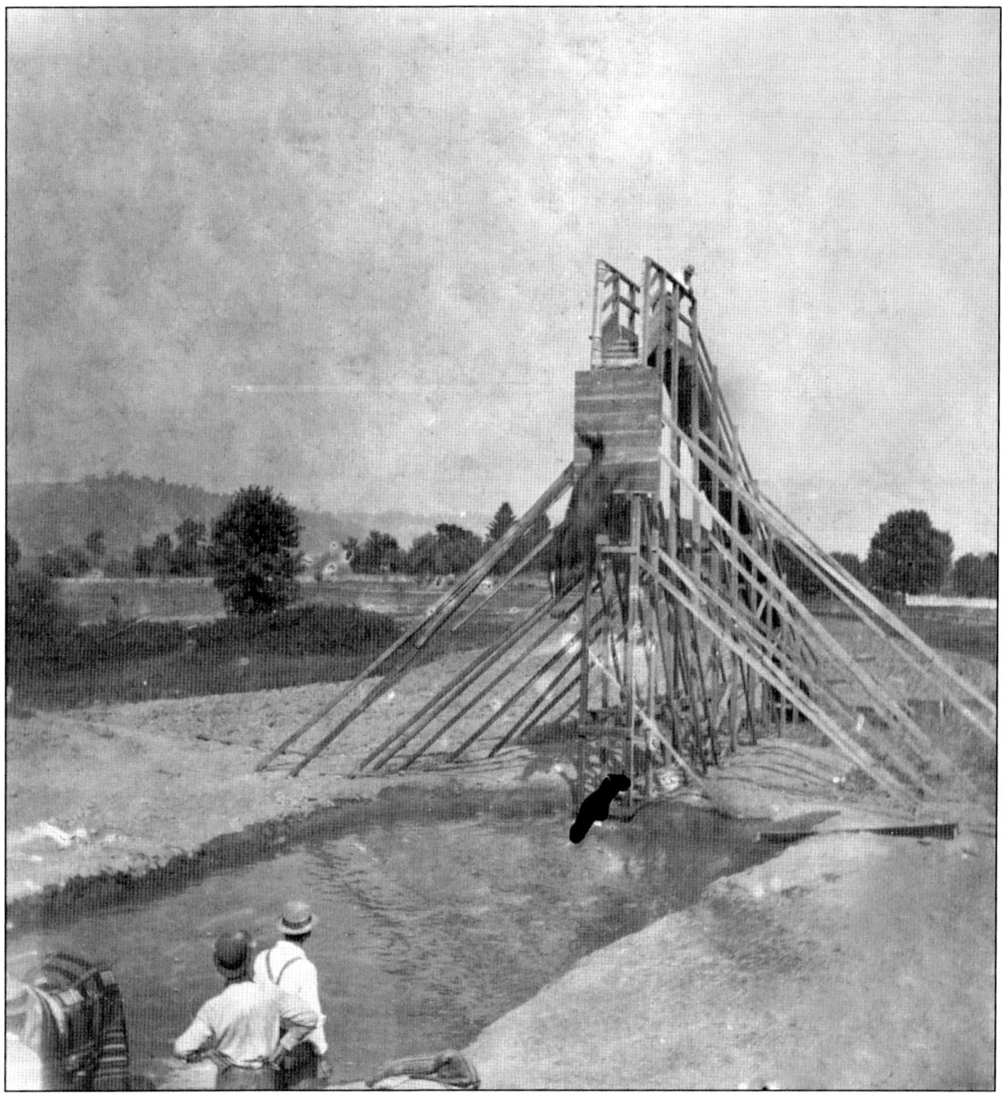

Diving Right in. This fascinating photograph, taken in the 1890s at a fair near Maysville, captures a horse in mid-fall after diving off the wooden platform. The diving horse act was the brainstorm of a man who saw his horse fall or dive off a collapsing bridge in the 1880s. The act became a permanent fixture at the Steel Pier in Atlantic City, delighting crowds for decades. The diving horse act was still being performed after World War II. As illustrated in this photograph at the much-smaller venue of a fair in Mason County, the act had gone "on the road" by the 1890s to more rural areas. One hopes the pond below was nice and deep. (KHS, MAS.1990ph2.15MAS1.)

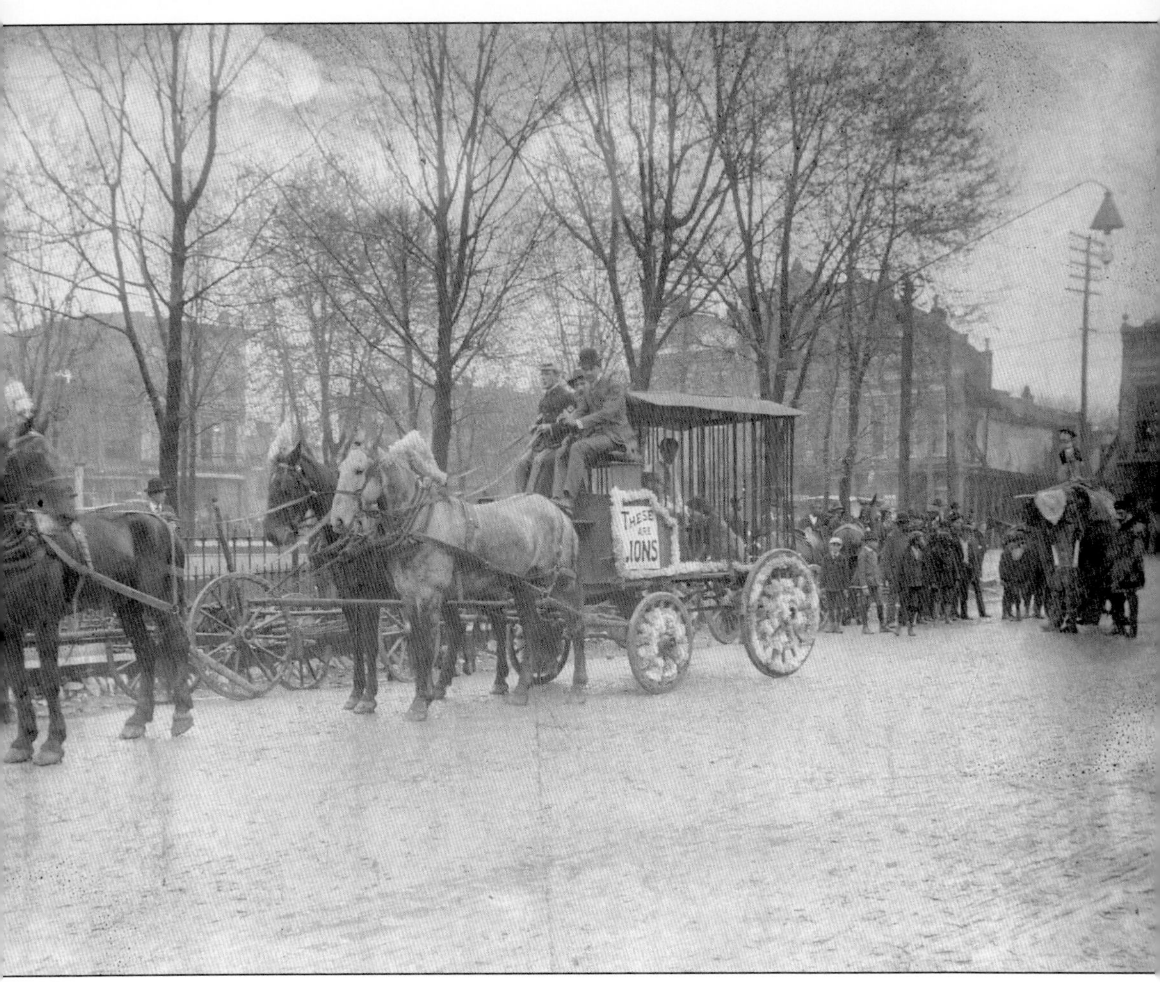

"These Are Lions." In the days before the Discovery Channel, people needed to be informed that the animals in the wheeled cage being pulled by four plumed horses were lions. This 1900 photograph of a circus parade at Fountain Square Park in Bowling Green includes not only the lions, but also an elephant, seen walking behind the lion's wagon. The elephant is accompanied by a costumed trainer and is the center of attention for the crowd of men and boys on the corner. It appears that a costumed dog is riding the elephant. Circus parades were living advertisements of the rare sights that customers would be able to see by parting with a hard-earned nickel for admission. Those who could not or would not pay up had to make do with the free parade. Even though lions and elephants were important to the circus, it was horses that provided the muscle to move everything to and from the railroad and to get everything set up. (WKU Special Collections.)

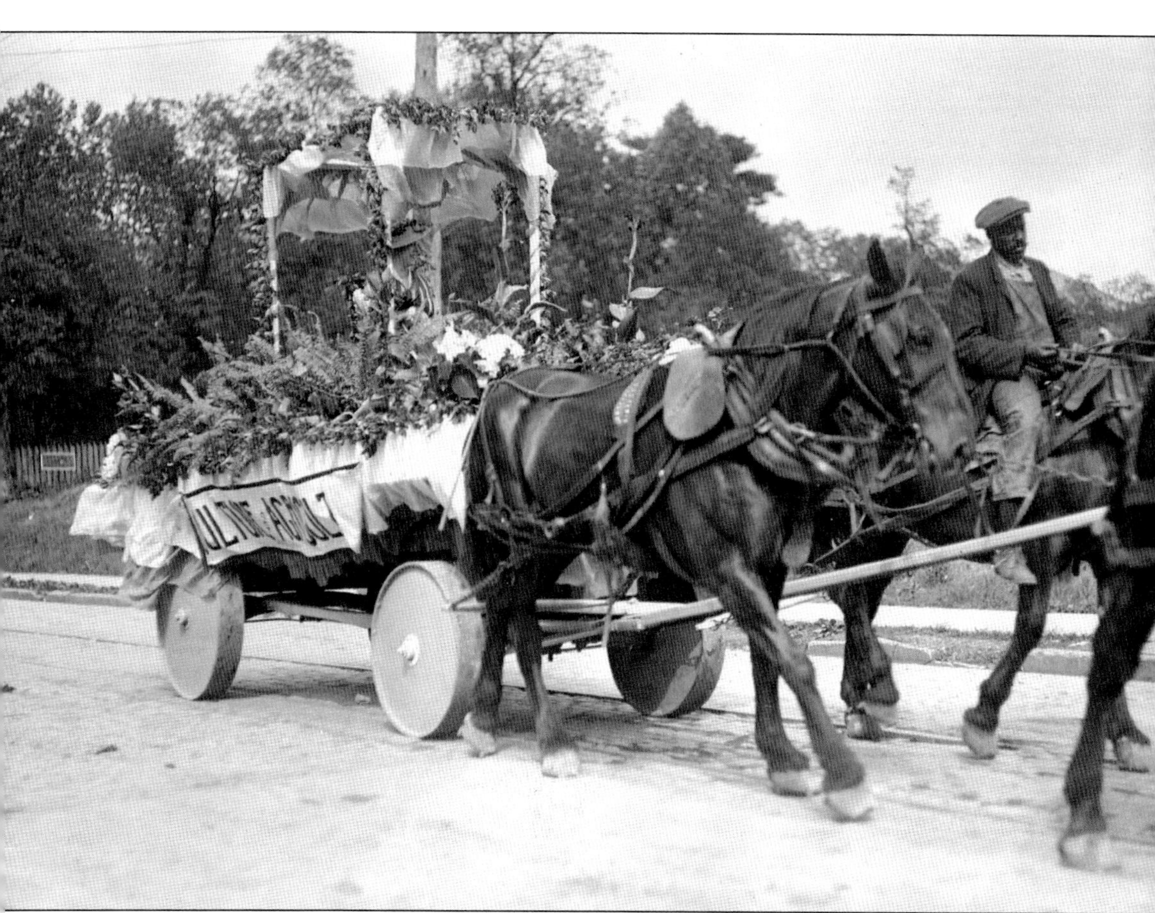

UK Golden Jubilee Float. Main Street parades in Lexington included floats designed by the freshman, sophomore, junior, and senior classes of the University of Kentucky and were part of the events celebrating the school's golden jubilee in 1916. That year was observed as the school's 50th anniversary, because it actually began operations in 1866 after the act establishing the Agricultural and Mechanical College (now the University of Kentucky) was passed by the Kentucky Legislature in 1865. The college will celebrate its sesquicentennial in 2015. This float is being drawn by four mules, one of which is being ridden by a driver. (UK Special Collections.)

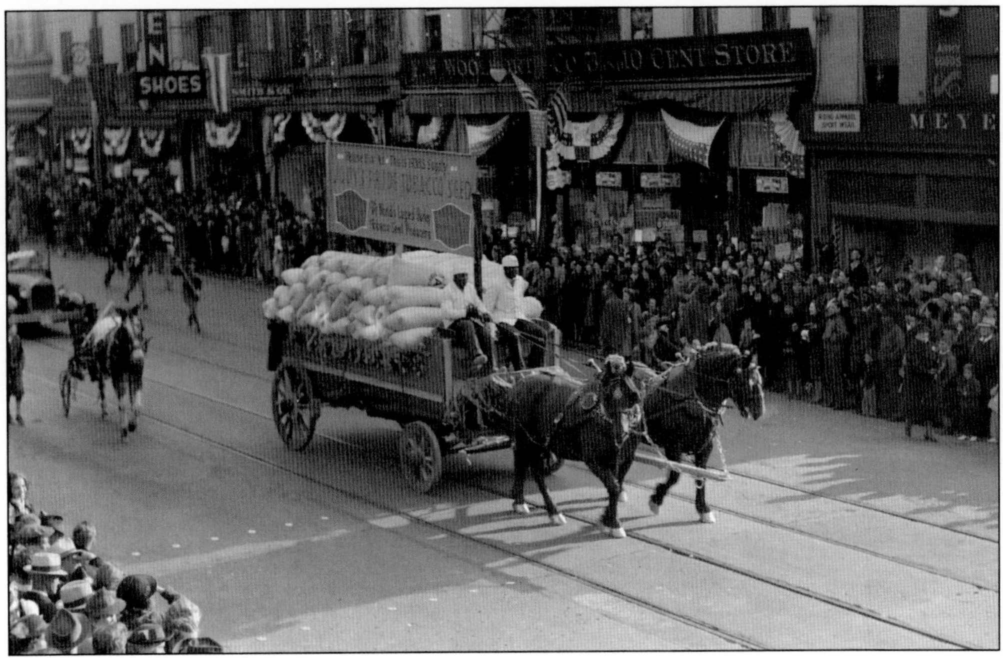

Hurray for Tobacco. This wagon, filled to the brim with Judy's Pride Tobacco Seeds, was pulled down Main Street in Lexington by a handsome team of draft horses as part of the 1938 Tobacco Carnival parade. A huge crowd lined both sides of the street. In the background, stores, including Woolworth's and Dan Cohen Shoes, are decked out in bunting. (UK Special Collections.)

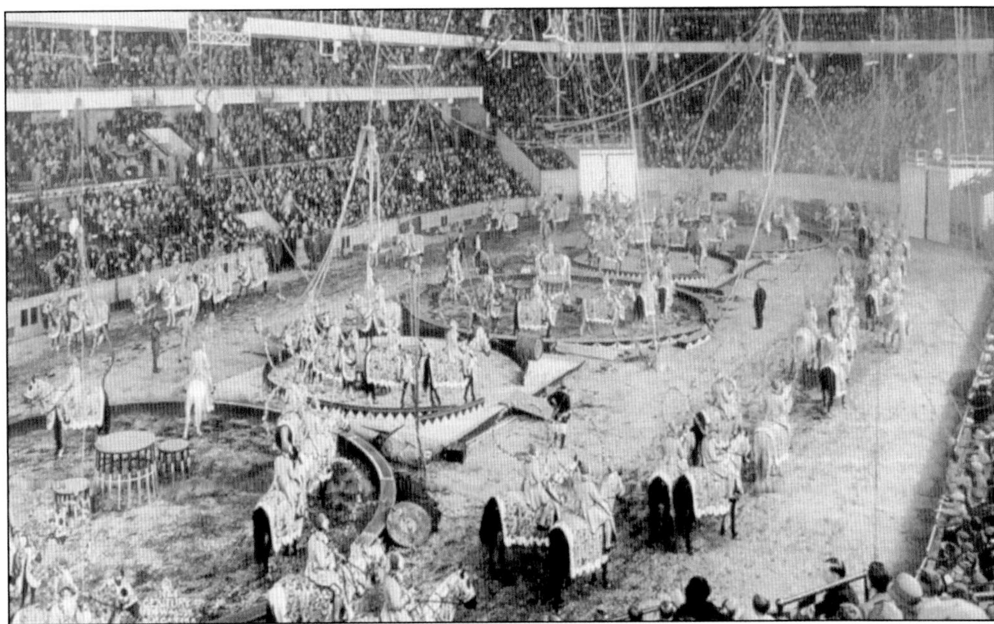

Five-Ring Circus. Forget the traditional three-ring circus, this 1929 photograph shows a parade of horses around five rings in a huge arena. This photograph was not taken in Kentucky, but it was taken by a Kentuckian, W.B. Griffin. He was a trumpeter who lived in Lexington but traveled extensively around the country playing in circus bands, especially for the Barnum & Bailey Circus. (UK Special Collections.)

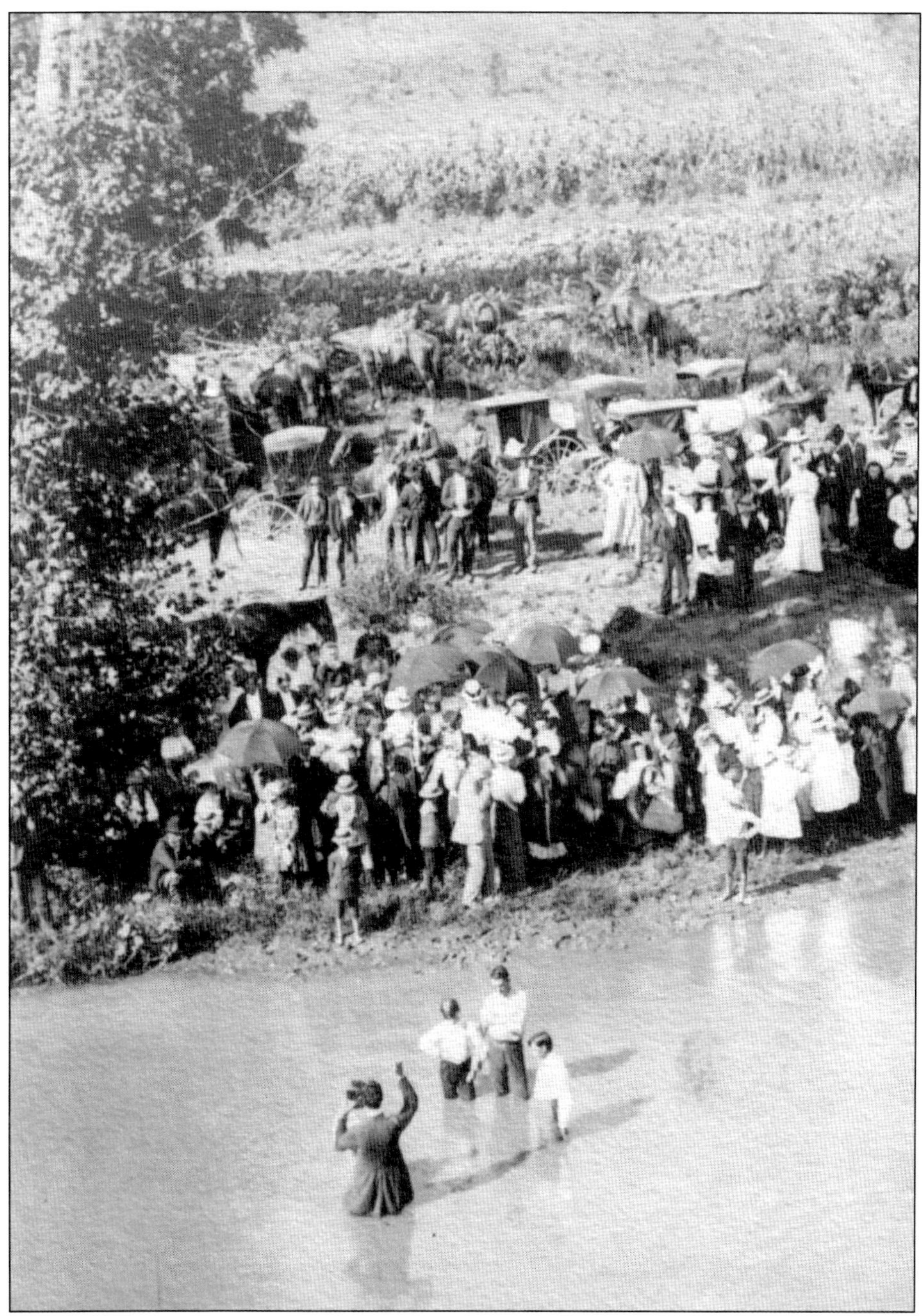

Gathered at the River. This large group of churchgoers turned out to see a man and two boys being baptized in the muddy waters of an unidentified Kentucky river. Many in the well-dressed crowd are standing back from the river bank in a likely futile attempt to keep their shoes clean. A pair of small boys in the front have abandoned their shoes and are probably enjoying feeling the squishy mud between their toes. The horses and buggies that transported the crowd to the riverbank can be seen in the background of this undated photograph. The photographer's location is not known; perhaps he or she was in a tree on the other bank of the river. (Berea College Special Collections.)

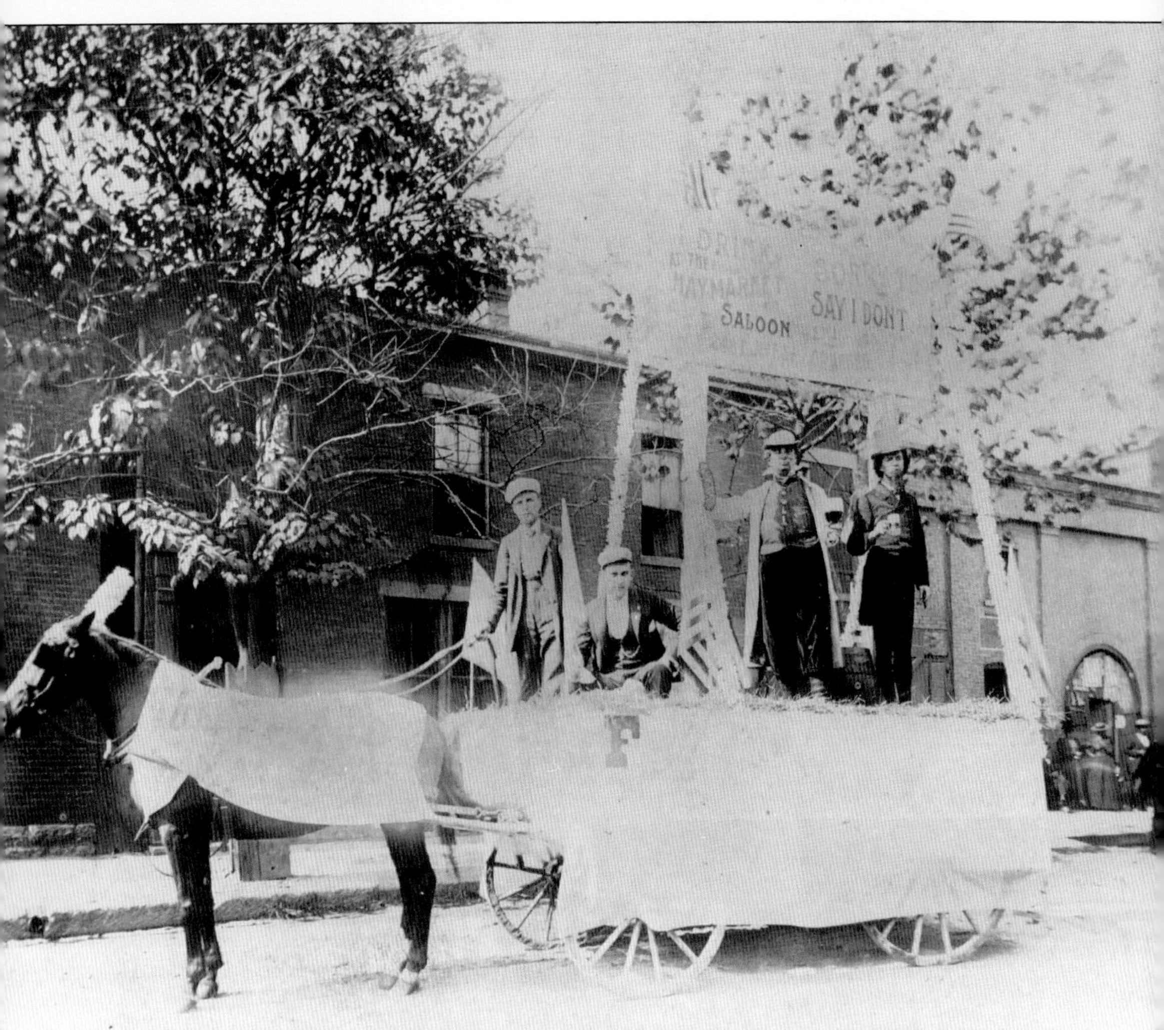

Saloon's Parade Float. The signage on this float, sponsored by the Haymarket Saloon in Louisville, is a little difficult to read. What is visible is the sign over the head of the two men riding on the float. The section on the left reads, "I drink at the Haymarket Saloon, 248 E. Jefferson St." Under that section, a well-fed man holds a large, half-full glass. Perhaps he is a customer who tried the "Three pint lager beer and fine lunch for five cents." The saloon's owner, Emil Graeser, advertised that special in a local newspaper aimed at Irish immigrants. At the rear of the float, under a sign that reads "Sorry to say, I don't," a thin man holds a very small mug, perhaps showing what happens to people who do not try the Haymarket Saloon. There are two drivers at the front of the float, one of them holding the horse's reins. (KHS, JFA.1990ph2.7JEFA11.)

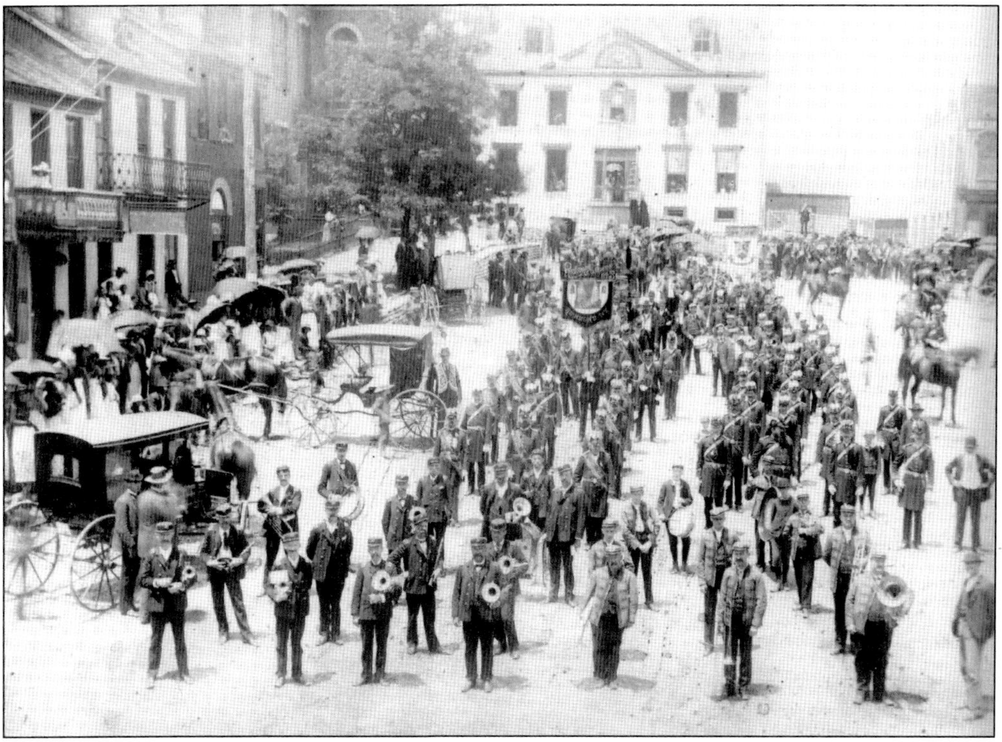

KNIGHTS OF PYTHIAS PARADE. The Knights of Pythias was one of many fraternal and benevolent associations formed after the Civil War. This photograph was taken in Paris, in Bourbon County, sometime in the late 1890s, when the group held its state convention there. The Knights are getting ready to parade down Main Street, led by their band. (Authors' collection.)

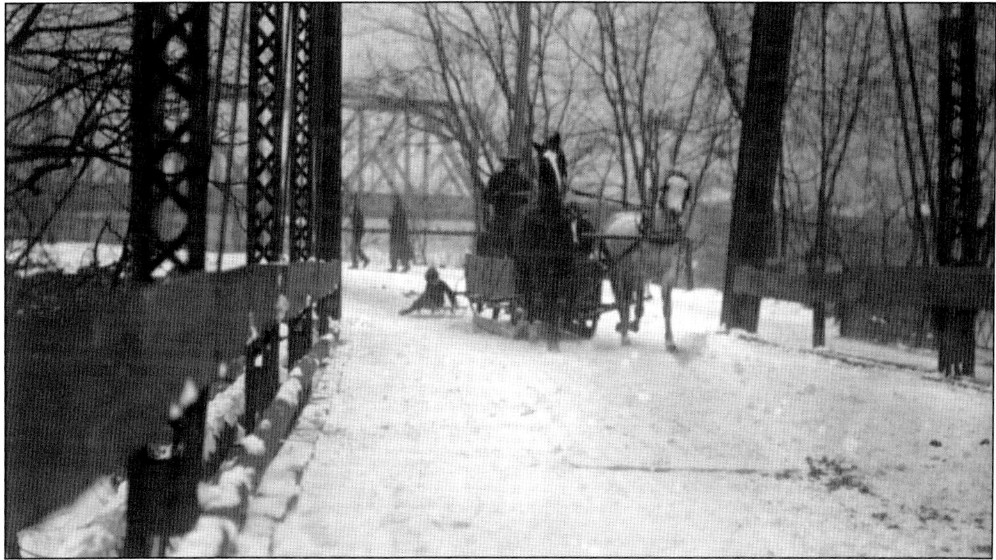

LOOKS LIKE FUN. A child on a sled is being pulled behind a sleigh drawn by a team of horses. This is the bridge over Benson Creek in Bellepoint, near Frankfort. Another iron bridge can be seen in the background. Horses were usually shod with a different type of horseshoe in the winter, helping them to better grip the road—a kind of equine snow chain. (Capital City Museum.)

Discover Thousands of Local History Books Featuring Millions of Vintage Images

Arcadia Publishing, the leading local history publisher in the United States, is committed to making history accessible and meaningful through publishing books that celebrate and preserve the heritage of America's people and places.

Find more books like this at
www.arcadiapublishing.com

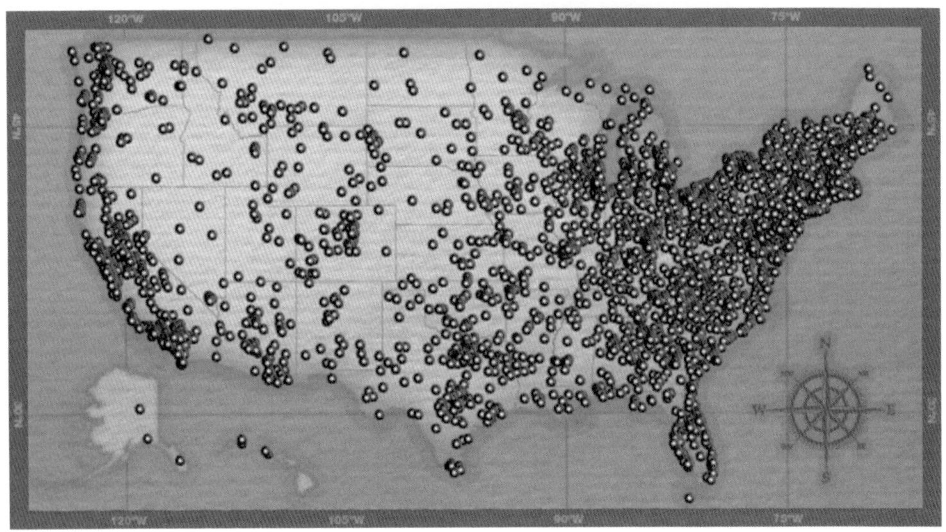

Search for your hometown history, your old stomping grounds, and even your favorite sports team.

Consistent with our mission to preserve history on a local level, this book was printed in South Carolina on American-made paper and manufactured entirely in the United States. Products carrying the accredited Forest Stewardship Council (FSC) label are printed on 100 percent FSC-certified paper.

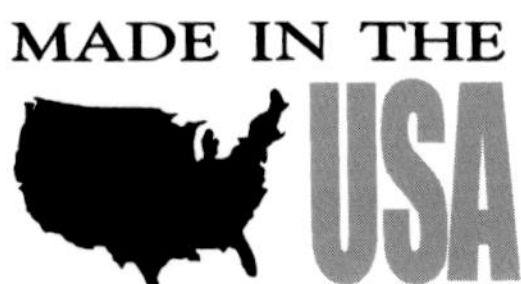